Transnational Enterprises

Other Titles in This Series

Westview Special Studies in Social, Political, and Economic Development

Transnational Enterprises:
Their Impact on Third World
Societies and Cultures
edited by Krishna Kumar

This book represents the first attempt to conceptualize the social and cultural impact of transnational enterprises on host nations and to provide empirical and analytical material on the subject. Well-known social scientists focus on three critical areas: social inequalities, knowledge systems, and lifestyles and values. Collectively, they advance their central thesis: TNCs not only affect the economic and political systems of a nation but by internationalizing production processes and facilitating the movement of products across national boundaries, they influence social structures and organizations, lifestyles, and the cultural identities of the people.

Dr. Krishna Kumar is a staff member of the East-West Center, Honolulu, where he coordinates a program of study and research on transnational interactions.

Transnational Enterprises: Their Impact on Third World Societies and Cultures

edited by Krishna Kumar

Westview Press / Boulder, Colorado

Westview Special Studies in
Social, Political and Economic Development

Copyright © 1980 by Westview Press, Inc.

Published in 1980 in the United States of America by
    Westview Press, Inc.
    5500 Central Avenue
    Boulder, Colorado 80301
    Frederick A. Praeger, Publisher

Library of Congress Cataloging in Publication Data
Main entry under title:
Transnational enterprises, their impact on Third World societies and
cultures.
    (Westview special studies in social, political, and economic development)
    Bibliography: p.
    1. Underdeveloped areas--International business enterprises--Social
aspects--Addresses, essays, lectures. I. Kumar, Krishna. II. Series.
HD2755.5.T69   338.8'88'1724   80-16759
ISBN 0-89158-852-3

Composition for this book was provided by the author.
Printed and bound in the United States of America.

Contents

Tables

Acknowledgments

Several friends and colleagues have helped me in bringing out this volume. The very idea of my undertaking this task came from Dr. Karl P. Sauvant of the U.N. Center on Transnational Corporations. Dr. Verner C. Bickley, Director of the Culture Learning Institute, was instrumental in overcoming my initial hesitation in this regard. I very much profited from the suggestions of my colleagues, Drs. Mark Lester, Sripada Raju, and Robert T. Snow. I also solicited the help of Mssrs. Lim Ma Hui, Maxwell McLeod, and Robert Mashburn in various matters. My wife, Dr. P. Tahbazzadeh, was most helpful in the selection of material for this book. I sought her advice on endless numbers of articles, documents, and research reports that I considered for inclusion in it. Ms. Jenny Ichinotsubo did an excellent job in typing the manuscript while Ms. Deborah Weiner provided valuable editorial assistance. I wish to record my deep gratitude to all these friends.

I would also like to express my thanks to Mr. Frederick A. Praeger and Ms. Lynne C. Rienner, publisher and associate publisher of Westview Press, for their encouragement and support.

Krishna Kumar

1
Social and Cultural Impact of Transnational Enterprises: An Overview

Krishna Kumar

The main purpose of this overview of the social and cultural impact of transnational enterprises (TNEs) is not to articulate a sociological paradigm which can help to organize ideas, research findings, and substantive discussions on the subject in a theoretical framework. Nor is it to identify all possible kinds of influences and effects which TNEs as distinctive economic bureaucracies, linking two or more nations in an economic relationship, can have on social and cultural elements and processes. Our objective is rather limited: we confine ourselves here to a brief discussion of only those impacts which have been stressed in the growing literature on transnational enterprises. The discussion is analytical rather than theoretical.

Two limitations of the present discussion can be mentioned here. In the first place, our focus is essentially on macro dimensions. Thus we do not examine the micro-level issues pertaining to what happens within the confines of a TNE in home or host nations, where people from different societies and cultures interact for rational, goal-oriented activity. In the second place, our emphasis is on developing nations. The term developing nations has undoubtedly lost some of its precise connotations and discriminating property in recent years for it has come to include nations such as Brazil, South Korea, and Taiwan which have sizable industrial sectors, as well as those countries which are yet to make any headway towards industrialization. However, despite its obvious limitation, we still find it of some heuristic value. We take it to be a residual category referring to those nations which cannot be

classifed as industrialized and which have not
opted for a socialist model of development.
This overview is organized as follows: we begin
with a working definition of transnational enterprises and briefly mention the recent trends and
patterns in direct foreign investment. The second
section examines the effects of TNEs on social
structures and inequalities while the third section
focuses on TNEs' impact on cultural systems.
Finally, we explain the organization of this volume.

TRANSNATIONAL CORPORATIONS:
RECENT TREND AND PATTERNS

Since scholars have offered a wide variety of
definitions of TNEs using different criteria-
variables, it is necessary to mention that we
follow the United Nation's definition which has
the widest acceptance. Following this definition,
TNEs are defined as the enterprises which "own or
control production or service facilities outside
the country in which they are based."[1] These
enterprises can operate in extractive, agricultural,
manufacturing, or service sectors and can be
private, semiprivate, or government-owned operations. Obviously, this definition excludes all
those firms which do not own or control production
and/or service facilities in foreign countries,
and yet are involved in substantial foreign
operations. The enterprises which operate within
the confines of national boundaries have been
termed as national enterprises (NEs).
There are no reliable figures about the
number of TNEs. However, a recent survey conducted
by the European Economic Community noted that
there were about 10,000 TNEs which were operating
in more than one country.[2] The actual number might
be slightly higher because the survey was made in
1973, and since then there has been further
internationalization of national firms both in
industrialized and developing nations. The conservative estimate of subsidiaries owned by TNEs
is 50,000, which attests to their importance in
the movement of the factors of production and
products across national boundaries.
The majority of TNEs are undoubtedly based
in a few highly industrialized nations. While the
number of countries in which TNEs are based has
increased with the economic development and
technological sophistication of these nations,

most of the largest firms continue to be domiciled
in the United States, U.K., Germany, Japan, and
France.[3] The current volume of direct foreign investment is estimated to be 287.2 billion dollars. (Out
of this amount, the U.S. share accounts for 137.2
billion, which is followed by the U.K. with 32.1
billion dollars.) The shares of Germany, Japan,
Switzerland, France, and Canada are 19.9, 19.4, 18.6,
11.9, and 9.8 billion dollars respectively. In
percentage terms it can be suggested that, taken
together, these nations account for 86.9 percent of
the direct foreign investment. Thus TNEs, despite
the adjective transnational, are in practice owned
and controlled by the nationals and governments of
a few countries.

There is also a degree of concentration of
foreign subsidiaries within a few large TNEs. It is
estimated that less than 200 TNEs control half of the
total direct foreign investment. According to
Sauvant and Mennis "approximately four-fifths of all
foreign affiliates are owned and controlled by parent
enterprises headquartered in five major investor
countries (the U.S., U.K., Germany, France, and
Switzerland) and although no figures are available
on the degree of foreign affiliate-concentration in
terms of major enterprises, it can be expected that
150 major TNEs control a substantial number of
them."[4] However, the recent trend seems to show a
slight decline in this concentration. A majority of
the subsidiaries are either wholly-owned or
majority-owned.

Although TNEs operate all over the globe, the
bulk of their investments are located in industrialized nations. In fact, over the last decade, the
U.N. data show that there has been an absolute and
proportional increase in the volume of TNEs' investment in these nations. About 76 percent of the
total direct foreign investment, that is, about
191.66 billion dollars, was in the industrialized
nations in the year 1975. In the case of developing
countries, while there has been a significant
increase in foreign investment (from 32.55 in 1967
to 67.34 in 1975), its relative share has declined.
It was estimated to be 31 percent in 1967 and only
26 percent in 1975. However, it should be noted
that the "presence of foreign multinational corporations in the developing countries is generally of
greater relative significance, since their economies
account for much less than half of that of
developed market economies."[5]

About 50 percent of the assets of TNEs are in

manufacturing, while the remaining are equally divided in extractive and service sectors.[6] There is, however, an asymmetry in the industrial distribution of TNE activities in industrialized and developing nations. "Whereas in developing countries half of the estimated stock of investment is in extractive industries and a little more than a quarter in manufacturing, in developed market-economies half of it is in manufacturing, and about 30 percent is in extractive industries."[7] However, these estimates were made in the early seventies and the situation has slightly changed since then. There has been a dynamic growth in the manufacturing sector in developing nations.[8] The most recent data show that the percentage of assets of the U.S. TNEs in the manufacturing sector has increased from 34.1 in 1971 to 39.1 in 1974 and those of the U.K. TNEs from 40.5 to 47.6 for the same period. Nearly half of the investment of Japan in developing nations is in the manufacturing sector.[9] The most pronounced growth in developing nations has been in the operations of service TNEs.

TNEs exercise effective control over their foreign affiliates, both directly and indirectly. Some of the earlier European and American TNEs were more like octopuses, who have little control and coordination over their limbs. The situation has drastically changed in recent years because of the remarkable developments in transport and communications, especially satellite communications. Several studies have indicated that the real power in relation to overall strategic decision-making is concentrated in a small group of decision-makers.[10] Large TNEs prefer to have an organizational structure based on product division. Thus, the status of the product rather than the distinctive characteristics of the host countries is the basis for global strategy. Paradoxically, there has also been a trend towards joint ventures in developing nations, as more and more nations are demanding equity participation. The Japanese TNEs in Asian countries were the pioneers in establishing joint ventures. However, it is doubtful that joint ventures are enjoying more freedom than the majority-owned subsidiaries in respect to planning their long-term goals and strategies.

The above features of direct foreign investment should be kept in mind while discussing the effects of TNEs on the societies and cultures of developing nations.

IMPACT ON SOCIETY

The TNEs' impact on the societies of developing countries can be conceptualized in various ways. The constraints of space and lack of data do not permit us to focus on all the important social institutions and processes. Therefore the discussion is confined to the impact on two major social classes--workers and entrepreneurs. In addition, we discuss their effects on ethnic stratification and economic inequalities.

Social Classes

A social class can be defined as an aggregation of persons who occupy similar positions with regard to economic roles. Broadly speaking, there are four important classes--the peasantry, a land-owning class which consists of absentee landlords and renters, workers, and entrepreneurs--in a less-developed society. All these classes can be affected by TNEs, in one way or the other.

However, the effects of TNEs on peasantry and land-owning classes are not discussed here, for there is little social science literature on the subject. Historically, by investing in extractive and agricultural sectors, TNEs have led to the transformation of peasantry into wage-earners in enclave economies. For example, Kabala M. K. K. Kabunda has shown that Unilever disrupted the existing social systems and contributed to the proletariatization of the peasantry in several regions of Zaire.[11] TNEs also attract peasants to urban areas in search of employment. Thus, they might be indirectly responsible for the peasants becoming wage earners (in case they are able to secure employment) or joining the ranks of the uprooted, unemployed labor force in the industrial centers of developing nations.

TNEs also dislodge landowners or enter into alliance with them by purchasing or leasing lands for their operations. Little is known about the long-term consequences of such transactions. However, in the literature on colonialism there are pointed references to the role of foreign investors who with the cooperation of colonial authorities established working alliances with the land-owning classes. Some scholars have also suggested that the economic integration of Latin American nations in the world economy during the nineteenth century brought significant transformations in their agrarian social structures. Thus, Cockcroft *et al.* attribute the growth of the *latifundista* system in Mexico with European and North American countries.[12] However, whatever might have been their role in the past, TNEs do not seem to have a significant impact on peasantry and land-owning classes in most of the developing nations. The overall investment by TNEs in extractive and agricultural sectors in these countries has been decreasing in recent years. In fact, more and more host governments are not enthusiastic about it. As a result, their direct impact on the above-mentioned classes is more a matter of intellectual curiosity rather than an immediate concern to policy makers.

Working class. The concept of the working class, as used here, refers to that segment of the population which is employed as wage earners in extractive, manufacturing, agricultural, or service sectors of the economy.

The contribution of TNEs to the growth of the working class is both direct and indirect. TNEs employ skilled and unskilled workers in their subsidiaries. More importantly, depending upon their integration in local economies, they have backward and forward linkages which create additional jobs. It has been estimated that about two million people are directly employed by TNEs in developing nations.[13]

Despite significant investments in extractive industries in developing nations, TNEs create limited job opportunities in this sector which has become highly capital-intensive in recent years. Technological developments over the last three decades have been responsible for a higher capital-labor ratio with the result that employment in some extractive industries has actually fallen in many countries. Taking 1970 as a base year for his computations, C. V. Vaitos found that employment in the tin industry in Malaysia declined from 100 in 1965 to 84 in 1973 and in Chile (for all extractive industries) from 140.6 in 1964 to 98 in 1973.[14] The same pattern is discerned in Gabon and Venezuela. Although the high manpower outlay required during the early stages partly explains this decline in employment, the main cause remains the increasing technological sophistication irrespective of the national or transnational nature of the enterprise.

In contrast, since the late fifties, there has been a continual rise in employment in manufacturing TNEs. During the import substitution phase, a growing number of TNEs established their subsidiaries in developing nations, creating additional employment. Thus, the employment in United States manufacturing TNEs increased "between 1966 and 1970--an average of 8.3 percent yearly (more than the total growth in employment in the manufacturing sector during the same period) and about 4 percent for all developing nations."[15] Data from Korea indicates that "between 1970 and 1973, the share of employment by foreign corporations increased from 3 to 11 percent."[16]

Mention must be made in this connection of the export processing zones (EPZs) which have been specifically designed to create job opportunities in developing nations. Because of higher wages in industrialized and relatively low labor costs in developing nations, TNEs have established their subsidiaries in the latter for assembling components imported from parent and sister firms. Most of the finished products are exported to the markets of origin. Several Latin American and Asian nations have offered special concessions for such operations which generally focus on electronic, garment, leather, toys, and similar labor-intensive indus- tries. Although the earlier expectations have not fully materialized, TNEs have generated signif- icant employment opportunities. It is estimated that in Malaysia (Penang area only), South Korea, and Taiwan, about 19, 22, and 64 thousand persons were employed in EPZs in the mid-seventies.[17] In other countries, such as India, the Philippines, and Indonesia, their impact on employment has so far been marginal.

The indirect effects of TNEs on the growth of the working class cannot be ignored either. Most TNEs use raw materials, semi-finished products, transport, and other services as inputs for their production activities. While some of these inputs are imported from abroad, others are procured from the local markets. With the increasing sophistication of the economies of developing nations, more and more inputs are locally available. Moreover, it is often cheaper for TNEs to use local rather than imported inputs. The host governments are also putting pressures on TNEs for utilizing local materials and facilities. Thus, TNEs indirectly generate employment in industries whose output they use. Besides, the

products and services produced by TNEs also enter
as inputs in other sectors of the economy. To
the extent they facilitate the growth of other
industries, they are also responsible for the
generation of additional employment. In addition,
the rents, wages, commissions, interests, taxes,
and dividends (in the case of joint ventures)
paid by TNEs have some multiplier effects on the
economy. Often indirect effects are even more
significant than the direct ones.

It may be stressed here that while TNEs
invariably create employment opportunities, it does
not necessarily follow that employment would not
have been created in their absence. In many cases,
TNEs have established their subsidiaries by buying
local enterprises. Moreover, it is quite possible
that the local entrepreneur might have established
similar production facilities to those which the
TNEs created.

A wider perspective is necessary for
examining the contribution of TNEs to employment
generation. None can dispute the fact that they
have created employment and what is more, have
great potential. However, when one views this
volume of employment against the unemployment
problem faced by developing nations, their record
does not seem so impressive. Even when we compare
their performance in the manufacturing sector
alone, we find that only 10 percent of the labor
force is employed by TNEs in countries like Brazil
and Mexico.[18] In countries like India, Indonesia,
and even the Philippines, which have significant
investment by TNEs, their overall contribution is
marginal. Only in a few countries such as
Hong Kong, Malaysia, Singapore, and Taiwan, have
TNEs accounted for about 40 percent of the labor
force employed in the manufacturing sector. The
actual percentage varies from 31 percent in
Malaysia[19] to 44.3 in Singapore.[20]

Thus, barring a few cases, the overall direct
and indirect effects of TNEs on the growth of the
labor force in developing nations are not very
significant: only a small segment of the working
population are employed by them.

The available evidence, though fragmentary,
unmistakably indicates that TNEs as a rule provide
higher wages than national enterprises in developing
nations. Their wages are high for all categories
of workers--blue collar and white collar as well as
management personnel. Grant L. Reuber's study of
direct foreign investment shows that TNEs claim to

follow a high wage policy in Asian, Latin
American, and African countries.[21] The most
comprehensive study of the wage policy has been
made by the International Labor Office (ILO)
which concludes: "In LDCs [less-developed
countries], the average level of earnings of
employees in multinational enterprises far exceeds
those of their counterparts in all national
firms. This gap is much larger than is found for
developed countries (in most cases being above 50
percent) and appears to be related to the stage of
economic development."[22]

Wage differentials between national enterprises (NEs) and TNEs are the result of several
factors: first, TNEs are concentrated in the most
modernized sector of the economy of developing
nations. Since they use more sophisticated
technology, it is reasonable to assume that they
employ a larger percentage of skilled and semi-
skilled manpower than NEs, which is responsible for
their high wage bills. Second, the profit margin
of TNEs is generally larger than those of NEs,
partly because of the economies of scale and
mainly because of their semi-monopolistic position.
NEs in developing countries are often small firms
carrying out a wide range of production activities
with little capital investment. Third, TNEs have
been known to establish their subsidiaries near
metropolitan areas where wages are relatively
high.

The fact that TNEs pay better wages has led
some scholars to suggest they contribute to the
emergence of a labor aristocracy. Historically
the concept of a labor aristocracy has been used to
explain the lack of revolutionary potential among
the working class in metropolitan nations. It is
based on the celebrated thesis of Lenin that
imperialist exploitation creates the economic
possibility for corrupting a segment of workers
who share in the "spoilage of imperialism."
When applied to developing nations, the thesis
implies that the operations of TNEs create a
privileged sub-class of the working populace, which
is linked to and dependent on the transnationalized
economy. Giovanni Arrighi argues that management
practices and technology introduced by TNEs have
led to the creation of a small, semi-skilled but
highly productive and well-paid labor elite in
tropical Africa, which has a general shortage of
skilled manpower.[23] Osvaldo Sunkel suggests that
the labor force engaged in the transnational sector

occupies a privileged position in Latin America.[24]
Richard L. Sklar mentions the special interest
group orientations of organized mine workers in
Zambia: "As Michael Burawoy says, the Zambian
mine workers are 'a labor elite' or 'aristocracy'....The special interest orientation of
organized mine workers within the Zambian
nationalist movement is a well-documented historical
fact. Recently, Burawoy and others have shown
that the ruling party elicits far less enthusiasm
from mine workers than from other, less-advantaged
sections of the proletariat."[25]

The implicit assumption of the above
formulation is that the elite working class develops
an interest in maintaining the *status quo*, since
it is beneficial to it or is, at least, perceived
to be such. While there are occasions for
tensions and conflicts between the elite labor
force and TNEs, these relate to marginal issues
rather than to the structural transformation of
the economy. A segment of the labor-elites
perceives the opportunities for upward mobility
in the system, and even begins to identify itself
with the lower-middle classes, instead of its
counterparts in NEs. Thus, the working class is
fragmented and loses its revolutionary potential.

In the absence of any empirical data about
the orientations of workers employed in TNEs, the
whole thesis looks highly speculative. Only the
empirical research about the differences in the
attitudes, perceptions, and behavior of workers
employed in national and transnational firms can
substantiate or refute it. However, two points
can be made in this connection. First, past
experience does not necessarily show that the
workers in TNEs have always sided with TNEs
whenever the latter have come into conflict with the
national government. Often, these workers have
demanded outright nationalization of TNEs. A good
example is provided by the nationalization of
companies in the extractive sector. By and large,
both white and blue collar workers have supported
the moves for nationalization. Whenever the
muted voices of protest have come in these countries, they have come from the management and
technical personnel. Giovanni Arrighi is aware
of this fact and has conceded that the labor
aristocracy might not be opposed to state ownership
and management of the means of production.[26]
Second, the very notion of a revolutionary potential
of the working class springing from their class

consciousness represents more an article of faith
than an empirically observable phenomenon in
developing nations. Workers are highly fragmented
in these nations; ethnic, cultural, political,
and sectoral cleavages and conflicts rather than
wage differentials may then appear to be posing
barriers to their mobilization, assuming that such
a mobilization is possible. Under these circumstances, the notion of labor aristocracy seems
to have limited analytical value, if any.

Closely related to the above thesis is that
of the docility of the working class. There is
substance to the hypothesis that sometimes TNEs
exert pressure on the governments of host
developing nations for following "labor repressive"
policies. Often, though not always, such a
pressure is unintended and is inherent in the
present international situation in which developing
nations compete with one another for attracting
foreign investment.

The governments of these countries are
undoubtedly sensitive to the fact that one of the
main considerations in TNEs' decisions about overseas expansion, is the availability of a docile,
disciplined working force. As a result, they are
tempted to "tame" their working class by curbing
trade unions and other activities, which might be
construed as "unfavorable" by TNEs. Some partial
confirmation of this hypothesis is provided by the
advertisements placed by several Latin American
and Asian nations in well-known business magazines
stressing the proverbial docility of their workers.
Otto Kreye has mentioned that one form of major
political incentive provided by the host developing
nations is "restrictions on and/or suspension of
the political and social rights of the labor force
that work in the export processing zones. This
means the suspension of applicability of the
labor laws that are otherwise observed in the
countries, the elimination of the minimum wage
laws, the exemption for the firms from payments
to social security, and the limitation of trade
union rights."[27]

Louis W. Goodman has pointed out that "in
extreme cases, corporations have demanded
guarantees of police action against the formation
of unions or the arrest of principal union
militants as preconditions for establishing a
plant in a host country."[28] Such direct pressure
is generally not favored by most of the TNEs for
diplomatic and humanitarian reasons.

Chomsky and Herman have alluded to the fact that countries such as Brazil, Chile, Dominican Republic, the Philippines, South Korea, Thailand, and Uruguay, which have received substantial United States aid and direct investment, follow "labor repressive policies."[29] They imply a direct causal relationship between foreign investment and labor repressive policies. Such a generalization is unwarranted, for the problem remains of determining which is the cause and which is the effect: whether these countries followed such policies because they desperately wanted TNEs' investment, or TNEs invested because these nations were following certain policies.

It is indeed an oversimplification to attribute the anti-labor policies of several developing nations to the presence of TNEs. Obviously, many of them adopt such policies not because of the pressures from TNEs but out of their own ideological and political commitments. The ruling elites in these countries often represent the dominant social and economic strata and are therefore apprehensive about labor movements and trade union activities. A section of them see in trade union activities the seeds of an economic and political revolution which will undermine the present order. A majority of them also believe that the only way in which their underdeveloped economies can make strides towards industrialization is through the accumulation of surplus by hard work and subsistence standards of living.

Thus, the validity of the thesis of labor docility seems questionable to us. While some TNEs undoubtedly prefer curbs on the political and trade union activities of their employees, others also realize that the best way to ensure industrial peace is not through coercion but by satisfying the economic needs of their employees and providing them suitable channels for expressing their grievances. It would not be out of place to mention that practically all expatriate managers of the U.S. subsidiaries the author interviewed in Asia showed a preference for a single united union with whom the company could bargain. They regarded unions as contributing to industrial peace. The indigenous executives were often the ones who expressed reservations about union activities. As the number of executives the author interviewed was small, no firm conclusions are warranted from his informal interviews. More empirical research

is therefore required before any generalization can
be made in this connection.

Entrepreneurial class. The concept of
entrepreneurs as used here refers to persons who
own, control, and manage means of production and
employ them for gainful economic activity. In
classical economic analysis, they are the leaders
who transform a tradition-bound agrarian order
into a prosperous industrial system. It is therefore necessary to briefly examine the effects of
TNEs on entrepreneurs in developing nations. We
primarily focus on two interrelated issues:
(a) growth--whether TNEs promote or inhibit the
growth of local entrepreneurial classes, and
(b) autonomy--whether the local entrepreneurs in
an economic system having considerable foreign
investment can exercise autonomy or remain
dependent on TNEs.

It has often been argued that the growth of a
local entrepreneurial class can be inhibited by
TNEs in several ways. The most obvious is that the
developing nation's entrepreneurs find it difficult,
though not impossible, to compete with them. TNEs
possess enormous technological resources and are
in a position to introduce new production technologies and products more rapidly and economically
than NEs. Even when they do not introduce a new
product, they are able to create an illusion
of innovation by efficient advertising. Besides,
since they can raise resources--nationally and
internationally--TNEs do not suffer from the
shortage of capital. In contrast, local
entrepreneurs generally find it difficult to
solicit loans from international banking
institutions. Nor are they in a position to take
risks. TNEs also have the advantage of familiar
brands, trademarks, and patents. Before they
establish a manufacturing subsidiary, their
products are well-known to the potential consumers.
The local entrepreneurs, on the other hand, have
no such visibility and do not have access to
assured markets. They are further hampered by the
fact that consumers in developing nations prefer
foreign brands over the domestic ones. Thus, the
cumulative effect is that, as a result of the
operations of TNEs, the position of the local
entrepreneur is constantly undermined and potential
competitors are discouraged.

Available evidence, though not entirely

reliable, indicates that the growth of TNEs in a
sector is marked by the decline of small, local, or
family enterprises.[30] Claes Brundenius has shown
that the domination of the mining sector by TNEs in
Peru has inhibited local entrepreneurs.[31]
According to him, the national entrepreneur has
been confronted by two unpalatable choices: to
collaborate with TNEs or face extinction by being
outcompeted. Franklin B. Weinstein observes that
Japanese joint ventures in the textile industry
have been responsible for the closure of a large
number of indigenous firms in Indonesia.[32]

It should be mentioned here that these
inhibiting effects are confined to sectors in which
there is a scope for competition between TNEs and
NEs. These do not necessarily occur in the other
sectors of the economy. However, there are some
undesirable effects on entrepreneurs in other
sectors which cannot be ignored.

Most of the developing nations have undergone
a period of foreign subjugation which has shaped
their self-images and identities and has created
a widespread feeling of inferiority and
inadequacy. The people have been socialized to
look at outsiders for guidance and support. In the
post-colonial era, the labels of "underdeveloped,"
"traditional," or "developing" which have been
indiscriminately applied to these nations have
hardly helped to improve their self-images.
Under these conditions, the widespread operations
of TNEs can tend to nourish the prevalent feelings
of inferiority and inadequacy instead of eradicating
them. Potential entrepreneurs, then, are
discouraged because they tend to assume that they
cannot be as "efficient," "innovative," or
"successful" as the foreigners are.

Finally, some social scientists have suggested
that TNEs, by virtue of their being "outsiders,"
are not in a position to remove or control the
prevalent institutional impediments to entrepreneurial behavior. They cannot press for the
necessary reforms. As Albert O. Hirschman has
pointed out: "The trouble with the foreign investor
may well be not that he is so meddlesome but that he
is so mousy! It is the foreign investor's mousiness
which deprives the policy makers of the guidance,
pressures, and support they badly need to push
through critically required decisions and policies
amid a welter of conflicting and antagonistic
interests."[33]

On the other hand, there are both logical and empirical grounds for hypothesizing positive effects of TNEs on entrepreneurship. TNEs have backward, forward, and lateral linkages with the economy, though their volume and extent differ in time and place. TNEs therefore create new entrepreneurs by generating demands for those goods and services which are used as inputs by them. Whenever they award subcontracts or purchase raw materials, TNEs tend to provide necessary training and incentives. These contractors and producers gradually gain expertise and confidence and begin to move to other sectors of the economy as well. Moreover, the goods and services produced by TNEs enter as inputs in other industries. TNEs' involvement in steel, chemicals, heavy machinery and tools, electronics, etc. have opened new opportunities for local entrepreneurs in several sectors. TNEs also create new national and international markets for local products. A good example in this connection has been provided by Sears when it opened its department stores in Mexico. As Werner Feld has mentioned, Sears created fresh national and international demand for local products. This led to the establishment of several new plants to meet the demand.[34]

TNEs directly or indirectly provide skills that are necessary for entrepreneurial behavior. They train their employees in management, marketing, public relations, production processes, and related skills. Taking advantage of their training and experience, some employees establish their own businesses or move to other firms. In addition, the mere presence of TNEs can have some favorable psychological effects as it makes people aware of modern management techniques and production skills.

In the past, foreign direct investment has contributed to the growth of entrepreneurs in several countries. A. I. Levkovsky has argued, though not very convincingly, that British capital in India was responsible for the rise of the Indian bourgeoisie.[35] While the British rule destroyed the artisan class which catered to the needs of the large urban centers in the early part of the nineteenth century, it led to the emergence of small and medium-size entrepreneurs whose interests were tied to foreign capital.

Raymond Vernon has mentioned that the Mexican mining and railway building boom in the nineteenth

century helped to establish a new entrepreneurial
class composed of traders, bankers, provisioners,
contractors, and small manufacturers.[36] He has
also suggested that the Peruvian boom of the
nineteenth century "though centered on some
isolated off-shore islands in the Pacific was
responsible for bringing a local contractor industry
into existence on the mainland--an industry which
lived off the public works that the guano boom
financed."[37] Case studies of several Asian and
Pacific nations also show that the influx of
foreign capital led to the creation of petty
entrepreneurs in the early part of the twentieth
century.

Udom Kerdpibule concluded in his study of the
effects of joint ventures that they "are positively
helping the formation of local entrepreneurship.
The experience of Thailand with multinational
corporations and the foreign-based companies so
far has been a reasonably good one for the formation
of local entrepreneurship."[38]

Some of the success stories of economic
growth in recent years come from nations which
registered considerable investment by TNEs.
Brazil, Hong Kong, Malaysia, South Korea, and
Taiwan provide good illustrations. In all these
countries, an entrepreneurial class has simultaneously grown with the increase in foreign investment. In fact, there seems to be a positive
correlation between the two. While these cases
do not prove any causal relationship, they do
point to the conclusion that TNEs have not unduly
inhibited local entrepreneurs.

In our views, the overall impact of TNEs on
local entrepreneurs depends upon factors such as the
level of industrialization of the host nation, the
sectors of the economy in which TNEs operate, and
the policies of the government. Perhaps it can
be argued that while in a traditional society
their impact is generally positive, TNEs can
inhibit the potential of entrepreneurs in a
country which has already made some progress
towards industrialization. Moreover, their effects
can differ from sector to sector depending on the
nature of their integration within the economy.
In extractive sectors or export processing zones,
which have few backward or forward linkages, the
positive effects are likely to be marginal. The
case of manufacturing firms, however, can be
altogether different. Manufacturing subsidiaries,

especially when they utilize local inputs, can help to promote local entrepreneurs.

However, the most significant factor is the role of government. The local entrepreneurs in developing nations need special protection and support for effectively competing with TNEs in established or new industries. Therefore, the policies of the government can promote or hamper the growth of local entrepreneurs. If it fails to protect them at an early stage, their growth can be slanted. On the other hand, if it bestows excessive protection and squeezes TNEs away, the country can be deprived of the economic benefits of direct foreign investment.

Another issue, which is basically related to the first, concerns the autonomy of entrepreneurs. *Dependencia* theorists have stressed that because of the operations of TNEs, the entrepreneurial classes which are emerging in developing nations are not independent but dependent. They lack the autonomy to play a critical role in the industrialization process--a role which has been played by entrepreneurs in West European and North American nations. Various labels such as *"lumpen-bourgeoisie,"* "compradore" classes, or "client classes" have been used to indicate the dependent status of local entrepreneurs.[39]

These social scientists are aware that the dependent status of local entrepreneurs is not necessarily the result of Machiavellian manipulations of TNEs or of the military and political power of their home countries. Rather, it is inherent in the present situation in which local entrepreneurs derive tangible benefits from their alliance with TNEs. As Dale L. Johnson points out, in Latin America "the new urban based oligarchies and national bourgeoisie, though essentially dependent, even client or compradore classes, profit from the structure of the international system and from their close financial and political relations with multinational corporations and those who hold power internationally."[40]

In the absence of comparative historical data, it is indeed difficult to make any valid generalization in this connection. However, the thesis cannot be taken at its face value. As mentioned earlier, there are several factors which condition the overall effects of TNEs on the local entrepreneurship--and these could possibly be also examined in this connection. Besides, the role

of surging economic nationalism should not be
underestimated in shaping the ideological
orientations of entrepreneurs in developing
nations.[41]

There is little doubt that during the initial
phase of industrialization pioneered by foreign
capital, the local entrepreneurs are highly
dependent on TNEs. The question then is whether
they are able to transform this relationship in
their favor with the passing of time.

Raymond Vernon has argued that the dependent
status of local entrepreneurs in developing
nations has drastically changed during the last
three decades. According to him, up to the
second world war the local businessmen in Latin
America, Asia, and North Africa largely served as
"adjuncts and partners of foreign entrepreneurs."[42]
The second world war, Raymond Vernon suggests,
was a turning point. It made local entrepreneurs
in several developing nations self-reliant by
cutting off their overseas sources of supply of
foreign markets. Since then, the local entrepreneurs have started asserting their independence.

At the end of the second world war,
Raymond Vernon notes, "selected sons of business
elites were sent off to the advanced countries to
study law, economics, engineering, or business;
and when they returned, their strivings for
autonomy seemed stronger than those of their
fathers. In a number of countries--including
notably Brazil, Mexico, India, Colombia, and
Algeria--the distributors and purveyors for the
foreign sector began turning to production and
distribution of their own. Of course, many of the
old partnerships with foreigners persisted, and
many new ones were created. But, on the whole,
one could see the emergence of a new breed of
tough local entrepreneurs prepared to make
partnerships or do battle with foreign enterprises
as their interests demanded."[43]

While one may not fully concur with
Raymond Vernon's analysis, he does bring to the
fore a basic sociological insight: as a country
treads the path of industrialization, its
entrepreneurial class undergoes a process of
differentiation. New cleavages and conflicts arise
within it. A section of it undoubtedly remains
allied to TNEs--and often in a junior position. It
generally consists of entrepreneurs who collaborate
with TNEs in the sectors requiring sophisticated
technology, huge capital investments, or access to

foreign markets. Some others seek to improve their position by challenging the domination of TNEs in the sectors in which technology has already been standardized. In several sectors such as banking, mining, and petroleum, the local entrepreneurs have more or less succeeded in dislodging TNEs. Still others remain unaffected by the operations of TNEs and are therefore indifferent towards them. Thus, the interests of all entrepreneurs are not identical. Nor do all of them remain in a dependent status. Even those who are allied to TNEs constantly try to improve their bargaining position.

One unmistakable lesson of the recent revolution in Iran, which successfully overthrew what once appeared to be an invincible monarchy, is that the local bourgeoisie in developing nations is neither too dependent upon outside economic interests to lose its identity nor too timid to challenge the political authority which it perceives to be favorably disposed towards foreign capital. In the case of Iran, the conspicuous presence of and widespread penetration by TNEs in almost every important sector of the economy caused anxieties and hostilities not only among *bazzaries* (national bourgeoisie) but also among the *mullahs* (clergy) and the secular intelligentsia. In fact, it was the alliance of these three groups which undermined the legitimacy and authority of the Shah's regime in the country. It is interesting to note that throughout the revolutionary struggle, the Shah of Iran was portrayed as an agent of foreign imperialism which was sacrificing vital economic interests. We are not concerned here about the validity of the charge but with the fact that the Iranian bourgeoisie, despite its linkages with TNEs, tried to assert its autonomy from foreign domination and did succeed in this attempt.

There are already signs on the horizon indicating that the balance is likely to tilt further in favor of local entrepreneurs. Increasingly, more and more developing nations are demanding greater equity participation in the subsidiaries established by TNEs. Often their contracts stipulate that within a fixed time, management and even majority ownership of the subsidiaries should pass on to the local partners. Moreover, the areas in which TNEs can operate are now being precisely demarcated. Measures like these will undoubtedly further enhance the

position of local entrepreneurs vis-a-vis TNEs.
Their dependence is likely to be significantly
undermined, if not totally removed.

Thus, we find that the operations of TNEs
have some effects on the two social classes
discussed above, i.e., the working class and the
entrepreneurial class. We now briefly examine
their impact on social inequalities.

Social Inequalities

The phenomena of inequality can be
conceptualized in different ways. We shall,
however, focus on two aspects--ethnic stratification
and economic inequalities. The absence of
empirical data on the effects of TNEs on the system
of stratification--differentiation, ranking,
evaluation, and reward--in developing nations
makes any sophisticated discussion of the subject
next to impossible.

Ethnic stratification. Developing nations are
often faced with the problem of ethnic stratifica-
tion--a situation in which one or more ethnic
groups have come to occupy a dominant position in
social, economic, or political affairs. Thus, the
question can be posed: how does the presence of
TNEs affect the existing ethnic stratification?
Do they contribute to the maintenance of existing
ethnic boundaries, and even consolidate them?
Or, do they provide opportunities to deprived
groups for upward mobility?

TNEs generally do not have a corporate policy
on this issue. Their primary interest lies in the
maximization of economic gains with the least
possible risk involved. As economic bureaucracies,
they are neither for nor against any ethnic
group (which, of course, does not mean that their
executives in host nations are free from ethnic
prejudices and stereotypes). What can be safely
suggested is that given adequate opportunities, the
same TNEs can effectively operate in South Africa
(where its policies will discriminate against
nonwhite ethnic groups) as well as in Uganda
(where the main benefit of its investment might
accrue to black ethnic groups). After all, most
TNEs do not perceive themselves as crusaders for
social or ethnic equality.

There is the possibility that under some
situations (such as when some ethnic groups in
host nations have close ties with the ethnic

groups of home countries), TNEs are under pressure
to favor specific ethnic groups. Several
examples can be given. The British TNEs have
largely depended upon English expatriates for
fulfilling middle and senior range positions in
the former colonies. Empirical investigation has
shown that Japanese firms in Hawaii have
demonstrated a marked preference for hiring
Japanese-Americans.[44] Chinese firms in ASEAN
countries are generally accused of hiring and
collaborating with people of Chinese ancestry.
Such cases are not uncommon. However, with a trend
towards the indigenization of management and
personnel, and a growing sensitivity for ethnic
tensions, only a few TNEs are likely to follow
such policies in the near future.

TNEs impact on ethnic stratification stems
not from conscious, deliberate policy, but from
a set of structural constraints which are imposed
on them. TNEs need employees and collaborators
who have economic resources, technical and entrepreneurial skills, and if possible, access to
bureaucratic and political leadership in the
government. In situations where an ethnic group
has monopolistic or quasi-monopolistic position
with regard to these factors, they have little
option other than depending on them. Under
these circumstances, this ethnic group is likely
to be the main beneficiary of direct foreign
investment and might even be able to consolidate
and improve its position.

Malaysia provides a good illustration in
this regard. In this country, TNEs have largely
entered into collaborative arrangements with
local Chinese firms. Moreover, in these
subsidiaries, the percentage of Chines employees
as compared to Malays is higher in technical and
management positions. The explanation is not that
TNEs like Chinese better than Malays or Indians,
but that Chinese have in the past owned retail
outlets and distribution networks in Malaysia.
Therefore, when TNEs begin establishing their
manufacturing plants, they form alliances with the
existing Chinese firms. Moreover, since the
Chinese have come to acquire entrepreneurial and
technical skills because of their preeminent
position in the economic affairs of the country,
they are in a position to capitalize on the job
opportunities offered by TNEs. Similar situations,
though on a smaller scale, exist in Indonesia.
Perhaps only governmental intervention, as

exemplified by the "Bhumiputra" policies in
Malaysia, can establish a more balanced situation in
these nations.

The presence of TNEs can have both stabilizing
and destabilizing effects on ethnic boundaries.
This is evident from the case of South Africa,
where TNEs have generally followed, though
perhaps reluctantly, the apartheid policies of the
government.[45] Some of them have not even hesitated
from exerting pressures on home countries for not
supporting "economic sanctions" against South
Africa. By all accounts, the huge investments
made by TNEs in South Africa have contributed to
its growing economic power and political
stability. However, while the main benefits
accrued to the white minority, it is wrong to infer
that Blacks and Asians did not derive any benefits.
In fact, TNEs have contributed, to a small extent,
to the emergence of nonwhite middle classes in
South Africa.[46]

In the face of mounting public pressure and
the growing power of Black nations in South
Africa, some TNEs are now formulating non-
discriminatory policies toward Blacks and Asians.
They recently signed a code of fair employment
practices, which commits them to eradicating racial
discrimination.[47] About 98 TNEs have been signatories to this code, and "task forces--one for each
point--are meeting regularly to compare notes
and develop new approaches."[48]

It is too early to evaluate the impact of this
code on ethnic stratification. It is by no
account a revolutionary attempt, however, it has
put some pressure on the administrative staffs of
the subsidiaries. The local managers of the U.S.
TNEs, Herman Nickel points out, "have to
address themselves seriously to each of the six
principles, report back to the home office what
they have been doing, and spell out concrete
objectives for the future. The result has been to
inspire a new kind of corporate competition."[49]

Thus, TNEs are showing some defiance to the
apartheid policies, which can hardly be
demonstrated by national firms in South Africa.

It should be pointed out here that past
history shows that when plural societies make
rapid economic advancement (even without foreign
investment), the resulting benefits are not
always evenly shared by all the existing ethnic
groups. Some, decidedly, profit more than others.
Therefore, while the effects of TNEs on ethnic

relationships cannot be ignored, it is quite likely
that they may not be different from those of NEs
in most cases.

Economic inequalities. There now exists a
widespread concern for increasing economic
inequalities in developing nations. Gini index (a
measure of economic disparities) data, whatever
its reliability, unmistakably indicates that
economic disparities, instead of being bridged, have
actually increased over the last decade in most of
the developing nations. The benefits of economic
growth registered in many nations have not reached
the needy segments of the population. It is sometimes suggested that the TNEs should also share
the blame for the present state of affairs. A
recent study undertaken by Bornschier *et al*. notes:
"The effect of direct foreign investment and
foreign aid has been to increase economic inequality
within countries. This effect holds for income
inequality, land inequality, and sectoral income
inequality."[50]
There are some ways in which the presence of
TNEs could contribute to economic disparities.
First, it has been mentioned that because TNEs
pay higher wages, they indirectly promote economic
disparities. As suggested earlier, the wages for
all the categories of employees--blue collar,
white collar, and professional--are higher in TNEs
as compared to NEs. The argument, despite its
intuitive appeal, is not very convincing. Wage
differentials between TNEs and NEs are not as
significant as to make a critical difference in the
existing economic system. Moreover, by no stretch
of the imagination are employees of TNEs
regarded as the most affluent strata of developing
nations. They constitute the lower, middle, and
upper middle stratas of the societies: they
are not the owners but the wage-earners.
Second, some social scientists have pointed
out that whenever TNEs have entered into
collaborative arrangements, they have strengthened
the position of dominant economic and political
groups. By Mamoru Tsuda has shown that well-known
Filipino business groups and figures are the
major beneficiaries of the direct foreign investment in the Philippines.[51] With the active support
of the government, they have made collaborative
arrangements with Japanese TNEs and have enriched
themselves. Still, in other countries, local
military or political officials have made

partnership in the joint ventures established by
TNEs and have amassed wealth in addition to
political power. Such an alliance has made the
existing economic stratification more rigid and
has blocked the channels of social mobility.

Third, the presence of TNEs can aggravate
regional economic imbalances in developing nations.
While NEs and TNEs are likely to determine the
location of their plants on the basis of more or
less similar criteria, past experience has shown
that TNEs prefer metropolitan sites, where an
economic infrastructure already exists.
Franklin B. Weinstein has reported that within the
Southeast Asian countries (with the exception of
Singapore) "the concentration of foreign enterprises near the chief metropolitan centers has
accentuated the disparity between rural and urban
areas."[52]

Sometimes, TNEs are also instrumental in
creating enclaves of prosperity amidst poverty,
especially in extractive and agricultural sectors.
The relative affluence of the employees and petty
entrepreneurs who flourish around such enclaves
offer a sharp contrast to the overall poverty
of the surrounding areas.

Finally, TNEs' effects on the consumption
patterns and life styles cannot be ignored in this
connection. TNEs produce a large range of
consumer items such as electronics, cosmetics,
soft drinks, canned foods, and cars, which are
within the reach of the majority of the populace
in the industrialized world. However, in developing
nations, because of the low income levels of the
masses and the skewed nature of income distribution,
only a small proportion are able to purchase them.
This sharpens the gulf between the standard of
living of the higher and lower income groups.
It makes economic disparities more conspicuous
and thus creates relative deprivation in the minds
of the deprived.

It should be recognized that the existing
disparities in a country can be aggravated by the
presence of TNEs even when those who occupy lower
positions in the stratification are not directly
affected by them. The mere fact that the income
levels of the higher strata rise when there is no
significant improvement in the earnings of the
poor segments can worsen the situation.

However, TNEs are not always contributors to
economic inequality. They have been quite
successful in operating in socialistic economies.

Not only East European nations but also countries such as China and Vietnam are at present greedily courting them. In such countries, the operations of TNEs are not likely to further disparities of wealth. Moreover, TNEs have formed joint ventures with the state-controlled sectors in developing nations, especially in extractive and heavy industries. Under these situations, it is governments rather than TNEs which shape the policies and output of the enterprise. In addition, suitable measures can be taken about the location of plants, wages and salaries paid to employees, and the nature of products produced, which can control the effects of TNEs in increasing economic disparities even in a free economy.

We have discussed above some of the TNE's effects on two social classes, namely entrepreneurs and workers, and social stratification. However, there remain several other institutions and groups, such as family, national elites, and civilian bureaucracies which can also be affected by the presence of TNEs in the host country.

IMPACT ON CULTURE

Despite the enormous literature (or perhaps because of it), culture remains an imprecise construct. For our own purposes, we have defined it with reference to the symbolic and expressive dimensions of a society. Culture in this sense refers to the prevailing values, ideologies, beliefs, knowledge, language, arts, literature, and the like. All these elements of a cultural system can be directly or indirectly affected by TNEs in host nations. However, we confine ourselves here to their effects on (a) consumption patterns and values, (b) knowledge and skills, and (c) cultural identity.

Consumption Patterns and Values

We make a distinction here between consumption patterns and a consumption-oriented value-system. The former refers to the habitual use of some products and services, while the latter to the emergence of a value system which evaluates individual and group life on the basis of the volume and quality of goods and services consumed. The two are interrelated but not one and the same. The construct of the consumption-oriented value-system indicates the standard for judging the individual and group life and not the consumption of specific items. We therefore discuss them separately.

TNEs generally introduce new products and product innovations in industrialized nations where they have large markets and effective sales organizations. The early consumers often come from the upper socioeconomic strata, for they are in a position to take the necessary risks. Others prefer to wait. However, once the product proves successful with the early consumers, the whole scene changes. People with low income levels start using it. It is at this stage that a firm often decides to manufacture the item in other nations. Since it has been producing it for some time, technical problems in the new environment are perceived to be minimal. Moreover, by this time, a section of potential consumers is also familiar with the product which they might be importing. In host nations, the early pattern of adoption repeats itself. The upper socioeconomic groups are the first users followed by middle and lower middle classes.

It is not out of place to note here that when the new product reaches the markets of host nations, especially those of developing countries, it often becomes out of date in home nations. The firm might introduce new refinements and differentiations if for no other reason than retaining its dominant position in the market. Other firms can come up with similar products which might be perceived more functional by consumers.

Thus, the point is that the products are developed by TNEs, not with reference to the needs of host nations, but to those of the home countries. The problem arises because the socio-economic milieu of developing nations is undoubtedly different from that of industrialized nations. Most of the people in the former live in utter poverty and penury; their elementary needs for food, clothing, and shelter remain unfulfilled. In all these countries, only a tiny minority can engage in the consumption of goods and gadgets which are commonly used in industrialized nations. Consequently, the social utility of the consumer products manufactured by TNEs remains doubtful.

Several studies can be mentioned here which illustrate the unsuitability of the consumer products of TNEs, not necessarily because of their intrinsic properties but because of the different socioeconomic contexts in which they are consumed. Robert J. Ledogar has presented some interesting data about soft drinks in Mexico and Brazil.[53] According to him, in Mexico where soft drink TNEs have successfully penetrated the market and now account for 75 percent of the output, per capita consumption of soft drinks comes up to 220 bottles a year. Thus, a person drinks about 4 bottles of soft drinks every week in a country where there is a shortage of protein and vitamins in the general diet. In the case of Brazil, a survey taken in 1973 by Anne Dias of the *Instituto de Nutrico*, has shown that soft drinks have become a regular part of the diet of children coming from rich and upper-middle classes, despite the fact that they suffer from vitamin deficiencies and show the symptoms of malnutrition.[54] Obviously, these children preferred soft drinks to natural juices or milk. Mexico and Brazil are not isolated examples. One discerns the same phenomena in most of the developing nations where soft drink TNEs operate. An ever-increasing number of people have learned to consume soft drinks at exhorbitant prices when inexpensive, nutritive, local drinks are available. Indeed, Coca Cola and Pepsi Cola are even regarded as status symbols.

Several TNEs produce baby foods and aggressively promote them as alternatives to breast feeding in developing nations. However, the majority of their customers are often too poor to purchase them in the required quantities. Nor do they possess adequate refrigeration facilities. The result is that bottle feeding has often contributed to malnutrition, leading to infant diseases and even mortality, especially among the poor. M. Müller has mentioned the case of West Africa where Nestlé was quite successful in persuading young mothers to rely on baby foods instead of breast feeding their newly born children.[55] Since the prices for baby foods were high, most of the mothers started diluting the milk to the point where it lacked adequate nutritive properties, causing infant mortality in many cases. In one of the most comprehensive studies in rural Chile, Plank and Milanesi noted that "the inverse relationship of the infant mortality rates to family income, environmental factors, and medical care, reinforce the

conclusion that the differential mortality
observed was attributable to bottle feeding and
neglect of supplementary food."[56] D. B. Jelliffe,
a nutrition expert, has used the expression
"commerciogenic malnutrition" to refer to the
starvation and death caused by the baby food
industry among the poor.[57] Many other scholars
have also stressed the harmful consequences of
bottle feeding promoted by the TNEs concerned
in developing nations.

Barnet and Müller have cited studies in
rural Mexico indicating that subsistence farmers
purchase white bread instead of their traditional
bread, which costs less and is at the same time
rich in protein.[58] Robert Girling has given the
example of the breakfast cereals in Jamaica,
where most of the people used to consume fish
and bananas for their breakfast, which were cheap
and plentiful. However, through advertising, the
idea has been sold that "breakfast cereals" are
better than the traditional foods, with the
result being that people now consume Kellogg's
products while "large quantities of bananas
spoil for want of markets."[59] Robert J. Ledogar
has documented the fact that pharmaceutical TNEs
in Latin America manufactured and marketed drugs
which were not considered safe in their home
nations.[60] Often the necessary warnings were
missing in the case of drugs which had significant
side effects.

The above discussion should not give the
impression that the consumer products manufactured
by TNEs are always of little intrinsic value or
are dysfunctional to the conditions of host
developing nations. This is hardly the case. In
many fields, despite shortcomings, TNEs have
made useful contributions to the welfare of the
people. Pharmaceutical firms, for example, have
undoubtedly helped these countries in their fight
against common diseases. They have been instrumental in making drugs locally available, which might
not have been otherwise possible. However, as the
U.N. Report points out: "Indeed, not enough has
been done by the multinational corporations
themselves or governments to channel corporate
production towards satisfying basic consumption
needs in nutrition, health, and housing."[61]

There is little incentive for TNEs to
manufacture products which satisfy the basic
physical needs of the majority. To them, it
remains more profitable to introduce products

which are well-known and for which they already
possess technical know-how rather than investing
in altogether different items which might be
more suitable to host nations. They know for
certain that if allowed to operate, they are
likely to create effective demand for their
product, whatever its utility. Therefore, it
is unrealistic to expect the Coca-Cola company
to develop a new drink utilizing local fruits
and sell it at a reasonable price, when it has
little difficulty in marketing Coca-Cola or other
drinks. Moreover, the fact remains that even if
TNEs make efforts to ivest in consumer foods
needed by the majority, it is questionable that
it will be a profitable exercise.

It has been pointed out that the TNEs not
only promote the consumption of certain goods and
services manufactured by them, but also help to
diffuse and reproduce the consumption-oriented
value-system of capitalistic economies. The
essence of this value system is that the
happiness, fulfillment, and development of an
individual or collectivity are measured in terms
of the quantity and quality of goods and
services consumed. Other things being equal, a
person who owns and consumes more goods and
gadgets is considered happier than the one who
possesses less of them. The countries with high
per capita consumption are "developed" while those
with low consumption are labeled as "underdeveloped." Thus, consumption becomes the measuring
rod, the standard for the evaluation of individual
and collective happiness.

The issue here is not the desirability of the
consumption-oriented value-system. The problem
which confronts us is how this value-system is
being produced and diffused in developing nations
and what is the role of TNEs in this regard, if
any. This is indeed a very intricate issue which
can hardly be discussed within the confines of a
few lines. However, at the risk of oversimplification, we would like to make two points.

The first concerns the modes of reproduction
and transmission of this value-system. In our
view, the most important role is to be assigned
to manufacturing technologies--imported or
indigenous. The fact remains that when consumer
goods are produced in a free economic system,
they create their own demands. People begin to
feel that they are desirable, if not indispensable.
For example, until television sets were invented,

people did not feel their need, but now they have
become common household items in industrialized
nations. In fact, the growth of a consumer-
oriented value-system in these nations has been
coterminous with the industrialization process.
Manufacturing technologies promoted it, and were
in turn, promoted by it. Besides technology,
transnational media--television, radio, news
agencies, books and magazines, and above all,
advertising--is also an important source of the
creation and diffusion of this value-system.

Secondly, one should not presume that the
developing nations in the past did not have
"subcultures" or social stratas, which subscribed
to this value-system. Most of these nations had
special groups, consisting of senior civil
servants, political elites, landlords, businessmen, and military officials, who engaged in
conspicuous consumption and relentlessly pursued
the quest for more and more materialistic goods.
The others were often too poor or too ignorant
to follow this course. The ideology of renun-
ciation, or self-imposed sacrifice, represented
more of a rationalization for their condition
than a guiding value-system.

The above two points should be considered
while examining the impact of TNEs on the growth
of a consumption-oriented value-system. Undoubtedly TNEs have some effects on the transnational
media as well as the nature and forms of technological transfers that take place. Therefore, there
is some justification for the premise that TNEs
directly or indirectly contribute to the inter-
nalization of the consumption-oriented value-
system. However, the effectiveness of their
impact remains an empirical question.

Knowledge and Skills

There is little data, much less empirical
studies, on the subject of the overall impact of
TNEs on the knowledge and skills of people in
developing nations. Consequently, the only course
open to us is to briefly discuss the ways in which
TNEs contribute to, or inhibit, the growth of
knowledge and skills in host nations.

TNEs widely recognize the need of extensive
training for their employees. Increasingly, they
are following the concept of treating manpower
development as an investment, that is, they
capitalize on training costs in the same fashion

as expenditures on plants and machinery. There
are, of course, significant variations among TNEs'
practices depending on the level of industrialization of the host nation, the sectors in which the
TNEs operate, the capital or labor utilized, the
intensive nature of the technology used and their
respective corporate and personnel policies.
However, it is safe to assume that the majority
of TNEs impart training to their employees and
that collectively their contribution is quite
significant. The OECD study conducted in 1967,
for example, noted that "of the 48 firms interviewed, 40 of them trained people from developing
countries at the home base in 1965. It may be
estimated that their total number of trainees
was at least 4,500 and may have been as high as
8,000."[62] The report concluded that "even allowing
for the fact that this survey includes several
of the biggest enterprises of the industrially
advanced countries, it may be safely assumed that
home-based training by private firms as a whole
substantially exceeded the amount of officially
(the governments of home countries) financed
training."[63] These figures do not include the
number of employees trained in developing nations
by TNEs, which is undoubtedly much higher.

From the host nation's point of view, what
is most critical is not the skills created within
the confines of a subsidiary, but their diffusion
to the wider society. In case the skills or
knowledge are used only within the specific TNEs,
the benefits to the host nation remain marginal
and other sectors of the economy are not benefited.
There are reasons to believe that this is the
situation. Dmitri Germidis notes that "empirical
studies, notably those conducted by the OECD
Development Center, have revealed a relatively
low mobility in the case of skilled workers, and a
practically negligible mobility in the case of
senior executives. Moreover, there sometimes
exist institutional obstacles to this mobility,
created by MNC's themselves, when competing
subsidiaries (in Brazil, for example) enter into
agreements among themselves to prevent executives
leaving any one of them from being recruited by
any of the other."[64]

TNEs award contracts to local contractors
and manufacturers for specific inputs. Sometimes
this involves providing them necessary training
and instructions. Such training is also useful in
the manufacturing of items not used by TNEs.

Corporations such as Heinz, Del Monte, and Dole
are known to provide necessary information and
expertise to independent growers of fruits and
vegetables. They also supply other inputs such as
seeds, fertilizers, and insecticides.

All available evidence points to the
conclusion that TNEs do not undertake significant
R & D activities in the host developing countries.
An investigation carried out by the National
Academy of Sciences in 1973 on the research,
development, and engineering activities of U.S.-
based TNEs concluded: "Except for the engineering
involved in scaling down production techniques
for markets of more limited size and in making
modest adjustments to consumer tastes, little R D
& E has actually been carried out in the LDCs."[65]
A more recent study by Daniel B. Creamer came to
the same conclusion: "...only a negligible share
of the U.S. Overseas R & D found its way to the
developing countries of the world, about 1.8
percent in 1966 but by 1972, a larger 3.3
percent."[66] Moreover, the intrinsic value to the
society of what little R & D TNEs have undertaken
in LDCs remains doubtful. For example,
Miguel Wionczek has found that "most of the
limited R & D by M.E. [TNE] subsidiaries in Latin
America is directed not only to adapting products
to consumer tastes, but also to changing these
tastes."[67]

Some TNEs have recently started operating
research facilities in a few developing nations.
However, they have followed the principle of
international specialization, with the result
being that facilities do not feed to the national
subsidiaries but are directly and vertically
related to the R & D wing of the parent company.
For example, the reasearch wing of IBM in India
did not directly feed its findings and output to
the Indian subsidiary, but to the headquarters.
Under such conditions, host nations hardly
benefit from research and development activities.
This "pseudo-decentralized" type of laboratory
and research, Dmitri Germidis suggests, "is not
slanted to the needs of the local market. It
meets first and foremost the imperatives of the
policy of recruiting high level staff at salaries
markedly lower than in the country of origin:
in other words, it results in a 'brain drain'
in situ and 'occupational training' ultimately
acts to the detriment of the developing host
nations."[68] Thus, IBM mainly utilized the local

talent in India at least at one-fifth of prevalent salaries in industrialized nations.

No discussion of TNEs' impact on knowledge and skills can be complete without the mention of the role of two communication TNEs--transnational news agencies and transnational book publishing firms. In recent years, there has been a growing controversy about the operations of transnational news agencies which provide news all over the world. Since the beginning of the present century, three or four agencies have dominated the world scene. They have been the main suppliers of international and national news to print and visual media as well as to the governmental agencies. Critics such as Fernando Reyes Matta, Herbert I. Schiller, Juan Somavia, and Jeremy Tunstall have suggested that by virtue of their origin and control by industrialized nations, they have been selective in their news coverage and have often articulated the viewpoint of these countries.[69] The result is that the elites in developing nations often learn to interpret current events from the point of view of industrial ones. However, few would deny that despite their limitations, they have been playing a significant part in making people aware of happenings and events in different parts of the world.

Perhaps, more important from our point of view is the contribution of book publishing TNEs which are gradually extending their operations to developing nations. They are bringing out local editions of scientific, technical, and general books. As labor costs are relatively less in these countries, these TNEs find it economical to bring out cheap editions which can be purchased by students and libraries. Often, governmental aid agencies have subsidized them in publishing cheap editions of well-known works. This has undoubtedly helped to build up the intellectual resources of host developing nations. It should be noted that most of them generally reprint the works of home countries, which has led to the criticism that they perpetuate a kind of intellectual dependency. As a result, they have started seeking manuscripts from local authors as well. In addition, other TNEs, specifically those involved in advertising, accountancy, and consultancy, have been responsible for the diffusion of technical know-how in host developing nations.

The above discussion shows that the role which TNEs play in the diffusion of knowledge and skills is much more than is usually covered under the fashionable title "technology transfer." The fact that social scientists have ignored it does not minimize its importance to the host nations.

Cultural Identity

Finally, a word about the impact of TNEs on cultural identity. This is indeed an important but neglected area. Although the broad formulation of the *dependencia* theorists is well known, little empirical work has been done in this regard. It need hardly be stressed that TNEs not only facilitate the movements of the factors of production and products across national boundaries but also the underlying ideas, philosophies, values, and behavior patterns. In fact, some social scientists have theorized that TNEs transmit "business culture" to host nations.[70] Besides, communication TNEs are partly responsible for the transnational diffusion of music, art, literature, and films of the metropole nations. They also promote consumption patterns and a consumption-oriented value-system in the host LDCs. The contribution of the U.S.- and U.K.-based TNEs to the promotion of English in trade and commerce is now widely recognized.[71]

Such cultural diffusions and reproductions, some social scientists have contented, undermine the cultural identity in developing nations.[72] The masses and the elites come to idealize the lifestyles, beliefs, value systems, worldviews, and the arts of the metropole nations: they begin to accept them uncritically and develop a feeling of inferiority about their own cultural systems. In fact, their own self-images are shaped by the images of them held by people in industrialized nations. Frantz Fanon, Paulo Freire, and William Ryan have cogently argued that the subjugated people internalize the values, beliefs, and prejudices of the dominant nations. This cultural dependence, it can be pointed out, sheds some light on the ambivalent attitudes of the dominant elites in developing nations towards the operations of TNEs. On the one hand, they want them as transmitters of not only capital and technology but also os "modern" values and behavior patterns. They seem to believe that the values, beliefs, and ideologies of industrialized

nations are the major causes of their economic
and political dominance, and their own nations can
progress only when they accept them. On the other
hand, they are not comfortable about their
dependence. They resent being manipulated by
outside economic institutions over which they have
little control. Their presence also makes them
aware of their own limitations.

While the validity of the above formulation
cannot be easily dismissed, we would like to
mention two points in this regard. First, one
should resist the temptation to reify cultural
systems whether of the industrialized or developing
nations. There is nothing sacrosanct about their
elements or processes that they be preserved at
all costs. In fact, for their own survival they
should be able to adopt the elements of the other
cultural systems and respond to the changing
economic, social, and political milieu. Therefore,
the intersystemic contact facilitated by TNEs
should not always be construed to be dysfunctional
to the cultural systems of the host nations.
Second, there now exists a greater sensitivity
to the cultural consequences of the operations of
TNEs. Social scientists, for example, are now
examining the effects of communication TNEs on the
elements of local cultural systems. Such a
concern may contribute to the formulation of
suitable policies and programs in the host
developing nations, which might mitigate against
some of the dysfunctional effects of TNEs on
cultural identity.

The above discussion shows that the operations
of TNEs tend to have significant effects on the
social and cultural systems of the host
developing nations. This volume is an attempt
to explore these effects from a multi-disciplinary
perspective. More specifically, it focusses on
the effects of TNEs on social classes and
inequalities, knowledge systems, and values and
life-styles. Our main objective is to raise a
set of conceptual and substantive issues which
deserve to be investigated. Thus, both empirical
studies and analytical articles have been included
in it.

ORGANIZATION OF THE BOOK

This volume is divided into four parts.
Part 1 deals with the impact of TNEs on social

classes and inequalities of development. Chapter 2 discusses the role of TNEs in the disintegration of social classes in Latin America. Chapter 3 presents a class analysis of the growth of TNEs and explores their relationship with "managerial bourgeoisie." Chapter 4 examines the effects of offshore-sourcing TNEs on the status and role of women employees in Malaysia and Singapore. Chapter 5 deals with the issue of whether TNEs contribute to inequalities of development.

Part 2 focusses on TNEs' effects on knowledge systems. Chapter 6 examines the role of book publishing TNEs in the diffusion of intellectual knowledge. Chapter 7 presents the findings of a study which examines the effects of transnational news services on the dissemination of information in Latin America. Chapter 8 deals with the effects of TNEs on educational and cultural processes in Africa. Chapter 9 discusses the role of TNEs in vocational training.

Part 3 seeks to examine the effects of TNEs on consumption patterns and values. Chapter 10 discusses the role of TNEs in the promotion of "bottle feeding" in developing countries, which has caused malnutrition and even infant mortality. Chapter 11 focusses on sociocultural consequences of TNEs in the context of North-South economic relations. Chapter 12 outlines a conceptual framework for the discussion of cultural and ideological dependence and duscusses the role of TNEs in this regard.

Part 4 presents a select bibliography on the subject of the social and cultural impact of transnational enterprises.

NOTES

1. U.N. Report 1973, p. 25.
2. *Business International*, 1976, p. 254.
3. There has been a significant change in the concentration of direct foreign investment in recent years. The U.N. Report (1978, p. 37) notes: "The share of the United States of America, the United Kingdom, and France in the total stock of direct investment declined..., while that of the Federal Republic of Germany, Japan, the Netherlands, Switzerland, and various small countries increased sufficiently." The U.N. data show that the percentage of U.S., U.K., and French shares of direct investment has declined from

53.8, 16.6, and 5.7 in 1967 to 47.6, 11.2, and
4.1 in 1976. On the other hand, the shares of
Germany and Japan have increased from 4.6 and
2.8 to 6.9 and 6.7 for the same period. Even then,
it is interesting to note that 11 countries
(the U.S., U.K., Germany, Japan, Switzerland,
France, Canada, Netherlands, Sweden, Belgium,
Luxembourg, and Italy) owned 94.2 percent of the
direct foreign investment in 1976.

    4.   Sauvant and Mennis, 1977, p. 3.
    5.   U.N. Report, 1973, p. 9.
    6.   U.N. Report, 1978, p. 65.
    7.   U.N. Report, 1973, p. 11.
    8.   U.N. Report, 1978.
    9.   *Ibid.*
  10.   See, for example, Brooke and Remmers,
1970, and Stopford and Wells, 1972.
  11.   Kabunda, 1975, pp. 309-311.
  12.   Cockcroft *et al.*, 1972, p. xvii.
  13.   ILO, 1976a, p. 1.
  14.   Vaitos, 1974.
  15.   ILO, 1976a, pp. 5-6.
  16.   U.N. Report, 1978, p. 92.
  17.   Takeo, 1978.
  18.   ILO, 1976a, p. 6.
  19.   Hui, 1976, p. 59.
  20.   Fan, 1973, p. 23.
  21.   Reuber, 1973.
  22.   ILO, 1976b, p. 49.
  23.   Arrighi, 1971.
  24.   Sunkel, 1973.
  25.   Sklar, 1975, pp. 205-206.
  26.   Arrighi, 1971, p. 256.
  27.   Kreye, 1977, p. 37.
  28.   Goodman, 1976, p. 14.
  29.   Chomsky and Herman, 1977.
  30.   ILO, 1976b, p. 16.
  31.   Brundenius, 1972.
  32.   Weinstein, 1976, p. 44.
  33.   Hirschman, 1972, p. 449.
  34.   Feld, 1972.
  35.   Levkovsky, 1966, p. 52.
  36.   Vernon, 1971, p. 198.
  37.   *Ibid.*
  38.   Kerdpibule, 1974, p. 26.
  39.   Johnson, 1972, pp. 71-114.
  40.   *Ibid.*
  41.   See, for example, Fayerweather, 1972.
  42.   Vernon, 1976, pp. 49-50.
  43.   *Ibid.*
  44.   Heller, 1974, p. 109.

38

45. U.N. Report, 1977.
46. Spandau, 1978, pp. 110-178.
47. See,for example, Nickel, 1978.
48. *Ibid.*, p. 70.
49. *Ibid.*
50. Bornschier, *et al.*, 1978, p. 677.
51. Tsuda, 1977.
52. Weinstein, 1976, p. 400.
53. Ledogar, 1975, pp. 111-126.
54. *Ibid.*
55. Muller, 1974.
56. Plank and Milanesi, 1973.
57. Jelleffe, 1972.
58. Barnet and Müller, 1974, p. 183.
59. Girling, 1976, p. 59.
60. Ledogar, 1975, pp. 6-51.
61. U.N. Report, 1973, p. 48.
62. OECD Study, 1967, p. 23.
63. *Ibid.*
64. Germidis, 1976, p. 3.
65. National Academy of Sciences, 1973,
pp. 1-2.
66. Creamer, 1976, p. 5.
67. Wionczek, 1976, p. 145.
68. Germidis, 1976, p. 9
69. See, for example, Reyes Matta, 1976;
Schiller, 1978; Somavia, 1976; and Tunstall,
1977.
70. Sauvant, 1976.
71. Sauvant, 1976, p. 56.

REFERENCES

Arrighi, Giovanni. 1971. "International corporations, labor aristocrats, and economic development in tropical Africa," *Imperialism and Underdevelopment: A Reader*. New York: Monthly Review Press, pp. 220-267.

Barnet, Richard J., and Müller, Ronald. 1974. *Global Reach: The Power of Multinational Corporations*. New York: Simon and Schuster. pp. 123-210, 363-388.

Brooke, Michael, and Remmers, H. Lee. 1970. *The Strategy of Multinational Enterprise: Organisation and Finance*. London: Longman.

Brundenius, Claes. 1972. "The anatomy of imperialism: The case of the multinational mining corporations in Peru," *Journal of Peace Research*. Vol. 9(3), pp. 189-207.

Business International. 1976. "More multinationals in the EEC than in the US." Vol. 23(32), Aug. 6, p. 254.

Chomsky, Noam, and Herman, Edward S. 1977. "Why American business supports third world fascism," *Business and Society Review*. No. 23, Fall, pp. 13-21.

Cockcroft, James D., Frank, Andre Gunder, and Johnson, Dale. 1972. *Dependence and Underdevelopment: Latin America's Political Economy*. New York: Anchor Books.

Creamer, Daniel B. 1976. *Overseas Research and Development by United States Multinationals, 1966-1975; Estimates of Expenditures and a Statistical Profile*. New York: The Conference Board.

Fan, Wan Shoung. 1973. "The multinational enterprise in Singapore," *Multinational Corporations and their Implications for Southeast Asia*, edited by Eileen Lim Poh Tin.

40

(Current Issues Seminar Series No. 1)
Singapore: Institute of Southeast Asian
Studies, pp. 13-26.

Fayerweather, John. 1972. "Nationalism and the
multinational firm," *The Multinational
Enterprise in Transition: Selected Readings
and Essays*, edited by A. Kapoor and
Phillip Grub. Princeton, N.J.: Darwin
Press.

Feld, Werner. 1972. *Nongovernmental Forces and
World Politics: A Study of Business, Labor,
and Political Groups*. New York: Praeger.

Germidis, Dmitri. 1976. *Multinational Firms and
Vocational Training in Developing Countries*.
Paris: United Nations Educational, Scientific
and Cultural Organization. SHC.76/CONF.635/
COL. 7.

Girling, Robert. 1976. "Mechanisms of imperialism: technology and the dependent state,"
Latin American Perspectives. Vol. 3(4),
pp. 54-64.

Goodman, Louis Wolf. 1976. "The social
organization of decision making in the multi-
national corporations," in *The Multinational
Corporation Social Change*, edited by
David Apter and Louis Wolf Goodman. New York:
Praeger, pp. 63-95.

Heller, Heinz Robert. 1974. "The Hawaiian
experience," *Columbia Journal of World
Business*. Vol. 9(3), pp. 105-110.

Hirschman, Albert O. 1972. "How to divest in
Latin America, and why," *The Multinational
Enterprise in Transition: Selected Readings
and Essays*, edited by A. Kapoor and
Phillip Grub. Princeton, N.J.: Darwin Press,
pp. 445-466.

Hui, Lim Mah. 1976. "Multinational corporations
and development in Malaysia," *Southeast Asian
Journal of Social Science*. Vol. 4(1),
pp. 53-76.

International Labor Office. 1976. *The Impact of
Multinational Enterprises on Employment and
Training*. Geneva.

International Labor Office. 1976. *Wages and
Working Conditions in Multinational Enterprises*. Geneva.

Jelliffe, D.B. 1972. "Commerciogenic malnutrition," *Nutrition Reviews*. Vol. 30(9),
pp. 199-205.

Johnson, Dale. L. 1972. "The national and
progressive bourgeoisie in Chile," *Dependence

and *Underdevelopment: Latin America's Political Economy*, edited by James D. Cockcroft, Andre Gunder Frank and Dale L. Johnson. Garden City, New York: Anchor Books, pp. 165-217.

Kabunda, Kabala, M.K.K. 1975. "Multinational corporaitons and the installation of externally-oriented economic structures in contemporary Africa: the example of the Unilever-Zaire group," *Multinational Firms in Africa*, edited by Carl Widstrand. New York: Africana Publishing Company, pp. 303-322.

Kerdpibule, Udom. 1974. "Thailand's experience with multinational corporations," Bangkok: Dept. of Economics, Kasetsart University (unpublished).

Kreye, Otto. 1977. "World market-oriented industrialization of developing countries: free production zones and world market factories," in *Die neue internationale Arbeitsteilung. Strukturelle Arbeitslosigkeit in den Industrieländern und die Industrialisierung der Entwicklungsländer*. By Folker Frobel, Jurgen Heinrichs and Otto Kreye. Hamburg: Rowohlt Taschenbuch Verlag.

Ledogar, Robert J. 1975. *Hungry for Profits: U.S. Food and Drug Multinationals in Latin America*. New York: IDOC North America.

Levkovsky, A.I. 1966. *Capitalism in India: Basic Trends in Its Development*. Bombay: Peoples Publishing House.

Muller, M. 1974. *The Baby Killer*. London: War on Want Pamphlet.

National Academy of Sciences. 1973. *U.S. International Firms and R, D and E in Developing Countries*. Washington, D.C.

Nickel, Herman. 1978. "The case for doing business in South Africa," *Fortune*. Vol. 97(12), June 19, pp. 60-74.

Organization for Economic Cooperation and Development. 1967. *Pilot Survey on Technical Assistance Extended by Private Enterprise*. Paris.

Plank, S.J., and Milanesi, M.L. 1973. "Infant feeding and infant mortality in rural Chile," *World Health Organization Bulletin*. Vol. 48, pp. 203-210.

Reuber, Grant L. 1973. *Private Foreign Investment in Development*. Oxford: Clarendon Press.

42

Reyes Matta, Fernando. 1975. "America Latina, Kissinger y la UPI: Errores y omisiones desde Mexico," in *Comunicacion y Cultura* (Argentina) Septiembre 1975, No. 4, pp. 55-72. Also, Stanford, Calif.: Institute for Communication Research, 24 pp.

Sauvant, Karl P. 1976. "The potential of multinational enterprises as vehicles for the transmission of business culture," in *Controlling Multinational Enterprises: Problems, Strategies, Counterstrategies* edited by Karl P. Sauvant and Farid G. Lavipour. Boulder, Colo.: Westview Press.

Sauvant, Karl P., and Mennis, Bernard. 1977. "Puzzling over the immaculate conception of indifference curves: the transnational transfer and creation of sociopolitical and economic preferences," paper presented at the Second German Studies Conference, Indiana University, Bloomington, 12-17 April 1977. Bloomington: Indiana University.

Schiller, H. I. 1976. *Communication and Cultural Domination*. New York: International Arts and Sciences Press.

Sklar, Richard L. 1975. *Corporate Power in an African State: The Political Impact of Multinational Mining Companies in Zambia*. Berkeley: University of California Press.

Spandau, Arnt. 1978. *Economic Boycott Against South Africa--Normative and Factual Issues*. Johannesburg: University of Witwatersrand.

Stopford, John M., and Wells, Louis T. 1972. *Managing the Multinational Enterprise: Organization of the Firm and Ownership of the Subsidiaries*. New York: Basic Books.

Sunkel, Osvaldo. 1973. "Transnational capitalism and national disintegration in Latin America," *Social and Economic Studies*. Vol. 22(1), pp. 132-176.

Takeo, Tsuchiya. 1977. "South Korea: Masan--an epitome of the Japan-ROK relationship," *Free Trade Zones & Industrialization of Asia*. Tokyo: Pacific-Asia Resources Center, pp. 53-66.

Tsuda, Ey Mamoru. 1977. "The social organization of transnational business and industry: a study of Japanese capital--affiliated joint-ventures in the Philippines," M.A. thesis submitted to the College of Arts and Sciences, University of the Philippines.

Tunstall, Jeremy. 1977. *The Media are American.*
    New York: Columbia University Press.
United Nations. 1977. *Activities of TNC's in
    Southern Africa and the Extent of their
    Collaboration with the Regimes in the Area.*
    New York: United Nations, Economic and
    Social Council, Commission on Transnational
    Corporations.
United Nations Department of Economic and Social
    Affairs. 1973. *Multinational Corporations
    in World Development.* New York: United
    Nations, ST/ECA/190.
United Nations, Economic and Social Council,
    Commission on Transnational Corporations.
    1978. *Transnational Corporations in World
    Development: A Re-examination.* New York:
    United Nations, E/C.10/38.
Vaitsos, C. V. 1974. "Employment effects of
    foreign direct investments in developing
    countries," *Tecnologia para el Desarrollo.*
    Mexico City.
Vernon, Raymond. 1971. *Sovereignty at Bay.*
    New York: Basic Books.
Vernon, Raymond. 1976. "Multinational enterprises
    in developing countries: Issues in
    dependency and interdependence," *The
    Multinational Corporation and Social Change,*
    edited by David E. Apter and Louis W. Goodman.
    New York: Praeger, pp. 40-62.
Vernon, Raymond. 1977. *Storm Over the Multina-
    tionals.* Cambridge, Mass.: Harvard
    University Press.
Weinstein, Franklin B. 1976. "Multinational
    corporations and the Third World: The case
    of Japan and Southeast Asia," *International
    Organization.* Vol. 30(3), pp. 373-404.
Wionczek, Miguel. 1976. "Notes on technology-
    transfer through multinational enterprises
    in Latin America," *Development and Change.*
    Vol. 7(2), pp. 135-155.

PART 1
IMPACT ON SOCIAL CLASSES AND INEQUALITY

Editorial Note

This section is composed of four chapters
which shed light on the impact of transnational
enterprises (TNEs) on social classes and inequality
in the host developing nations. Osvaldo Sunkel,
in the second chapter, suggests that TNEs, which
have undoubtedly emerged as the basic economic
institutions of the post-war world, are contributing
to national disintegration in Latin America. Their
operations lead to the prosperity of only those
social strata which are directly or indirectly
involved with them while segregating and marginalizing the rest of the populace. He identifies
four social classes--entrepreneur, middle class,
working class, and the marginalized population.
Sunkel points out that only a small fraction of the
first three social classes is integrated in the
activities of TNEs and therefore profits by them.
Some national entrepreneurs are incorporated as
executives in TNEs while others are marginalized;
some professionals forming part of the technical
staff get employment in them while others have
little future; and a small section of the qualified
labor force is absorbed in them while the others
swell the ranks of marginalized populace. Sunkel
thus concludes that the overall impact of TNEs
is the disintegration of social classes in
developing nations.

Richard Sklar, like Osvaldo Sunkel, presents a
class analysis of TNEs. However, his focus is on
the relationship between TNEs and what he calls
"managerial bourgeoisie" which consists of the
upper stratum of national bourgeoisie, executives
of public enterprises and high government
officials. According to Sklar, while sharing the
managerial approach and the life-styles of the
affluent, the "managerial bourgeoisie" is utterly

45

nationalist in its ideological moorings. The
"managerial bourgeoisie" in developing nations is
neither *compradore* nor clientele of the international capitalist class. Its strength is based
on factors internal to the society rather than
on its linkages with TNEs and their subsidiaries.
Its relationship with TNEs, Sklar points out, is
founded on the principle of domicile which means
that the subsidiaries of a TNE operate in
accordance with the requirements set by their
respective host governments. The "managerial
bourgeoisie" seeks to strike a balance between the
profit maximization goal of TNEs and the perceived
interests of host governments. Sklar also suggests
that TNEs have been contributing to the emergence
of a new international class consisting of three
layers: the top consisting of the international
executives of TNEs, the middle of the corporate
bourgeoisie of industrialized nations, and the
bottom of the "managerial bourgeoisie" of
developing countries.

Linda Lim in the fourth chapter examines the
effects of offshore-sourcing TNEs on the status
and role of women employees in developing nations.
Her data pertain to Singapore and Malaysia where
TNEs employ a large number of women workers who
are supposed to be malleable, obedient, and
hardworking. Her findings indicate that the wages
and employment conditions are hardly satisfactory.
Women workers in these TNEs earn only a small
fraction of what their counterparts in industrialized nations get for the same work. Besides,
women workers get low wages as compared to men
because of job segregation. There is little job
stability and the fringe benefits are minimal. The
prospects for upward mobility for most employees
are practically nil, since the skills acquired are
such that they cannot be used in other industries.
Thus Lim's findings seem to support her fundamental
hypothesis that women in developing nations are
being exploited by TNEs at three levels, as
workers, as workers from low wage nations, and
finally as women. Lim does not believe that the
job opportunities offered by offshore-sourcing
TNEs will improve the long-term economic position
of women, as they are confined to export-oriented
sectors whose future viability is questionable.
Nor does she think that factory employment is
creating a class consciousness among women
workers. However, she recognizes that widespread
employment in a transnational enterprise is likely

to have some liberating influence on women in the semifeudal, tradition-bound societies of Malaysia and Singapore.

Arghiri Emmanuel in the fifth chapter questions the widely held formulation of the *dependencia* theorists that TNEs contribute to economic stagnation in developing nations. He insists that this thesis is hardly justifiable on empirical grounds. According to him, if one looks at the figures for direct foreign investment, one cannot fail to observe that there is a positive correlation between foreign investment and the development of the host nation; the greater the foreign investment in a country, the higher its per capita income. Historically, both Marx and Lenin recognized that one unintended consequence of the influx of foreign capital in a periphery nation is the growth of a capitalistic system in it. Emmanuel therefore concludes that by exporting capital and modern technology, TNEs have been contributing to the development of less-developed nations. It is, of course, another matter that the "capitalist optimum" might not be "social optimum."

2
Transnational Capitalism and National Disintegration in Latin America

Osvaldo Sunkel

The principal "factors and processes in which the Latin American social scientist is immersed" are precisely: development, underdevelopment, dependency, marginality, and spatial imbalances; they constitute the "defined set of coherent phenomena" which we want to study in this essay with a view to formulating a global interpretation.

THE APPROACH OR "VISION"

We shall start with a preanalytic cognitive act or vision which is not arbitrary, but is in turn the product of substantial experience as well as of ideological, theoretical, and empirical conceptualization of the set of processes which have characterized our evolution. The essential elements of this approach have already been suggested by the author elsewhere, but it may be useful to repeat them here in a summary vein, since what follows is but a first attempt at an analytic elaboration of the overall approach referring especially to the evolution of Latin America during the last two decades.

The reality of our underdevelopment has been seen mainly from the vantage point of conventional theories of growth and modernization. The optimum functioning of the social system is therefore perceived in terms of the ideal theoretical framework of the mature capitalist economy, represented in practice by the developed countries; underdevelopment as an imperfect and earlier stage on the way towards the ideal prototype. However, the formative stages of development and the present structure of the underdeveloped countries are radically different from the assumptions implicit in such a theoretical logic.

It is necessary, therefore, to replace the idealized and mechanical vision implied by conventional theory with an approach which enables us to perceive in concrete terms the structure, functioning, and the problem of transformation of underdeveloped societies. Given such a position, it is possible and logical to direct our research towards the development of an analytical approach based on a historical study of the process of development of our societies. In order to produce the scientific base needed for the elaboration of a more comprehensive interpretation, such an approach will obviously have to make critical use of existing analytical tools.

The approach proposed here takes the characteristics of underdevelopment as a set of normal features inherent in the functioning of a given system. In other words, the structure of the system defines the manner in which it functions, and, therefore, the results which it produces. These results are well known in the case of under-developed countries: low income and slow growth, regional disequilibria, instability, inequality, unemployment, dependence on foreign countries, specialization in the production of raw materials and primary crops, economic, social, political, and cultural marginality, etc. The conventional student takes those symptoms of underdevelopment as deviations from the ideal, or the teething troubles of an infant economy which would be overcome with economic growth and modernization. He does not perceive that at the root of these characteristics there exists a system which normally produces and continues to produce those results as long as development policy continues to attack the symptoms of underdevelopment without dealing with the basic structural elements which give rise to under-development.

Historical insight is essential for the identification of such structural elements, explana-tion of the functioning of a system with a given structure, and analysis of structural change itself. This seems to be the more decisive aspect of development analysis, because if the results of the process are seen as a function of the structure of the system, these results will change only if the structure of the system undergoes change.

If one were to apply this orientation to Latin American countries, it becomes quite clear that external links and relationships have exercised a fundamental influence on the shaping of the structure of our systems, and, therefore, on their functioning and outcome, as well as on the process of structural transformation. Nevertheless, the importance attached to these external links should not lead us to underestimate the existence of structures of underdevelopment internal to the system. Although external influences probably tend to prevail as main factors in the long term process of transformation, structural transformation is the product of the interaction between external and internal variables.[1]

A realistic analysis of Latin American development should therefore be based on a conception which assumes our socioeconomic system to be formed by two groups of structural elements: internal and external. Among the internal factors are: the pattern of natural resources and population; political institutions, especially the state; sociopolitical groups and classes; the ideologies and attitudes of different groups and classes; the specific policies followed by the government; etc. The complex of internal and external structural elements, and the interrelations among them, define the structure of the system, and constitute, therefore, the framework within which the functioning of the national system and its processes of structural transformation take place.

The two different aspects of the dynamics of the system, already referred to above, are now clearly distinguishable. On the one hand, there is the functioning of the system with a given structure: the higher or lower intensity of the processes of capital accumulation, of mobilization and utilization of productive resources, of change in the location of economic activity, of changes in income distribution, etc. In conventional economic theory this is the subject of macro-economic growth theory.

But what is far more interesting from the point of view of the long term development process is the dynamics of the structural change of the system. The systematic study of the long term development process of Latin American economics suggests that such transformation takes place in two main ways. Firstly, in so far as a system

functions and grows during a certain period, and
capital accumulates, economic activity expands,
the composition of production and income changes,
economic activity is redistributed spatially, etc.;
this will necessarily induce significant transformations in the internal structure, that is, in
the pattern of natural resources and population,
institutions, and particularly the state, in socio-
economic groups and classes, in their ideologies
and specific policies, and also in the nature of
external relations.

Secondly, the internal structure of the system
suffers fundamental transformations as a consequence
of exogenous changes in the nature of the external
links of the country. These exogenous changes are
the product of the evolution of the system of
international relations within which the country
operates, and particularly of the evolution of the
hegemonic power of that system of international
relations. On historical examination, in effect,
it is quite clear that the great transformations
experienced in the past by European society and by
the United States are distinctly reflected in the
various phases of structural change which the
Latin American countries have undergone over time.

An adequate analytical framework for the
study of underdevelopment and development must rest
on the notions of process, structure, and system.
According to an approach of this kind, it is not
possible to admit that underdevelopment is a
moment in the evolution of a society which is
economically, politically, and culturally autonomous
and isolated. On the contrary, it is postulated
that underdevelopment is part and parcel of the
historical process of global development of the
international system, and therefore, that underdevelopment and development are simply the two
faces of one single universal process. Furthermore,
underdevelopment and development have been,
historically, simultaneous processes which have
been linked in a functional way, that is, which
have interacted and conditioned themselves mutually.

The evolution of this global system of under-
development-development has, over a period of time,
given rise to two great polarizations which have
found their main expression in geographical terms.
First, a polarization of the world between countries: with the developed, industrialized,
advanced, "central northern" ones on one side, and
the underdeveloped, poor, dependent, and
"peripheral southern" ones on the other. Second,

a polarization within countries, between advanced
and modern groups, regions, and activities and
backward, primitive, marginal, and dependent
groups, regions, and activities.

Development and underdevelopment should therefore be understood as partial but interdependent
structures, which form part of a single whole. The
main difference between the two structures is that
the developed one, due basically to its endogenous
growth capacity, is the dominant structure, while
the underdeveloped structure, due largely to the
induced character of its dynamism, is a dependent
one. This applies both to whole countries and to
regions, social groups, and activities within a
single country.

This approach focuses attention on two types of
polarization processes, one at the level of international relations, the other at the domestic level.
We shall now examine some of the more relevant
aspects of both processes from the dominant viewpoint of this paper, viz., the interaction between
the international and domestic levels of the dual
process of polarization.

INTERNATIONAL POLARIZATION

The theories which relate the national development process to the system of international economic
relations, and which underlie the interpretation of
past and present trends, may be classified in three
main groups: the neoclassical theory of international trade, the Marxist theory of capitalistic-
imperialist exploitation, and the theories of the
"backwash effect" of international trade.[2]

The liberal *laissez faire* approach is a rather
inappropriate basis for analysis and recommendations, because of the highly unrealistic and
restrictive assumptions upon which it is based, of
which one is particularly damaging. I refer to the
identification of the concepts of "economy" and
"country" which means that countries are conceived
as selfcontained economic units which exchange
products in the international market place, these
then being their "international economic relations."
Quite apart from the very partial aspect of international economic relations implicit in this approach,
such an approach fails to grasp one of the essential
characteristics of the international economy, viz.,
that it is basically made up of transnational
conglomerates, firms which operate simultaneously in

various *national* markets, thus constituting an international economic system which penetrates and overlaps with the national economic system.

The Marxist theory of imperialism is based precisely on the recognition of this fact, since it suggests that international monopolies penetrate national economies in search of raw materials and market outlets in order to use and add to their increasing economic surplus. Nevertheless, until relatively recently, the Marxist approach had restricted itself mainly to the role of *international monopoly capitalism*, neglecting to some extent an element which seems most essential from our point of view: the "spread" and "backwash" effects of the international extensions of some national economic systems into other national economic systems.

This analysis, which was associated originally with the names of Myrdal, Singer, Prebisch, and others, and which has been a central concern in important Marxist and non-Marxist contributions in recent years, suggests that in the interaction of industrial economies with primary producing economies, the former tend to benefit relatively more than the latter, and that this gives rise to cumulatively divergent trends in the development of the two groups of countries. Although there are many different arguments advanced in favor of this hypothesis, they essentially boil down to the following: (a) the nature of foreign owned or controlled primary production for export, which tends to be an "enclave" with little relation to or influence over the local economy but with substantial promotional effects over the home economy where most procurement, financing, storing, processing, research, marketing, and reinvestment take place; (b) the characteristics of the local economy, which lacks trained manpower, entrepreneurial talent, capital, and physical as well as institutional infrastructure, and is therefore unable to respond positively to the potential opportunities of an expanding export activity; (c) the relative behavior of the prices of raw material exports and manufactured imports--the worsening of the terms of trade of primary producers--as well as the instability of primary product prices; (d) the generally monopolistic nature of the primary export activity which, when the firm is foreign owned, implies an outflow of excess profits.

This approach introduces a most important perspective since it focuses attention on the

interaction between the external agents and the
domestic economic, social, and political structures.
Nevertheless, it is still somewhat partial and
requires further generalization and systematization.

Apart from other considerations, it is partial
because it has concentrated its analysis of the
differential effects of the interaction between
developed and underdeveloped countries exclusively
on the primary producing export activities of
the latter. One of the results of this bias in
the analysis was the conclusion that these
countries had to industrialize because industrialization would result in a cumulative process of
self-enforcing "spread" effects--Rostow's "take-off
into self-sustained growth." To a large extent this
seems to have been the consequence of applying the
European model of the industrial revolution to
the Latin America cases.

But the model of import substituting
industrialization that has characterized Latin
America seems to be something quite different. It
is in fact very difficult to understand if, apart
from the internal peculiarities of each country
reference is not made to the framework of external
links, conditioning factors, and pressures that
have influenced industrial development so decisively
in our countries. In fact, its dynamics, its
structure, and the nature of the productive
processes adopted, especially with reference to
technology, have been induced to a large extent
by external conditions.

When Latin American countries embarked on a
deliberate policy of industrialization, they were
confronted with the need for substantially
expanding specialized manpower, skilled human
resources, entrepreneurs, machinery and equipment,
raw materials and inputs, financial resources,
sales, marketing, credit and publicity organizations, as well as the technology and know-how
necessary for all these tasks. When industrial
development outgrows its initial stages, the
scarcity and urgency of all these elements become
more and more critical, particularly when industry
enters the more complex fields of basic manufactures
and consumer durables.

Under such conditions, the forces of
industrialization have had to rely heavily and
increasingly on external support, for know-how,
technology, administrative capacity, equipment,
financing, etc. These various international
contributions to domestic industrial development,

clearly indispensable in view of the precarious
base from which such development started, have
taken place in various forms manifesting different
modalities. External financial contributions, for
instance, have come as public or private loans,
portfolio investments, immigration of foreign
capitalists, foreign subsidiaries wholly or
partially foreign-owned. Skilled human resources
have also come in different ways: immigration
of qualified people, hiring of foreign experts,
training of personnel both at home and abroad.
Technological transfers also conform to different
modalities--through foreign subsidiaries which
bring their own technology by means of licenses,
patents, trade marks, technical assistance
contracts, etc., and by adapting or developing
technology locally.

It is therefore clear that the process of
industrialization via import substitution, although
stimulated and induced by the crisis in international relations and international crises in
general and balance of payments problems in
particular, and also by a deliberate policy of
protection, has not taken place in isolation, as
a spontaneous process. On the contrary, it has
meant new and very important, though different,
links with the international economy, and particularly with the United States. Industrialization
did not reduce foreign dependence; a primary-
exporting economy is fatally condemned, by its very
structure, to depend almost entirely on its basic
exports, unless and until industrialization
changes that situation, which import substituting
industrialization has not been able to do.

In other words, at a higher level of
abstraction, the phase of import substituting
industrialization, just as the period of primary
export expansion that preceded it, constitutes, in
the final analysis, a new way of integration of the
underdeveloped economy, at a different level of
evolution and through different means, into a new
type of international capitalist system. Although
this new system is again organized in terms of
developed and dominant economies on the one side,
and underdeveloped and dependent economies on the
other--ever more closely interrelated--it is
necessary to take into account that this new model
of international economic relations is based
operationally on the transnational conglomerate,
a new kind of business organization that has
experienced an enormous growth during the last

decades. This is particularly the case in the
United States, mainly as a consequence of the
enormous expansion of government expenditure--
especially in armaments and space exploration--and
of the resulting spectacular technological
progress.[3]

In the factories, laboratories, design and
publicity departments, and in the centers of
decision, planning, and finance which constitute
its superstructure and which is always situated in
a developed country, the transnational corporation
develops: (a) new products, (b) new ways of
manufacturing these products, (c) the machines and
tools necessary for manufacturing them, (d) the
synthetic and natural raw materials and inputs
needed for their production, and (e) the publicity
needed for the creation and dynamization of the
market for these goods.

On the other hand, the final stages of assembly
and production of these goods take place in the
underdeveloped economy through an industrialization
process that proceeds by means of the importation
of new equipment and inputs and the use of the
corresponding marks, patents, and licenses, both by
public and private national firms, as well as by the
wholly or partially owned foreign subsidiaries
of the transnational conglomerate. This process is
of course supported by public and private international finance as well as by international
technical assistance, which constitute efficient aid
for the expansion of the international markets of
the American, European, and Japanese transnational
conglomerates.

In a world of protected markets but helpless
consumers, a new international division of labor
appears with its new agent: the international
manufacturing oligopoly. As in earlier stages,
there is also a new international specialization
in the generation of scientific and technological
knowledge in the metropolitan countries, and of
its routine "consumption" in the peripheral
countries. If the above line of argument is valid,
then we are now again in a period of organization
of a center-periphery model of a new kind, despite
our prior belief that import substituting industrialization was leading us away from it.

We should not be surprised by the consequences
of such a process, with which we are only too
familiar: (a) a persistence and even worsening
of the primary exporting character of the economy;
(b) exogenous source of the economy's dynamism;

(c) exogenous character of most of the fundamental centers of decision in finance, economic policy, science and technology, access to foreign markets, etc.; (d) acute and persistent tendency to foreign indebtedness, denationalization, and subsidiarization; (e) a great danger of Latin American integration efforts ending up in favor of transnational conglomerates: a definitive liquidation of the remaining local enterprise; (f) a growing income gap between developed and underdeveloped countries, etc.

THE INTERNAL POLARIZATION

Let us now return to the central theme of this essay--the hypothesis that we are in the midst of a simultaneous process of dual polarization, international and national. We have just described the first, we shall now turn to the second.

The internal process of polarization can be seen as a growing division between modern dominant and advanced economic activities, social groups, and regions on the one hand, and backward, marginal, and dependent activities, groups, and regions on the other. In fact, the geographic, economic, social, political, and cultural centers of modernity and development are closely associated with the rise and fall of the activities linked more closely--directly or indirectly--to the developed countries. This is the case of regions, cities, or ports which are subject to the direct influence of the investments and expansion of the traditional export activities, and also of those other cities or regions which, either because they are administrative centers or areas producing inputs for the export sector are able to capture part of the income generated in the export sector and redistribute it to other regions and social groups.

In the import-substituting industrialization phase, the activities which concentrate a large part of the investments and which expand fastest are of course manufacturing, i.e., the activities which produce their inputs and the infrastructures most necessary for industrial development. As this industrialization is basically orientated towards consumer goods, it tends to concentrate around the larger population centers, thereby reinforcing the tendency of urban concentration so characteristic of Latin America. This

tendency is frequently further accentuated by
the stagnation and/or modernization of the
traditional export sector and of domestic agriculture, a phenomenon which is usually accompanied
by a growing concentration of ownership of the
means of production in these activities. All three
elements--stagnation, modernization, and concentra-
tion--accelerate the exodus of the population
directly or indirectly related to export and
agricultural activities.

When this polarization of population corresponds to the decline of economic activity in
traditional export and/or agricultural activity,
it leads to acute and growing spatial imbalances.
We might in this respect recall that some of the
most underdeveloped areas of Latin America today
are precisely zones which once were regions of
exceptional wealth, social prestige, political
importance, and cultural splendor: the Northeast
of Brazil; the areas of precious metals in Mexico,
Peru, Boliva, Brazil, and Chile; the nitrate
fields of Chile; *henequén* fields of Yacatan; the
abandoned banana fields of Central America, and
the old coffee and cocoa plantations of Brazil.

The great urban concentration in the two or
three main cities of each country, which is the
other side of the coin, poses a striking internal
disequilibrium. The phenomenon of the primacy of
a few important gigantic cities in which
practically the entire economic, social, administrative, and cultural infrastructure is concentrated
is of course well known. But a brief reference
should be made to the process of urban polarization
or segregation which occurs, particularly in those
few great cities where the largest part of the
population surplus is accumulating, and which has
given rise to a large portion of the literature
on the phenomenon of marginality. It is perhaps
precisely in the ecological characterization of
the main cities of Latin America that the
phenomenon of internal polarization becomes most
dramatic and explicit: the marginal population,
which constitute a belt of infernal misery around
the city and also infiltrating into it; the factory
districts which coincide more or less with the
residential areas of the proletariat; the
administrative, financial, and commercial center,
around which lower middle class residences are
located; and the residential areas of suburbia of
the middle and higher income groups which coincide
with the physical area of most of the luxury

spending, both in private and public goods and services, and where population density is probably lowest. This is in the end the spatial urban expression of the process of polarization and segregation which affects income distribution, the pattern of public and private expenditure--both in consumption and investment--social stratification and the distribution of power, prestige, and culture.

Given the structural and institutional characteristics of Latin American underdevelopment--concentration of property and wealth in all its forms; acute inequality of incomes; discrimination in the access to education; great technological and productivity differentials between various activities; oligopolistic goods and factor market structure; etc.--and the characteristically unstable dynamism of dependent economies, with their recent historical periods of export growth and import substitution, it seems convenient to base the analysis of the causation of the process of internal polarization or segregation--normally called marginality--on the factors which determine personal incomes.

The income generated by additional investments in the modern sector mainly enlarges the incomes of middle and higher income groups, whose demand expands proportionally to a greater extent in consumer durables and modern services where highly capital-intensive technologies prevail. This fact, together with the high marginal import propensity of these groups considerably reduce the employment-creating effect of investments in the modern sector. In this way, the multiplier effects of employment creation at the modern level will probably be lower than the unemployment caused by the replacement of economic activities at the primitive level and its negative multiplier effects.

It is not possible here to systematically apply this general working hypothesis to the various types of economies found in Latin America, nor to the different stages of export growth and import substitution that most of them have experienced or are experiencing. Nor is it possible to examine how the suggested process influences the availability of and access to the main sources of income: employment, property, independent activities, and income transfer systems. But a few examples may contribute to a better understanding of our approach.

The effect on the labor market of the
relatively fast growth of the modern activities
and the consequent disruption of the more primitive
activities is quite clear: the demand for skilled
human resources grows very rapidly while the
demand for unskilled manpower slackens. As a
consequence, a tendency towards improvement of
wages of qualified personnel (except under conditions of rapid expansion of higher and technical
education) and a relative stagnation or decline
in the wages of unskilled labor is observable.
This phenomenon has been perceived clearly in the
agricultural sector and in the traditional export
sector. These activities react to the decline in
demand with reduction of production and employment;
the decline in demand is still followed by
processes of technological modernization which
substantially reduce the level of employment. This
gives rise to an important outflow of unskilled
manpower which adds to the ranks of the urban
marginal groups.
    The same phenomenon can be examined from the
point of view of the different types of occupation
which provide access to sources of income. The
expansion of the modern sector normally implies
the installation of relatively large enterprises,
and this will increase the number of large firms.
But given the oligopolistic conditions which
generally prevail, this will also limit the
possibilities of expansion of medium and small-
sized firms, as well as of artisanal work.
Frequently, the expansion of large firms in extractive, commercial, industrial, or other activities
will result from the penetration of foreign
subsidiaries. This may have the effect of
limiting or excluding medium and small, and even
large, national entrepreneurs, particularly when
this process involves an acute tendency of
concentration of the ownership of markets or means
of production, land, water, foreign exchange,
credit, technology and know-how, etc.
Furthermore, inequalities in the labor market and
the concentration of property will tend to
accentuate the unequal distribution of income,
with the consequent reinforcement of a structure
of demand which contributes to the dynamization of
capital-intensive activities. This process involves
an acceleration of obsolescence of existing products
and processes, leading to unnecessary and premature
replacements of installed capacity, generally with
considerable savings of manpower. In this and many

other ways, impolicy, or lack of policy, contributes
to a restriction of the access of the population
to sources of income.

If what has been suggested in the foregoing
analysis is correct, the problem of marginality looks
much more serious and unmanageable than is normally
assumed, both because it probably will worsen in the
near future and also because such partial policies
as popular participation or integration as well as
such global policies as population control or indis-
criminate acceleration of economic growth do not
reflect the true dimensions and nature of the problem. An adequate consideration of the question of
marginality requires an approach that incorporates
this phenomenon as one of the inherent processes of
dependent underdevelopment, where appropriate
consideration is given to those questions of technology, institutions, income distribution, concentration of property, structure of consumption and
production, etc., which have a more pronounced and
direct influence on the accessibility of the
population to the sources of income.

THE RELATIONSHIPS BETWEEN THE PROCESSES OF INTERNATIONAL AND NATIONAL POLARIZATION

The examination of the internal and international processes of polarization clearly suggests
a further step in the analysis. If we look at
countries as composed of developed and underdeveloped functions, groups, and regions, and
remember the basic characteristics of the international economy--the penetration of the underdeveloped economies by the economies of the developed
countries through the extractive, manufacturing,
commercial, and financial transnational conglom-
erates--it becomes apparent that there must be a
close correlation and connection between the
extension of the developed economies into the
underdeveloped countries, and the developed, modern,
and advanced activities, social groups, and regions
of these countries.

From such a perspective of the global system,
apart from the distinction between developed and
underdeveloped countries, components of importance
can be observed:

    1. a complex of activities, social groups, and
       regions in different countries which conform
       to the developed part of the global system

and which are closely linked transnationally
through many concrete interests as well as
by similar styles, ways, and levels of
living and cultural affinities;
2. a national complement of activities, social
   groups, and regions partially or totally
   excluded from the national developed part
   of the global system and without any links
   with similar activities, groups, and regions
   of other countries.

In this conception of the phenomena associated
with the development-underdevelopment continuum
which implicitly claims to incorporate the aspects
of domination-dependence and marginality which
form an inherent part of it, the so-called developed
countries would be those where the developed
structure--economic, social, and spatial--prevails,
while the backward and marginal activities, social
groups, and regions would appear as exceptional,
limited, and secondary situations.
    Conversely, the so-called underdeveloped
countries would be those in which the phenomenon
of marginality affects a significant proportion of
the population, activities, and areas, and therefore would appear as an urgent and acute problem,
not only in relative terms but also for the reason
that large segments of population are affected by
it at extremely low absolute levels of living.
The modern activities, social groups, and areas
would, on the other hand, constitute more or less
restricted portions of these countries.
    Starting from the basic categories which have
been combined here to reach this formulation--
national capitalistic economies characterized
internally by a heterogeneity of levels of
development, the international differentiation
between developed and underdeveloped, or dominant
and dependent countries, and an international
capitalist system which defines the relationships
between national economies--we shall now present a
graphic model combining the different elements.
    Firstly, it is assumed that the international
capitalist system exists in isolation, since the
preliminary step of this analysis is not vitiated
by ignoring the fact of the coexistence of the
socialist and the international capitalist systems.
It is obvious that in a more advanced stage of
research, this factor will have to be incorporated
into the analysis, especially in view of the policy
implications involved. It is further assumed, for

64

the sake of simplicity, that our model of the
international capitalist system consists of only
one dominant developed country and two underdeveloped and dependent countries. The existence
of a number of subsystems of this type within the
international capitalist economy--where relations
exist among dominant powers of each subsystem,
between dominant powers of each subsystem and
dependent economies of the other subsystems, and
among the dependent countries within each
subsystem--constitutes, of course, a fact of
enormous importance. Although, for the sake of
convenience, it is not introduced at this stage,
it must be taken fully into account at a subsequent
stage.

Under the above stated assumptions, we would
have the following diagram (Figure 2.1):

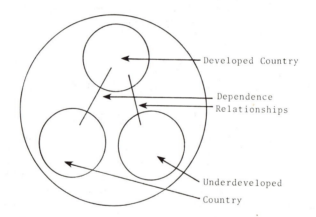

Figure 2.1 The Capitalist System

It is assumed that each country within the
system--both the developed and the underdeveloped
ones--manifests a certain degree of heterogeneity
in the levels of development, modernity, progress,
and incomes. Solely for the sake of convenience and
fully cognizant of the need for removing this
assumption from one final analysis we shall reduce
heterogeneity to its simplest expression, viz.,
duality. This would enable us to distinguish
between integrated and marginal or segregated
sectors (see Figure 2.2).

Finally, overlapping with the two previous figures, and in accordance with the basic categories of our analysis, we shall assume that at the heart of the international capitalist system is an international or transnational kernel or nucleus, consisting of (1) a matrix of national integrated sectors, (2) segregated individual national segments formed by the segregated or marginal sectors of each country, and (3) the relationships between (2) above and the integrated segments. The diagramatic expression corresponding to this idea is shown in Figure 2.3.

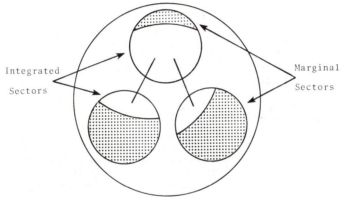

Integrated

Sectors

Marginal

Sectors

Figure 2.2

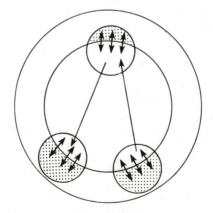

Figure 2.3

The interpretation so far advanced suggests that the international capitalist system contains an internationalized nucleus of activities, regions, and social groups of varying degrees of importance in each country. These sectors share a common culture and "way of life," which expresses itself through the same books, texts, films, television programs, similar fashions, similar groups of organization of family and social life, similar style of decoration of homes, similar orientations to housing, building, furniture, and urban design. Despite linguistic barriers, these sectors have a far greater capacity for communication among themselves than is possible between integrated and marginal persons of the same country who speak the same language. An advertisement in *Time* magazine expresses this idea with the perfection to be expected from publicity aimed precisely at the international market constituted by the nucleus of internationalized population:

> *Time's* 24 million readers are apt to have more in common with each other than with many of their own countrymen. High incomes. Good Education. Responsible positions in business, government, and the professions. *Time* readers constitute an international community of the affluent and influential, responsive to new ideas, new products, and new ways of doing things.[4]

For this international community, inhabiting different countries--developed and underdeveloped--to have similar patterns of consumption, it must also have similar patterns of income. However, it is well known that the average levels of income *per capita* of developed nations are greater by a factor of considerable magnitude than that of underdeveloped countries. But these averages are highly questionable, particularly if the national universe which they claim to represent is highly heterogeneous, as is particularly the case in underdeveloped economies, where income distribution is very unequal. In fact, depending upon whether greater or lesser weight is attached to the modernized, integrated, or internationalized segment of each underdeveloped economy, more or less significant proportions of the population in these economies will accumulate substantial shares of total income, thereby obtaining *per capita* incomes similar to those prevailing in the developed

countries. In the case of Chile, for example, with
an average *per capita* income of about U.S. $600,
the privileged 10 percent of the population which
receives about 40 percent of the total income has
a *per capita* income of U.S. $2,400, a figure
significantly higher than the average for any
European economy.

We shall now consider the trends of *per
capita* income of the integrated and segregated
segments of population. Although empirical
evidence on this matter is extremely scanty, it is
generally agreed that while income distribution
in the developed countries has been more or less
constant or slightly improved, in the underdeveloped
countries income inequalities, at least between
the extremes, has probably widened. It may well
be that the total income accuring to the middle
and higher income sectors grows faster than the
national average, since--as will subsequently be
shown--it is directly or indirectly associated with
the activity of the transnational conglomerates
which grow at substantially faster rates than
national economies--both developed and underdeveloped. In contrast, the population growth of the
higher income sectors tends to be substantially
below the national average both in developed and
underdeveloped countries. Therefore, *per capita*
incomes of these sectors must increase much faster
than the national average in both types of
countries. The marginal groups, on the contrary,
experience population growth rates higher than
national averages and income growth rates which are
lower than the national averages, and therefore,
per capita incomes would have to grow at rates
lower than national averages; and this would hold
again for both developed and underdeveloped
economies. Therefore, according to this analysis,
income distribution should deteriorate in both
types of countries. However, this tendency may be
overcome in the developed countries by means of
income redistribution policies which may have a
significant effect because of the relatively small
size of the lower income groups in an economy
relatively characterized by generally high average
levels of income. In contrast, in the underdeveloped countries such income redistribution
policies do not have similar results because the
relative size of low income sections of the population is very big. This may be one of the main
reasons why income redistribution policies, when
applied by these countries, tend to favor well

organized middle and lower middle income groups
rather than the poorer sectors of the population.

TRANSNATIONAL INTEGRATION AND
NATIONAL DISINTEGRATION

In the previous sections, an effort has been
made to interpret the five concepts, problems, and
processes that engage us in this essay--development,
underdevelopment, dependence, marginality,
and spatial imbalances--in such a way as to render
their interrelationships apparent. We believe
that we have suggested that they are not only
interrelated, but that in fact they are different
manifestations of a single global process, which is
simultaneously a process of transnational
integration and national disintegration.

The main actor in this process is the transnational conglomerate, in the sense that this is
the basic economic institution of the post-war
capitalist world, an institution of tremendous
dynamism, which is bringing about a fundamental
transformation of the structure and functioning
of that system, not only in the central countries
but in the whole world, creating in the final
analysis a new model of civilization represented
by the superconsumption society exemplified by the
U.S.

For our present purpose it is necessary to
stress only two aspects, viz.: (a) the TRANCOS
do in fact constitute a new economic system--both
national and international; and (b) this new
system favors the development of local segments
integrated into the internationalized nucleus of
the capitalist system, in particular, those
segments which are more directly connected with
the TRANCOS, while at the same time tending to
disrupt the rest of the economy and society,
segregating and marginalizing significant sections
of the population.

That part of the American economy which is
made up of "a few hundred technically dynamic,
massively capitalized, and highly organized big
corporations" is termed the "Industrial System"
by Professor J. K. Galbraith, who clearly perceives
that a system dominated by a few very large
corporations is qualitatively different from the
classical conception of the capitalist system
consisting of a large number of small and
independent enterprises.

Galbraith's argument is as follows: the tremendous development of modern technology requires an increase in the capital committed to production and in the time for which it is committed. The commitment of time and money tends to be more and more specialized in a great variety of different tasks. Therefore, requirements of specialized manpower increase greatly, and as specialization advances, efficient organization becomes essential. In order to maximize long run profits and reduce uncertainty and risk, the corporation engages in planning.

In addition to deciding what the consumer will want and is willing to pay, the firm must take every possible step to see that what it decides to produce is wanted by the consumer at a remunerative price. It must see that the labor, materials, and equipment that it needs will be available at a cost consistent with the price it will receive. It must exercise control over what is supplied. *It must replace the market with planning* [emphasis supplied]... The market is superceded by what is commonly known as vertical integration. The planning unit takes over the source of supply or the outlet. Where a firm is specially dependent in an important material or product (such as an oil company on crude petroleum, a steel company on ore, an aluminium company on bauxite) there is always the danger that the requisite supplies will be available only at inconvenient prices...From the point of view of the firm, the elimination of a market converts an external negotiation, and hence a partially or wholly uncontrollable decision, to a matter for purely internal decision...The size of General Motors is in the service not of monopoly, or the economies of scale, but of planning. As for this planning--control of supply and demand, provision of capital, minimization of risk-- there is no clear upper limit to the desirable size. It could be that "the bigger the better." The corporate form accommodates to this need. Quite clearly it allows the firm to be very, very large.[5]

The nucleus of the TRANCO is its headquarters, which is located in the metropolis, and which is the central planning bureau of the corporation.

The headquarters is something quite distinct from its productive activities, which can be classified in three main types--extractive, industrial, and marketing--and which are located also in the metropolitan country, but with subsidiaries, branches, or affiliates in the peripheral countries. The headquarters consists essentially of a group of people who plan and decide what will be produced and sold, how, where, how much, and over what period of time. In order to perform the decision-making process rationally, it has developed a highly efficient system of communications through which the necessary information, personnel, scientific, and technological knowledge, finance, and decisions flow.

Between the productive activities of the TRANCO there develops a flow of goods and services within an institutional framework of vertically and horizontally highly integrated oligopolistic enterprises--both nationally and internationally. In this manner, the TRANCO replaces to a large extent the market--again both national and international--since it takes over the sources of supply of its inputs and the outlets of its production. Moreover, it is able to influence significantly the demand for its goods and services through the pressure it is able to exercise over the individual consumer as well as over governments. As can be seen, the new industrial system also entails the disappearance of the classical entrepreneur, the suppliers of capital and capital markets, and their replacement by the top planners and managers who constitute the corporate techno-structure. These same technocrats who, according to Barber, will rule the world in the near future, are in fact replacing the national entrepreneurial class in the underdeveloped countries, as we shall see presently.[6]

For the reasons indicated above, and since the expenditures in research, design, and technology have become a major item in the TRANCO fixed cost structure, it has every interest in spreading these costs over an ever increasing total output, including the output sold in the metropolitan markets and overseas markets. Therefore, the capturing of more and more consumers at home and abroad is absolutely central to the long term profitability of the TRANCO. According to Galbraith, in underdeveloped countries the introduction of new consumer goods--cosmetics, motor scooters, transistor radios, canned foods, bicycles, phonograph records, movies, American cigarettes--is recognized as of the highest importance in the strategy of economic development. And he reminds us that, in the golden days, commodities such as tobacco, alcohol, and opium which involved a physical and progressive addiction were considered useful trade goods. It is clear then that this strategy of economic development is really a long term strategy of maximization of the TRANCO's profits, involving the spreading of its subsidiaries and of a homogenized consumer culture throughout the world.

Nearly every country in the world has in the past made efforts to attract foreign private capital for everywhere experienced the acute need for the contributions that foreign capital was supposed to make (capital, technology, markets, entrepreneurship, etc.). But the nature of traditional enterprise based on foreign capital was different from the new international industrial system built around the TRANCO. It is now becoming increasingly clear that the claims traditionally made regarding the contributions of foreign private capital are not necessarily valid.

In fact, the contributions of new additional capital are rather small, as the subsidiaries finance themselves in large measure with local resources. Remittances abroad of profits, interest, royalties, payments for technical assistance, foreign inputs, etc., are normally several times larger than the net inflow of capital, with the consequence of a substantial net outflow of resources (this amount is generally underestimated because of the possibility of overpricing in the case of each of the items of payments abroad, facilitated by the transnational integration of the firms).

Technological transfer also manifests some very special peculiarities. As it occurs within the framework of the TRANCO, it is not to be expected that any substantial effort will be made to adapt techniques to local conditions or to stimulate local scientific and technological activity; therefore, we learn to "consume" new techniques through this kind of transfer, but not to adapt or generate science and technology. Something similar occurs with the national entrepreneur--he is converted into an international technocrat or bureaucrat, or becomes marginalized. Finally, with respect to the opening of new foreign markets, experience, at least in the case of manufacturing, has been entirely negative.

On the other hand, multinational business through the proliferation of subsidiaries has grown so large and influential that nation-states, through which its influence extends itself challenging national decision-making processes, are becoming increasingly restless.

Some of the effects of the process of trans-national conglomeration on the underdeveloped countries are the following:

1. The increasing capacity of the TRANCO to take the fullest possible advantages of size and diversification--economies of scale, large accumulations of capital, long range planning, market power, scientific and technological research, predominantly internal sources of finance, reduction of uncertainty and risk, choice of best opportunities over a very wide economic horizon, etc., accrues mainly to the country where the basic functions of the TRANCO are located, constituting a kind of external economy which integrates, increases the degree of complexity and specialization, and dynamizes the rest of the economy of the metropolis. The subsidiaries and affiliates of the TRANCO located in the peripheral country--not only in the primary producing sectors but in all activities of the underdeveloped economy--do not create a similarly integrated industrial complex with the rest of the local economy, but on the contrary, remain integrated with the TRANCO. Moreover, they even have some disintegrating effects, among other factors, in view of the parallelism of productive activities which they tend to produce. This is due to the fact that TRANCOS never leave the market to competitors (which means excess capacity in small markets), and also to the massive introduction of highly capital-intensive technologies displacing local activities, including their entrepreneurs, workers, etc. Since the subsidiaries remain as closely tied to the TRANCO as possible in terms of inputs, technology, personnel, property, administration, product, and process innovation, etc., the effects of the spread over the local economy tend to be less important than the backwash effects or the spread effects over the economy of the metropolitan country.

2. Since, for various reasons, the TRANCO needs permanently to expand its markets, under-developed countries are subject to a massive offensive of the consumerism characteristic of

developed societies. There is of course a ready
market for these goods among the small segment
of higher income groups which are integrated into
the developed part of the global system, but the
demonstration effect also trickles down to the
lower income groups. This introduces serious
distortions and irrationalities into the structure
of demand and in the allocation of private and
public investment resources, while at the same
time reduces savings.

3. The activities in which TRANCOS operate
are frequently of a highly oligopolistic nature.
A few primary exporters may buy from a large
number of small agricultural or mining firms, while
a few producers of consumer durables may sell to a
large number of independent consumers. Under these
conditions, the TRANCOS could well underpay
local producers and overcharge local consumers,
obtaining excess profits on both accounts and
either sending them back to the headquarters or
reinvesting them locally, initiating a process of
cumulative accentuation.

The above analysis leads us to the following
tentative conclusion: the capitalist system of
world economy is in the process of being
reorganized into a new international industrial
system whose main institutional agents are the
TRANCOS, increasingly backed by the governments of
the developed countries; this is a new structure
of domination sharing a large number of
characteristics of the mercantilist system, which
concentrates the planning of the deployment of
natural, human, and capital resources and the
development of science and technology in the
"brain" of the new industrial system (i.e. the
technocrats of TRANCOS, international organizations,
and governments of developed countries), and which
tends to reinforce the process of economic, social,
political, and cultural underdevelopment of the
Third World deepening foreign dependence and
exacerbating internal disintegration.

The example of Canada may be illustrative:

The following is a sketch of Canada's slide
into a relationship of economic, political,
and cultural dependence upon the U.S. It
seeks to explain the process whereby national
entrepreneurship and political unity have
been eroded to a point beyond which lies the
disintegration of the Canadian nation-state.

Canada was discovered, explored, and
developed as part of the French, and later,
the British mercantile system. It grew to
independence and nationhood in a brief
historical era in which goods, capital, and
people moved in response to economic forces
operating in relatively free, competitive
international markets.

Present day Canada has been described as the
world's richest underdeveloped country. Its
regression into a state of extreme economic
and political dependence cannot possibly be
attributed, as is fasionable in some quarters,
to an unfavorable endowment of resources. Nor
can its present scarcity of independent
dynamic be laid at the door of a traditional
culture. Here we are forced to seek the
explanation of underdevelopment and fragmenta-
tion in the institutions and processes of
modern society. We suggest that such an
explanation is to be found in the dynamics of
the new mercantilism of American corporate
economy.[7]

In relation to Latin America, the following
quotation from Furtado suggests a similar process:

The penetration of the TRANCO in Latin
American industry started after the Great
Depression. After the Second World War, this
penetration becomes very intensive, particularly in countries which had already achieved
some substantial industrial development
(Argentina, Mexico, and Brazil mainly).
In this way,...the process of formation of
a national class of industrial entrepreneurs
was interrupted. Given their strong financial
position, TRANCOS progressively extended their
control over the most dynamic sectors of
industrial activity. The best talents that
emerged from local industries were absorbed
into the new managerial class....National
independent entrepreneurship was, in the
process, restricted to secondary activities
or to pioneering ventures which, in the long
run, simply open up new fields for the future
expansion of the TRANCO....The elimination
of the national entrepreneurial class
necessarily excludes (therefore) the
possibility of self-sustained national

development, in the line of classical
capitalist development.[8]

Furtado's observation may be generalized to
all groups and social classes in order to gain a
clearer perception of the process of national
disintegration. To do this, we must incorporate
a class structure into the scheme presented in
previous graphs, as in Figure 2.4.
As can be seen, the classification of
integrated and segregated groups now overlaps with
a class structure, so that integrated and non-
integrated groups appear among entrepreneurs,
middle class, and workers, as well as in a segment
of "absolutely" marginalized population. It should
be emphasized that the classification used here and
the relative importance of the seven segments into
which society has been divided are mainly of an
illustrative nature. This compartmentalization of
society will assume different forms, depending upon
the actual situation prevailing in different
countries.
The hypothesis that has been elaborated in
this essay suggests that this social structure
derives an important part of its dynamism from the
influence that the internationalized or integrated
sector receives from the central countries. At
the level of the productive structure, this
influence makes itself felt through the massive and
extraordinarily dynamic penetration of the transnational conglomerate and its subsidiaries and

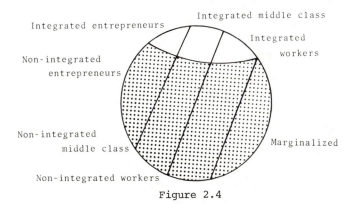

Figure 2.4

76

affiliates; at the technological level, by the
large scale introduction of highly capital-
intensive techniques; at the cultural and
ideological level, by the overwhelming and
systematic promotion and publicity of the superconsumption civilization, and at the concrete level
of development policies and strategies, by the
pressure of national and international public and
private interests in favor of the production of
higher income consumption goods and services and
the process of transnational integration.

As was indicated in the section on the
international process of polarization, modernization
implies the gradual replacement of the traditional
productive structure by another of much higher
capital intensiveness. In the conditions that were
specified then, this process appears to produce
two opposed tendencies. On the one hand, the
process of modernization incorporates into the new
structures the individuals and groups that are apt
to fit into the kind of rationality that prevails
there; on the other hand, it expels the individuals
and groups that have no place in the new productive
structure or who lack the capacity to become
adapted to it. It is important to emphasize that
this process does not only prevent or limit the
formation of a national entrepreneurial class, as
indicated by Furtado, but also of national middle
classes (including national intellectuals,
scientists, technologists, etc.) and even a
national working class. The advancement of
modernization introduces, so to speak, a wedge
along the area dividing the integrated from the
segregated segments (see Figure 2.5).

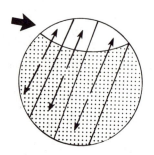

Figure 2.5

In this process, some national entrepreneurs
are incorporated as executives into the new
enterprises or those absorbed by the TRANCO, and
others are marginalized; some professionals,
forming part of the technical staff and the segment
of employees, are incorporated, and the rest are
marginalized; part of the qualified labor supply
and those that are considered fit to be upgraded
are incorporated, while the remainder are
marginalized.

The effects of the disintegration of each
social class has important consequences for social
mobility. The marginalized entrepreneur will
probably add to the ranks of small or artisanal
manufacture, or will abandon independent activity
and become a middle class employee. The
marginalized sectors of the middle class will
probably form a group of frustrated lower middle
class people trying to maintain middle class
appearance without much possibility of upward
mobility and terrorized by the danger of proletar-
ianization. The marginalized workers will surely
add to the ranks of absolute marginality, where,
as in the lower middle class, growing pools of
resentment and frustration of considerable
demographic dimension will accumulate.

Corresponding to this downward mobility there
will probably also be an upward mobility of a
selective and discriminatory character. Some
absolute marginals will be incorporated into the
working class, some workers will rise to the lower
ranks of the middle class, and some sectors of
the middle class may become medium or small
entrepreneurs. This upward movement will probably
tend to depress the wage level, at least of the
unskilled workers, and will increase the anguish
of the lower middle class.

Finally, it is very probable that an international mobility will correspond to the internal
mobility, particularly between the internationalized
sectors of developed and underdeveloped countries,
which, as we have indicated before, constitute the
nucleus of the international capitalist system, and,
therefore, probably also constitutes an international market for skilled resources. Part of this
international mobility is the so-called "brain
drain," the counterpart of which is the reverse flow
of experts and administrators sent to the underdeveloped countries in order to orientate and
administer the process of development and
modernization described in this paper. An attempt

is made to illustrate this complex of internal and external social mobility process (see Figure 2.6).

The process of social disintegration which has been outlined here probably also affects the social institutions which provide the bases of the different social groups and through which they express themselves. Similar tendencies to the ones described for the global society are, therefore, probably also to be found within the state, church, armed forces, political parties with a relatively wide popular base, the universities, etc. The crises which each of these institutions is experiencing in Latin America will also have special characteristics according to the combination of social forces which they represent, and of which they are made up, but also according to the intensity with which they are affected in their structure and functioning by the process of transnational integration and national disintegration.

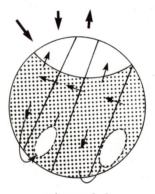

Figure 2.6

NOTES

1. The distinction between "internal" and "external" factors should be taken essentially as a preliminary simplifying classification. It will be seen later that the so-called "internal" structures are in turn the outcome of earlier historical processes of interaction between the external and the internal, and that "external" links have in fact very concrete and powerful internal manifestations.

2. The expression "backwash effect" is used here in the Myrdalian sense, to represent the deforming, inhibiting, and exploitative effects of specialization in primary exports on underdeveloped economies.

3. Celso Furtado, "*La concentración del poder económico en los Estados Unidos y sus proyecciones en América Latina*," *Estudios Internacionales*, October 1967-March 1968, *Año 1*, Nos. 3-4, Santiago, 1968 and *La reestructuración de la economía internacional y las relaciones entre Estados Unidos y América Latina*" in O. Sunkel (ed.) *Integración Política y Económica: La Experiencia Europea y el Proceso Latinoamericano*, Editorial Universitaria, Santiago, 1970. Also, Ch. Cooper and F. Chesnais, "*La ciencia y la tecnología en la integración europea*" in O. Sunkel (ed.) *Integración Política y Económica: La Experiencia Europea y el Proceso Latinoamericano*, Santiago, Editorial Universitaria, 1970.

4. *The Economist*, May 16-22, 1970, p. 81.

5. John Kenneth Galbraith, *The New Industrial State*, Boston, Houghton Mifflin, 1967.

6. A. Barber, "Emerging New Power: The World Corporation," *War/Peace Report*, October 1968, p. 7.

7. Kari Levitt, "Canada: Economic Dependence and Political Disintegration," *New World Quarterly*, Vol. IV, No. 2, Jamaica, 1968.

8. Furtado, *op. cit.*

This was abridged by the editor from an article appearing in *Social and Economic Studies*, Vol. 22, No. 1, (March 1973), pp. 132-176. Reprinted by permission.

3
A Class Analysis of Multinational Corporate Expansion

Richard L. Sklar

New frontiers for substantive research
frequently give rise to theoretical challenges.
More often than not, these will in fact be old
challenges revived or rediscovered in a new context.
Political scientists may well discover a fertile
field for research in the phenomenal expansion of
multinational business enterprise. Yet the
challenges they encounter may not differ in principle from those that have been presented in the past
by the growth of corporate enterprise in particular
nations. Indeed, the failure of political science
to comprehend the modern business corporation is
well enough known. As Grant McConnell has written,
"the existence of the modern corporation does not
accord with longstanding conceptions of political
organization, and no theory exists by which it
can be reconciled with such conceptions."[1] The
unmistakable relevance of transnational corporations
to basic issues of political development and international relations creates a new opportunity for
political scientists to face challenges that have
been posed but, largely and lamentably, ignored in
the past.

In this essay, three issues that arise from
the problem of corporate power in political theory
are identified with reference to pioneering works
on corporate power in modern industrial society.
These issues, involving economic oligarchy,
managerial authority, and class formation, are then
transposed to the transnational plane of study.
Recent works on transnational enterprise and the
problems of development in nonindustrial societies
indicate that these questions may now be studied
on a broader scale than heretofore, at possibly
deeper levels of theoretical comprehension.

81

I

No challenge to political science excites a
more defensive reaction than that implied by
Adolf A. Berle's view that the business corporation
is "essentially, a nonstatist political institution."[2] This idea casts doubt upon the separation
of economic power from political power for
analytical purposes, a presupposition that is
widely accepted in standard political science.[3] It
also severely restricts the claim of democracy
that can be made on behalf of political orders in
societies that rely upon oligarchic forms of
economic organization. As this observation implies,
there may be an ideological basis for the characteristic attribution of economic and political
power to different causes or generative activities
by the vast majority of Western political scientists. Yet the pioneers of scientific political
analysis did not uniformly balk at the challenge
to conceive their subject as a unified field of
power. Upon that provocative premise
George Catlin has proclaimed the conceptual
identity of political science and sociology,
envisioning from that point of view a transdisci-
plinary domain which, as Charles Hyneman observed,
might be extended to encompass much of the
discipline of economics as well.[4] It may not be
amiss to suggest that Berle's apparent iconoclasm
is, essentially, traditional common sense.
    The classic analysis of corporate power in the
modern era was published by Berle and
Gardiner C. Means in 1932.[5] This work set forth
a theory of managerial autonomy within the modern
business corporation based upon the authors'
debatable finding that the evolution of corporate
organization entails the divorce of ownership from
control and the lodgement of decisive power in the
hands of managers rather than owners. By 1940,
other authoritative studies had shown, contrary to
Berle and Means, that large nonfinancial
corporations in the United States were likely to
be controlled by their leading owners.[6] Nevertheless, the age of managerial authority, whether it
be inseparable from legal ownership or coexistent
upon separate foundations, had been proclaimed.
It was a short step from there to announce the
appearance of a managerial class, created by the
organizational imperatives of the corporation
itself. Thus, in 1941, James Burnham, recently
estranged from Trotskyite Marxism, declared that

a managerial ruling class, nurtured by the
corporation, was emerging in the United States
and other industrial countries.[7]

As a rule, those who conceive social class to
be a function of property ownership have rejected
the notion of a bureaucratic or managerial "class"
in capitalist societies.[8] However, the managers of
business enterprise and those who serve business in
a professional capacity, in addition to their
professional and social counterparts in other
employment sectors, are often classified with
property owners to constitute the bourgeoisie as a
whole.[9] As a recruitment agency to the ranks of
"middle management," bureaucratic organization
promotes the growth of a social stratum that
identifies firmly with the interests of property.
Andrew Hacker has argued that the American corporation has produced a "new middle class" of junior
and senior executives. This class is "large,
national, and propertyless." Following
William S. White, Hacker labels the species
homo Americanus," or the "Consensus American."
Its mode of social thought is cosmopolitan (within
national limits) rather than narrowly sectional;
its political style is passive and nonpartisan
rather than earnestly participative and staunchly
partisan, as the old middle class had been.[10]

Apart from Hacker, H. H. Wilson, and a few
others, political scientists have been remarkably
reticent about inquiring into political aspects of
the corporate presence in modern industrial
societies.[11] Among the many questions that bear
investigation, three issues to which I have alluded
in connection with the pioneering works of Berle,
Means, and Burnham appear certain to capture the
attention of those who study the multinational
corporation. First, Berle's conception of the
corporation as "a nonstatist political institution"
points, as we have seen, toward oligarchy as the
probable political future of the industrial
capitalist societies. This may be contested by
those who visualize a significant redistribution of
corporate power from managers to employees,[12] and
by those who are satisfied to define democracy as
a system of imperfect competition between opposing
groups of politicians.[13] For Berle himself, the
legal separation of corporate from state power was
a virtue of paramount importance, since it would
allow for the perfection of libertarian institutions
under modern industrial conditions.[14] At the
supranational level, the impression of oligarchy

as a consequence of corporate enterprise may be
intensified by the absence of an international
state which might countervail oligopolistic
corporate power. Richard J. Barnet and
Ronald E. Müller refer to the leading executives
of multinational corporations as "World Managers."[15]
Do the actions of multinational corporate executives
serve to secure and perpetuate the domination of
some countries by others? In other words, the issue
of oligarchy entails the question of imperialism.

Second, at the supranational level, the old
issue of autonomous managerial authority becomes
crucial to calculations about the potential exercise
of corporate statesmanship in world affairs. In
particular, it relates directly to the often
vaunted ability of corporate managers to act in
accordance with broad political and social values in
addition to their normal economic objectives.
John K. Galbraith has argued that the principled
pursuit of noneconomic goals by a "mature
corporation" is entirely consistent with its con-
current pursuit of overriding economic and technological goals. In fact, he contends, social goals
for the corporation are needed to maintain the
loyalty and morale of the many mental, as distinct
from manual, workers who serve it.[16] This theme has
been amplified by various expositors of multinational enterprise. Thus, Howard V. Perlmutter
believes that the senior executives of the leading
multinational corporations are the most important
"social architects" of the new era. He postulates
the "geocentric man" as the ideal executive for the
"geocentric corporation"--a multinational enterprise whose national affiliates operate on the basis
of economic equality.[17]

Third, beyond the issue of managerial autonomy, we may conceive the formation of a transnational class comprising at its core those who
manage multinational corporations. To substantiate
this thesis, it would be necessary to show that the
members of any such presumed class tend to think
and act as a collective entity. Social classes are
sustained and strengthened by many different
generators of vitality. A transnational ruling
class would be especially difficult to overthrow
inasmuch as its power would be fortified by the
appropriation of diverse resources in many
countries. Its significance as a power group might
transcend the conception of imperialism. These
three issues--imperialism, managerial autonomy,
and transnational class domination--will be

discussed in relation to the penetration of
nonindustrial countries by multinational
corporations.

II

The multinational corporation (or enterprise
or firm) may be suitably defined according to these
criteria: it consists of a parent company and
subsidiary companies, the latter of which are
located in a few or more countries and are engaged
in the performance of basic economic, typically
productive, activities in addition to trade. The
various national components of the enterprise are
mutually supportive and subject to central
direction. The management of each component is
designed to promote the overall interests of the
group as a whole.[18] If, for example, it should
appear to be in the interest of the enterprise as
a whole to move certain productive operations from
one country to another in quest of cheaper labor
or lower taxes, the inclination to do so is likely
to prevail. Inevitably, it will be suggested that
the interests of the whole normally coincide with
the interests of the controlling part. Since the
parent company does have a national identity and
since it is normally controlled by directors of a
specific nationality, or a small set of national-
ities, the spread of multinational enterprise
appears to result in the perpetuation and intensi-
fication of hegemonic domination by the industrial
capitalist powers. In short, the national and
organizational loyalties of transnational businessmen may be expected to fuse with imperialistic
force. This argument has been made from a Marxist-
Leninist standpoint as a matter of doctrine:

> Capital without a state is...unthinkable.
> But in the world as it is constituted today
> only nations have states: there is no such
> thing as a supranational state. If, for
> example, the state of the nation to which it
> belonged were to collapse, capital would lose
> its indispensable protector. It would then
> either be incorporated into the capital of
> another nation, or cease to be capital, by
> coming under the jurisdiction of a revolu-
> tionary regime dedicated to the abolition
> of the entire set of relations of production
> of which capital is one part....[T]he

historic course of the global capitalist
system is leading to one of two outcomes:
world empire or world revolution.[19]

An empirically based demonstration of the
thesis that multinational corporations promote
imperialism by economic means has been presented
by Stephen Hymer.[20] The basis of his argument is
his insistence upon the differing effects of the
technological and organizational determinants of
economic development. In his view, technological
diffusion alone does not produce or serve to
perpetuate imperialist domination. This condition
is plainly the result of corporate organization,
which typically distributes the functions of
planning, coordination, and routine operation
according to the principle of hierarchy. The
result is a proliferation of subsidiary firms,
whose actions are coordinated at regional levels
by higher subsidiaries of parent corporations,
themselves located in the major geographical
centers of corporate power and planning.[21]
Marxists in general assume that domination (of
the underindustrialized countries by the industrial
capitalist countries) and exploitation go hand in
hand--that in the course of multinational corporate
expansion, relatively poor and weak countries are
compelled by various means to pay for the benefits
that accrue to the advanced capitalist countries.[22]
Few people today would bother to challenge this
assumption by resuscitating the late Victorian
doctrine of beneficent, paternalistic imperialism.[23]
However, another somewhat paradoxical thesis to
the effect that imperialism is not only injurious
to subjugated peoples but also harmful to the
imperialist nations themselves--John A. Hobson's
distinctive viewpoint[24]--has been reiterated by
anti-imperialists of diverse ideological orientations. Thus, Barnet and Müller hold that by means
of "transfer pricing" and other exploitative/manip-
ulative devices, multinational corporations systematically cheat, and thereby retard the economic
development of, poor countries. At the same time,
they contend, in the spirit of Hobson, that such
corporations are directly responsible for
retrogressive tendencies in their industrial "home"
countries, especially the United States, as shown
by symptoms of economic, political, and social decay
that are reminiscent of conditions in underdeveloped
countries. American workers, they state, are
especially liable to suffer from the transfer of

productive and distributive operations from the
United States to low wage "host" countries.[25]
     These observations suggest that the domination
of one people or nation by another, which, strictly
speaking, defines the concept of imperialism,
should not be confused with the calculation of
benefits and costs that result from such domination.
Benefit/cost calculations involve an assessment of
outcome rather than power. Until the mid-twentieth
century, it was widely assumed that exploitative
economic relations between countries at different
levels of economic development were established and
maintained by means of imperial domination. With
the advent of colonial freedom in Asia and Africa,
and the emergence of communist powers comparable
in strength to their capitalist adversaries, it
became reasonable to expect that the causes of
economic exploitation would be clearly identified
and progressively eliminated. Proponents of
multinational enterprise do hold that this, in
fact, is the direction of movement within the
noncommunist sphere. Responding to the charge of
exploitation, they say that multinational
corporations diffuse modern skills, technologies,
and urgently needed capital resources to the nonindustrial countries, that they contribute
handsomely to governmental revenues in such
countries, and that they provide secure access to
world markets for their exports. Since there are
both benefits and costs on either side of all
international economic relationships, the calculation of *relative* benefit and cost is crucial to
this argument. If it can be shown, contrary to the
case for transnational enterprise, that the economic
position of given industrial nations is enhanced
relative to (or at the expense of) particular non-
or less-industrialized nations, the relationships
in question may be deemed to promote or perpetuate
imperialist domination. In fact, the debate about
relative benefit and cost in relationships mediated
by multinational corporations has been intense; it
is also likely to be interminable and inconclusive,
as powerful arguments are marshalled on both
sides.[26]
     Advocates of the exploitation-imperialism
thesis have had to assume an added theoretical
burden in addition to the weight of their evidence
on costs. They need to explain the persistence of
exploitation despite the passing of colonialism
and other overtly imperialistic forms of political
control.[27] Obviously, it will not suffice merely

to infer domination from a (usually rebuttable) demonstration of exploitation. To this author's mind, the elements of controversy about imperialist domination (whether and why it persists) have not been identified with anything like the clarity that recent studies have shed upon the question of relative benefit and cost. For want of satisfactory formulations of specific matters of controversy relating to the question of domination, the debate about imperialism in the age of multinational enterprise has not been properly joined.

III

Whereas the benefit/cost calculation, upon which a finding of "economic" imperialism[28] depends, does not directly bear upon the bases and exercise of power, the issue of managerial authority is directly and indubitably pertinent to the study of corporate power. Managers exercise authority. But the heralds of managerial autonomy misperceived the evolving relationship between management and ownership-interest as a case of divorcement. Recent evidence relating to the major American "global" corporations has been summarized by Barnet and Müller thus: "...in the upper reaches of America's corporations there is no 'technostructure' made up of managers with interests distinct from those of the owners. Increasingly, the managers are the owners, deriving an increasing proportion of their income not from their managerial skills but from the stock they own in their own corporations."[29] Paradoxically, the thesis of managerial autonomy may be revived in connection with multinational corporate expansion mainly as a result of conditions in the nonindustrial and newly developing countries, where corporate enterprise has been established upon foundations of foreign capital.

To be sure, the detection of managerial rule in nonindustrial societies would not mark the first removal of this idea from its original setting. Heretofore, expositors of the "managerial revolution" have cited developments in socialist countries, especially the Soviet Union, to corroborate their thesis.[30] Trotsky's harsh judgment, in *The Revolution Betrayed*,[31] has been repeated and refined by Marxist critics of "bureaucratic" autocracy in the Soviet Union, some of whom identify a "new class," comprising a party-bureaucratic formation,[32] while others, who are

equally critical, do not.[33] Charles Bettelheim
uses the term "state bourgeoisie" to describe and
condemn the ruling stratum in the Soviet Union,
holding, in a Maoist vein, that its existence
actually portends nothing less than the restoration
of capitalism.[34]

As in the socialist countries, bureaucratic
cadres in the nonsocialist, newly developing
countries have increasingly come to the forefront
of public affairs. Typically, the bureaucratic
elites of such countries enjoy incomes and social
privileges far beyond the dreams or expectations
of all but a few of their relatively impoverished
compatriots. In his moving critique of social
inequality and poor economic performance in newly
independent African states, the French agronomist,
René Dumont, observes that "a new type of bourgeoisie is forming in Africa...a bourgeoisie of the
civil service."[35] The concept of a "bureaucratic
bourgeoisie" as the new ruling class has been
applied effectively in African studies.[36] But it
does not appear to match the social realities of
countries such as Nigeria, where an entrepreneurial
bourgeoisie is well established; nor has this term
been widely adopted by students of those Asian and
Latin American societies where private enterprise
is the principal economic form.

As in the study of industrial societies, so
also in the study of nonindustrial societies the
relationship between bureaucratic and entrepreneurial class power becomes a matter of serious
controversy. The theoretical problems are com-
pounded by widespread uncertainty as to the
approximate degree to which the private enterprise
sectors of most newly developing countries are
dependent upon state patronage and support.
Invariably, a degree of dependence that is deemed
to be either too great or too small will automatically activate theoretical defense mechanisms
against the specter of an indistinct analytical
boundary between the bureaucratic and entrepreneurial spheres of life. In this circumstance,
a complex idea is needed to comprehend businessmen,
members of the learned professions, leading
politicians, and upper level bureaucrats as members
of a single class. Perhaps the term "managerial
bourgeoisie" will suggest an idea of merit.
Inasmuch as this term clearly refers to the private
business elite as well as to the managers of public
enterprises and to high government officials, it
may be preferred to either "bureaucratic" or

"state" bourgeoisie. Moreover, this term, in
contrast with the term "entrepreneurial bourgeoisie," reflects the apparent disposition of
bourgeois elements in the nonindustrial and newly
developing countries[37] to manage the production
and distribution of wealth rather than to create
new wealth-producing enterprises.[38]

In many postcolonial and nonindustrial
countries, as C. B. Macpherson has observed, the
state is conceived and appraised mainly in terms
of its contribution to development.[39] Development
itself is a value-laden idea, connoting progress
toward the achievement of desired goals.[40] The
political aspect of development, as distinct from
those value premises that involve political goals,
may be understood to signify the improvement of a
society's ability to control the rate and direction
of change. The concept of control is crucial to
this definition, since it implies the ability to
formulate and implement strategies for solving
problems and achieving goals. In newly developing
countries, drastic changes in the organization of
authority--organizational revolutions[41]--are
frequently required to facilitate the effective
exercise of social control. These political transformations are themselves contingent upon the
recruitment of unprecedented numbers of trained
people to staff the new and rejuvenated state
agencies. To this end, certain democratic and
egalitarian devices, such as equal educational
opportunity, are useful if not indispensable.
However, the new organizational men and women, taken
together with their immediate families and social
peers, constitute a minor fraction of the population, about 5 to 10 percent. The organizational
revolution, spurred by material incentives, is a
forcing house for class formation and privilege.

In all societies, "revolutions from above"
are prone to develop deeply conservative tendencies.
In newly developing countries, modern conservatism,
as distinct from traditionalism, normally connotes
a disposition to arrest the transformation of
organizational revolutions into social revolutions
or shifts in the class content of power. Typically,
the managerial bourgeoisie, virtually born (as a
class) to authority, takes care to contain
radicalism and maintain its position as the predominant class. Insecure as it is and not strongly
committed to liberal principles, this class has
shown a marked disposition to take refuge in various
forms of political monopoly, such as the one-party

state and the "caesarist" military regime. Populist
and socialist rhetoric may be "poured on" to obscure
and excuse the imposition of political monopoly.
Normally, however, this kind of arrangement serves
to protect and consolidate the rule of the
bourgeoisie.[42]

To what extent does empirical evidence sustain
the hypothesis of widespread class domination of
the nonindustrial countries by the managerial
bourgeoisie, as herein defined? The evidence is
not inconsiderable, although Maurice Zeitlin has
correctly noted the present need for studies of
"dominant classes" in underdeveloped countries.[43]
Regional studies would be especially valuable. In
African studies, the hypothesis in question is
supported by a formidable body of literature;[44] in
Asian studies, a few works on India and Iran have
corroborative value;[45] and in Latin American
studies, evidence relating to Brazil is particularly
relevant.[46]

It would not be correct to hold that the
presence of a managerial bourgeoisie as the
dominant class necessarily means that a given
country will be receptive to capitalist principles
of development. Anticapitalist--including Marxist--
strategies of development may be chosen, as in the
case of Tanzania.[47] Thus far, however, the vast
majority of such governments have chosen to adopt
mixed economy strategies in conjunction with
various forms of foreign investment. Increasingly,
"partnerships" between state investment agencies
and multinational corporations serve to promote
the organizational revolution and, by extension,
the class interests of the managerial bourgeoisie.
Leading members of the bourgeoisie are constantly
tempted to imbibe the capitalistic and managerial
attitudes of their foreign business associates.
Some of them may aspire to careers in the wider
business world. Given the obviously bourgeois
life-styles of individuals in this elite social
stratum, they may be expected to embrace an elitist
ideology. The influence of international
capitalism functions to reinforce immanent
tendencies toward embourgeoisment of the state
bureaucratic elite.

No one should assume that a policy of
partnership with the agencies of international
capitalism portends the abandonment of nationalist
principles on the part of governments in the
nonindustrial countries. It is the singular
failing of many "radical," including Marxist,

analyses, of such countries to underestimate the
strength and historic importance of bourgeois class
formation as well as the nationalist integrity of
that class. Too often, the generic term
"bourgeoisie" is casually qualified with the
contemptuous adjective "*comprador*," a synonym for
"puppet"--entirely dependent and subservient.[48] It
is thereby suggested that the emergent bourgeoisie
is a "clientele" class that betrays the national
interest of its own country to foreign capitalist
powers. This notion is fundamental to the closely
related doctrines of "dependency" and "neocolonialism."[49] Indeed, these doctrines purport to
supply a theory of postcolonial domination that
cannot be derived from the traditional economic
theories of imperialism. Beholden as they are to
Marxism, these doctrines are disabled, as is
standard Marxism itself, by the inadequate conception of class upon which they are founded. As
Stanislaw Ossowski has observed, in his Marxist
criticism of the Marxist conception of class, the
relevant determinants of class include relationships
to the means of production, consumption, *and*
compulsion.[50] Given its control over the means of
consumption and compulsion, the managerial
bourgeoisie, as herein identified, must be compre-
hended, contrary to the doctrines of dependency and
neocolonialism, as an autonomous social force--the
veritable ruling class in most of those countries
that comprise the so-called "Third World." The
identity of this class becomes more firmly
established with each passing year.[51] Its ardent
desire for autonomy is unmistakable. And it yields
to no other class in the intensity of its
nationalism.

Intense nationalism on the part of the
managerial bourgeoisie poses an historic challenge
to the leaders of international capitalism. Will
they be able to harmonize their practices with the
nationalistic values of bourgeois governments in
the newly developing countries? Only, we may
answer, if it is in their perceived interest to do
so. Adam Smith taught successive generations that
businessmen who pursue their own interests serve
the general interest as well. The business creed
comprehends this even more plausible corollary:
he who serves another benefits himself.

Is it not logical to expect the subsidiaries
of a multinational business group to harmonize
their policies with the interests of various host
governments insofar as they seek to survive and

prosper in the host countries concerned? Corporate policies of precisely this nature are described in my study of multinational mining companies that operate in the several states of central and southern Africa. In particular, I have observed that South African and American controlled mining corporations domiciled in the Republic of Zambia complied faithfully with Zambian national policies of economic disengagement from the white-ruled states of southern Africa even before the Zambian Government acquired majority ownership of those companies in 1970. They did so at considerable cost to themselves and despite the fact that the Zambian policies in question were largely inconsistent with economic values and policies espoused by the directors of the parent companies in South Africa and the United States. On the other hand, these companies made no apparent concession to the Zambian point of view in implementing their policies of equally good corporate citizenship on the part of subsidiaries domiciled in other states, including the white-dominated states of southern Africa.[52]

These observations suggest a corporate doctrine of domicile, meaning that individual subsidiaries of an international business group may operate in accordance with the requirements of divergent and conflicting policies pursued by the governments of their respective host states. Ultimately, the aim of local adaptation is to promote the interests of the enterprise as a whole. Meanwhile, the policy of good corporate citizenship will appeal to the leaders of newly developing host countries who would like to establish stable relationships with international business organizations. Positing a mutuality of interest, the doctrine of domicile justifies transnational corporate expansion while it also legitimizes large-scale foreign investments in the eyes of the host country. Furthermore, it commands subservience to the local authority of the managerial bourgeoisie.

My formulation of the doctrine of domicile as a tenet of corporate ideology is based upon political and logistical evidence from a turbulent and, in many ways, atypical region. It will be tested again within that region by relations between the giant corporations and the newly independent, avowedly anticapitalist governments of Angola and Mozambique. In southern Africa, as elsewhere, it would be far more difficult to make out a prima facie case for compliance with host country

interests at the expense of corporate group
interests with evidence derived from routine
business practices. Having surveyed the "transfer
pricing" practices, "cross subsidization" strategies, and sundry exploitative devices to which
multinational enterprises normally resort, Barnet
and Müller conclude that comprehensive regulatory
policies by the governments of the capitalist
states themselves will be required to discipline
and humanize the global corporations.[53] Other
commentators, more sympathetic to multinational
enterprise, have discerned a greater capacity for
the exercise of corporate statesmanship in the
quest for policies that will satisfy transnational
corporate managers and the nationalist governments
of newly developing countries at one and the same
time.[54] Joint ventures, involving the transfer of
substantial, even majority, ownership to agencies
of host states have become increasingly familiar.
Rarely do such schemes silence the cry of exploitation; nor do they settle the question of control,
since minority owners may yet retain effective
control of a given venture, while the reality of
self-management by the host state is contingent
upon many circumstances, including the attainment
of technical competence in diverse fields. Nonetheless, joint ventures do facilitate the
"revolution from above," and thereby help to
produce the institutional conditions and climate
of opinion that enhance the authority of the
bourgeoisie and promote its growth as a class.

IV

Within its sphere of control--specifically,
a newly developing, nonindustrial, and nonsocialist
country--the managerial bourgeoisie rises above a
larger, normally far larger, national bourgeoisie,
the diversity and extent of which depends mainly
upon the size of the country and its level of
economic development. In effect, the managerial
bourgeoisie is the ruling stratum of the national
bourgeoisie.[55] Its distinctive identity as a sub-
class is manifest behaviorally in the collective
actions and attitudes of its members. The action
which, more than any other, sets this subclass apart
from the bourgeoisie as a whole is its tendency
to coalesce with bourgeois elements at comparable
levels of control in foreign countries. To the
extent that the doctrine of domicile becomes a

maxim of corporate action, it helps to reconcile the
staunch nationalism of the managerial bourgeoisie
with the cosmopolitan values of bourgeois leaders
abroad who have global interests and perspectives.
Thus, it functions to promote transnational class
cohesion.

It may be enlightening to think of the worldwide corporate and managerial bourgeoisie as a class
in formation that now comprises three overlapping
entities, as shown in Figure 3.1. The corporate
bourgeoisie, based mainly in the industrial
capitalist countries, includes a corporate international segment. The managerial bourgeoisie of
the newly developing, nonsocialist countries also
overlaps with the corporate international bourgeoisie. These transnational extensions of, and
linkages between, comparable segments of the
bourgeoisie depend upon the creation and perfection
of transnational institutions. The multinational
corporation is probably the most effective institution for this purpose. It should, therefore, be
analyzed and understood in terms of transnational

Figure 3.1 Elements of Worldwide Corporate and
Managerial Bourgeoisie

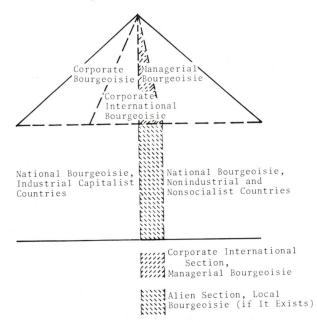

96

class development. In this process, the bourgeoisie, true to its epoch-making tradition, has taken
the lead.

Corporate internationalism is a social movement and a rising class interest. With its advent
as a major social force, the working classes of
the world confront a corporate bourgeoisie in
industrial capitalist countries, and a mana erial
bourgeoisie in newly developing countries.56 Where
the transition of a given developing country to the
stage of industrial capitalism is sustained, indigenous elements of the corporate bourgeoisie will
emerge. In the long run, if capitalism in that
country is preserved, the corporate bourgeoisie
may be expected to supersede the managerial
bourgeoisie as the ruling class. This essay
presents a short-term analysis. It draws attention
to the coalescent relationship between two dominant
classes--the managerial bourgeoisie and the corporate international bourgeoisie. In so doing, it
seeks to make the hypothesis of transnational class
formation credible.57

Wars of redistribution between rival capitalist
powers, specified by Lenin as the distinctive
product of imperialism,58 may yet disrupt and abort
the transnational evolution of the bourgeoisie.
But that danger is counteracted by the emergence of
the managerial bourgeoisie as a cohesive ruling
class in newly developing countries in conjunction
with the growth and spread of multinational enterprise. Increasingly, power in world affairs comes
to be organized in accordance with class rather
than national interests and values. Imperialism,
as a stage of capitalism, gives way to corporate
international capitalism. We may anticipate
severe ideological strain between the doctrinaire
liberalism of the corporate bourgeoisie59 and the
paternalistic authoritarianism of the managerial
bourgeoisie. However, the fate of the bourgeoisie--
corporate and managerial--will probably be
determined by domestic struggles, not by anti-
imperialist struggles that pit insurgent nations
against foreign powers.

NOTES

*I am grateful to Professor William Tordoff
for many valuable discussions and for his ever
constructive criticisms of my work during the term
of my appointment as Simon Visiting Professor at

the Victoria University of Manchester, where his
essay was written. Acknowledgments are due also
to Edward Merrow and Martin J. Sklar.

1. Grant McConnell, *Private Power and
American Democracy* (New York, 1966), p. 129.
2. Adolf A. Berle, Jr., *The Twentieth Century
Capitalist Revolution* (New York, 1954), p. 60; and
Berle, *Power Without Property* (New York, 1959),
pp. 17-24.
3. Systems theorists, in particular, normally
separate the economic and political spheres of life
for analytical purposes. See, for example,
David Easton, *A Framework for Political Analysis*
(Englewood Cliffs, 1965), p. 60; Easton, *A Systems
Analysis of Political Life* (New York, 1965),
pp. 21-23; and Karl W. Deutsch, *The Nerves of
Government* (New York, 1966), pp. 119-124. For an
example of this bent in "group theory," see
David B. Truman, *The Governmental Process: Polit-
ical Interests and Public Opinion*, 2d ed. (New
York, 1971), pp. 257-260.
4. See esp. George E. Gordon Catlin,
*Systematic Politics: Elementa Politica et
Sociologica* (Toronto, 1962), pp. 34-38, 45-47;
and Charles S. Hyneman's important defense of the
"power" approach to political science espoused by
Catlin and Harold D. Lasswell. See Hyneman, *The
Study of Politics: The Present State of American
Political Science* (Urbana, 1959), pp. 142-150.
5. Berle, Jr. and Gardiner C. Means, *The
Modern Corporation and Private Property*, rev. ed.
(New York, 1968).
6. These studies have been reviewed by
Maurice Zeitlin, "Corporate Ownership and Control:
The Large Corporation and the Capitalist Class,"
American Journal of Sociology, LXXIX (March 1974),
1084. A vigorous debate persists on the issue of
management- versus owner-control of large American
corporations. See the exchange between
Michael Patrick Allen and Zeitlin in ibid.,
LXXXI (January 1976), 885-903.
7. James Burnham, *The Managerial Revolution*,
new ed. (Bloomington, 1960). Note esp. the
author's preface to the Midland Books Edition.
8. H. H. Gerth and C. Wright Mills, "A
Marx for the Managers," LII *Ethics*, (January 1942),
200-215. Franz L. Neumann, a leading political
scientist in the Marxist tradition, held that in
capitalist societies economic power is translated
"into social power and thence into political
power." He doubted the alleged shift of political

98

power from social groups to bureaucracies; he also distinguished bureaucratic behavior from class action. Neumann, "Approaches to the Study of Political Power," *Political Science Quarterly*, LXV (June 1950), 161-180. On the "problem of bureaucracy" in Marxist social thought, see Daniel Bell, *The Coming of Post-Industrial Society: A Venture in Social Forecasting* (New York, 1973), pp. 80-99.

9. The theoretical basis for this view is Stanislaw Ossowski's exposition of "synthetic gradation" in his *Class Structure in the Social Consciousness* (New York, 1963), pp. 44-57. Representative statements include Leonard Reissman, *Class in American Society* (London, 1960), pp. 217-218; and Zeitlin, 1078-1079. For an alternative view, see Gerhard Lenski, *Power and Prestige: A Theory of Social Stratification* (New York, 1966), pp. 352-361.

10. Andrew Hacker, "Politics and the Corporation," in Hacker, ed. *The Corporation Take-Over* (Garden City, 1965), pp. 239-262. The similarly baleful and convincing portrait of recruits to the managerial vocation drawn by William H. Whyte, Jr., should also be cited (*The Organization Man* [New York, 1956]).

11. My own appreciation of the need for political studies of the business corporation derives from the inspired teaching of Professor H. H. Wilson at Princeton University in the mid-1950s. Among the pioneering analyses of corporate power by political scientists and sociologists, two are particularly noteworthy: Mills, *The Power Elite* (New York, 1956); and Earl Latham, "The Body Politic of the Corporation," in Edward S. Mason, ed. *The Corporation in Modern Society* (Cambridge [Mass.], 1959), pp. 218-236. The relevant literature has been reviewed by Edwin M. Epstein, *The Corporation in American Politics* (Englewood Cliffs, 1969). More recent studies of particular significance include Richard J. Barber, *The American Corporation* (New York, 1970), and Karen Orren, *Corporate Power and Social Change: The Politics of the Life Insurance Industry* (Baltimore, 1974).

12. Peter Bachrach, *The Theory of Democratic Elitism: A Critique* (Boston, 1967), pp. 102-105.

13. Joseph A. Schumpeter, *Capitalism, Socialism, and Democracy*, 2d ed. (New York and London, 1947), pp. 269-273, 283.

14. This appears to be the main basis of Berle's preference for the American corporate system to the Soviet system. Berle, *Power Without Property*, pp. 141-158. Similarly, Raymond Vernon, a foremost authority on multinational enterprise, has declared: "The challenge in social organization is to ensure that the large units on which our future societies are likely to be based act as countervailing political powers, not as mutually reinforcing ones." See his *Sovereignty at Bay: The Multinational Spread of U.S. Enterprises* (New York, 1971), p. 273.

15. Richard J. Barnet and Ronald E. Müller, *Global Reach: The Power of the Multinational Corporations* (New York, 1974).

16. His original term for this element is the "technostructure." Efficiency of operation, he contends, depends upon the congruence of corporate and social goals with the personal values of most individual members of the technostructure according to the "principle of consistency." See John Kenneth Galbraith, *The New Industrial State* (New York, 1967), pp. 169-188.

17. Howard V. Perlmutter, "The Tortuous Evolution of the Multinational Corporation," in Courtney C. Brown, ed. *World Business: Promise and Problems*, (New York, 1970), pp. 81-82.

18. These criteria are derived from the following works, which mention all of them, but vary in their emphases: Jack N. Behrman, *National Interests and the Multinational Enterprise: Tensions among the North Atlantic Countries* (Englewood Cliffs, 1970), pp. 1-2; John H. Dunning, "The Multinational Enterprise: The Background," in Dunning, ed. *The Multinational Enterprise* (London, 1971), pp. 16-17; Vernon, p. 4; and Isaiah A. Litvak and Christopher J. Maule, "The Multinational Firm: Some Perspectives," in Gilles Paquet, ed. *The Multinational Firm and the Nation State* (Don Mills, Ontario, 1972), p. 22. Samuel P. Huntington contends that "transnational corporation" is a more suitable term for the business organization with these characteristics. His clarifying definitions of "transnational," "international," and "multinational" organizations should be consulted. ("Transnational Organizations in World Politics," *World Politics*, XXV [April 1973], 336). Barnet and Müller prefer to use the term "global corporation" (*Global Reach*, pp. 17-18).

19. Harry Magdoff and Paul M. Sweezy, "Notes on the Multinational Corporation," in K. T. Fann and Donald C. Hodges, eds. *Readings in U.S. Imperialism* (Boston, 1971), pp. 100, 113. One way for the polemicist to live with an awkward phrase that has "caught on" is to define it so that it suits an approved purpose. "Third World" is a case in point. This term has been provocatively (and to my mind sensibly) defined by Marxist-Leninists for partisan purposes to designate "that large and in many ways diverse collection of colonies, semi-colonies, and neo-colonies which form the base of the global capitalist pyramid." Ibid., p. 94.

20. Stephen Hymer, "The Multinational Corporation and the Law of Uneven Development," in Jagdish N. Bhagwati, ed. *Economics and World Order from the 1970's to the 1990's* (New York, 1972), pp. 113-140.

21. Although Hymer's standpoint is avowedly Marxist, his thesis on corporate organization and the location of subsidiaries is derived from non-Marxist sources and implies an un-Marxian organizational determinism. Similar views are set forth in two significant essays: Norman Girvan, "Multinational Corporations and Dependent Under-development in Mineral Export Economies," *Social and Economic Studies* XIX (December 1970), 490-526; and Johan Galtung, "A Structural Theory of Imperialism," *Journal of Peace Research* , VIII (1971) 81-117.

22. See the excellent summation of this view by Michael Barratt Brown, *The Economics of Imperialism* (Harmondworth, 1974), pp. 201-255.

23. See the analysis of this outlook by Bernard Semmel, *Imperialism and Social Reform* (Cambridge [Mass.], 1960), pp. 53-72; and Richard Koebner and Helmut Dan Schmidt, *Imperialism: The Story and Significance of a Political Word, 1840-1960* (Cambridge, 1964), pp. 166-220. See also the dispassionate survey of benefits and costs by John Plamenatz, *On Alien Rule and Self-Government* (London, 1960).

24. John A. Hobson, *Imperialism--A Study* (1902; Ann Arbor, 1971); and see Semmel's keen summation of "the Hobson-Schumpeter theory," in *The Rise of Free Trade Imperialism* (Cambridge, 1970), pp. 222-226.

25. Barnet and Müller, *Global Reach*. See their chapters entitled, "The Latinamericanization of the United States," and "The Obsolescence of

American Labor." See also the trenchant critique
of American foreign investment as an alternative
to domestic investment and foreign trade, written
to clarify "the American national interest,"
in Robert Gilpin, *U.S. Power and the Multinational
Corporation* (New York, 1975).

26. The following statements exemplify these
opposing positions. The case for exploitation is
argued from a Marxist standpoint by Barratt Brown,
The Economics of Imperialism, and from a non-
Marxist standpoint by Müller, "The Multinational
Corporation and the Underdevelopment of the Third
World," in Charles K. Wilbur, ed. *The Political
Economy of Development and Underdevelopment* (New
York, 1973), pp. 124-151. The case against
exploitation is put by Peter F. Drucker, "Multi-
nationals and Developing Countries: Myths and
Realities," *Foreign Affairs* LIII (October 1974),
121-134; and by Mira Wilkins, who presents a
succinct summary of the positive effects of U.S.
direct investment in less developed countries, in
*The Maturing of Multinational Enterprise: American
Business Abroad from 1914 to 1970* (Cambridge
[Mass.], 1974), pp. 398-401. See also the carefully
balanced assessments by Raymond F. Mikesell,
"Conflict in Foreign Investor-Host Country
Relations: A Preliminary Analysis," in *Foreign
Investment in the Petroleum and Mineral Industries:
Case Studies of Investor-Host Country Relations*
(Baltimore, 1971), pp. 29-55; Paul Streeten,
"Costs and Benefits of Multinational Enterprises,"
in Dunning, ed. *The Multinational Enterprise*,
pp. 240-258; and Vernon, *Sovereignty at Bay*.

27. The recent doctrines of dependency and
neocolonialism are addressed to this problem.
They will be commented upon at a more relevant
point in this essay.

28. I place the word "economic" in quotes
because I take "imperialism" to be a political
conception, implying the domination of one people,
nation, or country by another. (I think that
John Strachey's definition is sound in *The End
of Empire* [London, 1961], pp. 7-8, 319-342.)
This may be effectuated by various means, including
buying, selling, and lending, as well as by
coercion and influence. To my mind, the institutions involved in these processes are "political,"
as is the resulting relationship among peoples.
See also Benjamin J. Cohen, *The Question of
Imperialism: The Political Economy of Dominance
and Dependence* (New York, 1973), pp. 15-16.

29. Barnet and Müller, pp. 294, 246, 458.

30. Burnham, p. vi.

31. Leon Trotsky, *The Revolution Betrayed*, trans. Max Eastman (1937; New York, 1945).

32. Molovan Djilas, *The New Class* (New York, 1959).

33. Herbert Marcuse, *Soviet Marxism* (New York, 1961).

34. Sweezy and Charles Bettelheim, *On the Transition to Socialism* (New York and London, 1971), p. 43. See also Sweezy's appreciative discussion of Bettelheim's recent book about class struggle in the Soviet Union, "The Nature of Soviet Society," *Monthly Review*, XXVI (November 1974), 1-16; (January 1975), 1-15. The extrapolation of class relationships from the situation of bureaucratic control is, at best, tangential to the Marxist tradition of class analysis. Its theoretical basis is Ralf Dahrendorf's doctrine to the effect that class relationships are essentially relationships of authority rather than of property: *Class and Class Conflict in Industrial Society* (Stanford, 1959), pp. 137, 165.

35. René Dumont, *False Start in Africa*, 2d ed., rev., trans. Phyllis Nauts Ott (New York, 1969), p. 81; also Frantz Fanon, *The Wretched of the Earth* (1963; rep. New York, 1968), p. 179.

36. For example, Ian Clegg, *Workers' Self-Management in Algeria* (New York and London, 1971). A study of similar import is Claude Meillassoux, "A Class Analysis of the Bureaucratic Process in Mali," *Journal of Development Studies*, VI (January 1970), 97-110.

37. I classify a country as industrial if a large part of its population--well over half--is engaged in occupations that depend upon a nonhuman and nonanimal power-driven machine technology. The basic measures of industrialization include the following: per capita consumption of standard energy units; percentage of labor force employed outside of agriculture; and possession of an engineering capacity to produce tool-making tools. According to these criteria, countries like India and Brazil are classified as nonindustrial despite the large industrial sectors of their economies. Most Indians and Brazilians do not live and work within the industrial sectors of their countries. Among nonindustrial countries, the range of difference between the least industrialized and those that are considered to be entering the industrial stage is immense.

38. This passage is partly derived from
Richard L. Sklar, *Corporate Power in an African
State: The Political Impact of Multinational
Mining Companies in Zambia* (Berkeley, Los Angeles,
and London, 1974), p. 199, where these ideas are
substantiated by a case study. See also
Martin Kilson's interesting perspective on the
"emergent African bourgeoisie" in "African
Political Change and the Modernization Process,"
Journal of Modern African Studies, I (December
1963), 425-440, esp. p. 439.
39. C. B. Macpherson, *The Real World of
Democracy* (London, 1966).
40. See Gunnar Myrdal, *Asian Drama: An
Inquiry into the Poverty of Nations* (New York,
1968), pp. 49-69.
41. Cf. Harold D. Lasswell and Abraham Kaplan,
*Power and Society: A Framework for Political
Inquiry* (New Haven and London, 1950), pp. 272-273.
42. Two classic expositions of this idea are
Karl Marx, *The Eighteenth Brumaire of
Louis Bonaparte* (Marx did not like the analogy
between nineteenth century bonapartism and classical
caesarism), and Fanon, pp. 148-205. See the keen
comparison of Marx and Fanon with reference to this
matter in Colin Leys, *Underdevelopment in Kenya:
The Political Economy of Neo-Colonialism* (Berkeley
and Los Angeles, 1974), pp. 207-212.
43. Zeitlin, p. 1112.
44. Evidence pertaining to class relationships
between the party political, state bureaucratic,
and entrepreneurial leaders of Nigeria has been
summarized by Sklar and C. S. Whitaker, Jr.,
"The Federal Republic of Nigeria," in
Gwendolen M. Carter, ed. *National Unity and
Regionalism in Eight African States* (Ithaca, 1966),
pp. 27-30, 65-67, and 110-115. See also Sklar,
*Nigerian Political Parties: Power in an Emergent
African Nation* (Princeton, 1963); Whitaker,
*The Politics of Tradition: Continuity and Change
in Northern Nigeria, 1946-1966* (Princeton, 1970);
and Sayre P. Schatz, *African Capitalism:
Development Policy in Nigeria* (Berkeley, Los
Angeles, and London, forthcoming). For a pene-
trating class analysis of Ethiopian politics, see
John Markakis, *Ethiopia: Anatomy of a Traditional
Polity* (Oxford, 1974). Comparable studies of
other African countries include: Leys, *Under-
development in Kenya*; Michael F. Lofchie, "The
Political Origins of the Uganda Coup," *Journal of
African Studies*, I (Winter 1974), 464-496;

Robert Molteno and Tordoff, "Independent Zambia:
Achievements and Prospects," in Tordoff, ed.
Politics in Zambia (Berkeley and Los Angeles,
1974), pp. 363-401; Sklar, *Corporate Power*,
pp. 192-216; the convincing thesis on "caesarist
bureaucracy" in Zaire by Jean-Claude Williame,
Patrimonialism and Political Change in the Congo
(Stanford, 1972); Meillassoux, "A Class Analysis
of the Bureaucratic Process in Mali"; Clegg,
Workers' Self-Management in Algeria; Gérard Chaliand
and Juliette Minces, *L'Algérie indépendante* (Paris,
1972); Manfred Halpern, *The Politics of Social
Change in the Middle East and North Africa*
(Princeton, 1963), pp. 51-78; Anouar Abdel-Malek,
Egypt: Military Society, trans. C. L. Markmann
(New York, 1968), pp. 167-186. These references
are limited to intensive studies relevant to my
identification of the bourgeoisie as the dominant
class. There is also an extensive literature of
commentary upon and speculation about class conflict
in Africa, but it is not especially relevant to
the argument of this essay.

45. On the commitment of the bourgeoisie to
"state capitalism" in India, see Bettelheim, *India
Independent*, trans. W. A. Caswell (New York, 1971).
Similarly, Michael Kidron maintains that the rule of
the Indian bourgeoisie is consolidated by mutually
supportive relationships among the state sector,
foreign enterprise, and domestic private enterprise.
See his *Foreign Investments in India* (London, 1965).
James A. Bill's class analysis of Iran (*The Politics
of Iran: Groups, Classes, and Modernization*
[Columbus, 1972]) should be noted. See also his
suggestive essay, "Class Analysis and the
Dialectics of Modernization in the Middle East,"
International Journal of Middle East Studies, III
(October 1972), 417-434. Marvin Zonis, *The
Political Elite of Iran* (Princeton, 1971) is also
relevant.

46. On the political and social implications
of multinational enterprise as the predominant
industrial force in Brazil's economy, see
Fernando Henrique Cardoso, "Associated-Dependent
Development: Theoretical and Practical Implications," in Alfred Stepan, ed. *Authoritarian
Brazil: Origins, Policies, and Future* (New Haven
and London, 1973), pp. 142-176. Of the twenty
largest enterprises in Brazil, ranked according to
the values of their assets, fourteen are state-
controlled, five are controlled by multinational
corporations, and one by Brazilian private

investors (*Expresso* [Lisbon], 7 June 1975).
Vernon cites impressive statistics on the heavy
recruitment of local managers by U.S.-owned
corporations in Brazil and elsewhere in Latin
America in his *Sovereignty at Bay*, p. 149.
    47. The continuing attempt by noncommunist
leaders to build socialism in Tanzania has been
extensively studied. Lofchie has analyzed the
leading issues that arise in several such studies,
in "Agrarian Socialism in the Third World: The
Tanzanian Case," *Comparative Politics*, VIII (April
1976), 479-499. See also Reginald Herbold Green,
"Political independence and the national economy:
an essay on the political economy of decolonisa-
tion," in Christopher Allen and R. W. Johnson, eds.
*African Perspectives: Papers in the history,
politics and economics of Africa presented to
Thomas Hodgkin* (Cambridge, 1970), pp. 273-324;
John S. Saul, "African Socialism in One Country:
Tanzania," in Giovanni Arrighi and Saul, *Essays on
the Political Economy of Africa* (New York and
London, 1963), pp. 237-335; Issa G. Shivji, et al.,
The Silent Class Struggle (Dar es Salaam, 1974).
    48. A locus classicus is Paul A. Baran,
The Political Economy of Growth (New York and
London, 1957), pp. 194-196. A characteristic
example of the genre is Andre Gunder Frank,
*Lumpenbourgeoisie: Lumpendevelopment: Dependence,
Class, and Politics in Latin America*, trans.
Marion David Berdecio (New York and London, 1972);
also Samir Amin, *Accumulation on a World Scale:
A Critique of the Theory of Underdevelopment*,
2 vols., trans. Brian Pearce (New York and London,
1974), pp. 20-25, 359-394.
    49. For an incisive discussion of neocolo-
nialism that is nonetheless sympathetic to the idea
itself, see Barratt Brown, pp. 256-284. For a
comparable discussion of the dependency doctrine,
see Susanne Bodenheimer, "Dependency and
Imperialism: The Roots of Latin American Underdevelopment," in Fann and Hodges, eds. *Readings in
U.S. Imperialism*, pp. 155-181. The Chilean
origins of this doctrine and certain of its
inherent conceptual weaknesses are shown by
Theodore H. Moran, *Multinational Corporations and
the Politics of Dependence: Copper in Chile*
(Princeton, 1974). Aspects of the "dependency"
thesis are specifically tested by
Charles T. Goodsell, *American Corporations and
Peruvian Politics* (Cambridge [Mass.], 1974). For
a realistic appraisal of capitalist development in

"third world" countries--one that rebuts a basic
tenet of the standard dependency thesis from a
Marxist standpoint, see Bill Warren, "Imperialism
and Capitalist Industrialization," *New Left
Review*, Number 81 (September-October 1973),
3-44. For an incisively critical appraisal of
the dependency doctrine, see Cohen, pp. 189-227.
 50. Ossowski, pp. 185-186.
 51. In an earlier study, mainly concerned
with the political implications of class
formation in Nigeria, I used the descriptive term
"new and rising class," defined with reference
to four objective criteria--high status occupation,
high income, superior education, and ownership or
control of business enterprise--and linked with
reality by means of behavioral evidence of class
action and incipient class consciousness. See
Sklar, *Nigerian Political Parties*, pp. 474-505.
Subsequently, I adopted the term "political class,"
as proposed by Gaetano Mosca, to designate those
persons who control the dominant institutions of
society, in "Contradictions in the Nigerian
Political System," *Journal of Modern African
Studies*, III (August 1965), 203-204. For the
reasons given in this essay and in Sklar,
Corporate Power in an African State,
pp. 198-209, I now think that "managerial
bourgeoisie" is the most appropriate term for
the modern ruling class of a nonindustrial and
newly developing but nonsocialist country.
 52. Ibid., pp. 144-148, 164-178, 182-188.
 53. Barnet and Müller, pp. 363-388.
 54. Vernon, pp. 265-270; Mikesell, pp. 48-51.
 55. This generalization should be qualified
with reference to Zeitlin's call for the study of
dominant classes in underdeveloped countries
(n. 43). My sketch of a major pattern for ruling
class development in nonindustrial countries must
be read with the realization that every country
has its own mix of bureaucratic, entrepreneurial,
and traditionally oligarchic elements.
 56. In socialist countries, the working class
may well confront a "state bourgeoisie," as
Bettelheim contends (n. 34). Similarly,
Immanuel Wallerstein argues that, in effect if not
in form, there is but one world economic system
which will remain essentially capitalistic until
it is transformed as a whole. See Wallerstein,
"Dependence in an Interdependent World: The
Limited Possibilities of Transformation within the
Capitalist World Economy," *African Studies Review*,

XVII (April 1974), 1-26; "Trends in World Capitalism," *Monthly Review*, XXVI (May 1974), 12-18; and "The Rise and Future Demise of the World Capitalist System: Concepts for Comparative Analysis," *Comparative Studies in Society and History*, XVI (September 1974), 387-415.

57. See also the suggestive comments by Irving Louis Horowitz, "Capitalism, Communism, and Multinationalism," in Abdul A. Said and Luis R. Simmons, eds. *The New Sovereigns: Multinational Corporations as World Powers* (Englewood Cliffs, 1975), pp. 123, 129-130.

58. See V. I. Lenin's rebuttal of Karl Kautsky's thesis of interimperialist cooperation, *Imperialism: The Highest Stage of Capitalism* (1917; New York, 1939), pp. 88-98. A portion of Kautsky's provocative article of 1914 has been republished in the *New Left Review*, Number 59 (January-February 1970), 41-46. The contemporary relevance of this debate has been noted by Barnet, *Roots of War* (Baltimore, 1973), p. 229; and Barratt Brown, pp. 323-325.

59. On the ideology of corporate liberalism in the United States, see James Weinstein, *The Corporate Ideal in the Liberal State: 1900-1918* (Boston, 1968); and Weinstein and David W. Eakins, eds. *For a New America: Essays in History and Politics* from *'Studies on the Left,' 1958-1967* (New York, 1970).

4
Women Workers in Multinational Corporations: The Case of the Electronics Industry in Malaysia and Singapore

Linda Y. C. Lim

Much of the recent research on women's work in developing countries has concluded that women are most often the losers in the process of economic development in Third World countries.[1] It is argued that women are systematically excluded from participation in wage labor in the modern capitalist sector. Instead, they are increasingly confined to work in the home and in marginal service jobs in the informal sector. In some cases, female labor force participation has even declined with development.[2]

The history of Western capitalist industrialization shows a different pattern of female labor force participation in the manufacturing sector. While initially women were heavily represented in labor-intensive manufacturing industries, e.g., textiles, they were eventually displaced by technological development. As these industries became more capital-intensive, they turned increasingly from unskilled or semi-skilled female labor to higher-wage, skilled male labor.

A similar pattern of industrial transformation has occurred in some developing countries,[3] but in the main it has been argued that "under industrial growth conditioned by the needs of monopoly capitalism, the period of a large industrial work force composed in large part of women is skipped."[4] That is to say, rather than rising first and then falling, women's participation in industrial wage labor falls almost as soon as modern industrialization, most often led by foreign investment from the West, begins in developing countries.[5]

The sources cited thus far focus on the "second stage" of foreign investment in ex-colonial

countries of the Third World. The "first stage,"
or traditional colonial mode of production, saw
a concentration of foreign investment in primary
industries, both in agriculture and mineral
extraction, for export to the metropolitan
countries. While this type of investment still
predominates in the Third World, political
independence and increasing economic nationalism
has led to the second stage of investment: the
establishment of manufacturing industries with
tariff protection to substitute for direct imports.
It is this second stage of foreign industrial
investment which tends to be capital-intensive.
Thus, the labor-intensive and female-intensive phase
occurring in early Western industrialization is
"skipped" when Western manufacturing is transferred
to the Third World.

A "third stage" of foreign investment in
developing countries has so far received little
attention in the literature on women's employment
in these countries.[6] It involves labor-intensive
manufacturing for export under the aegis of multinational corporations. This is called offshore
sourcing in economic terms.[7] Electronics represents
the best example of an offshore sourcing industry.
In many Asian and Latin American countries
electronics has in the past 10 to 15 years become
not only the most rapidly growing manufacturing
industry, but it also has the highest proportion
of women employed.

The fundamental hypothesis of this paper is
that women in Third World countries are exploited
on three levels: as workers, as workers from low-
wage developing nations, and finally as women.
Before proceeding further, it is necessary to
clarify the concept of exploitation as used in
several schools of economic thought. For the
neoclassical economists, exploitation exists if
a worker is paid less than the value of his/her
marginal product. This occurs in all market
structures except the pure (and generally
unattainable) case of perfect competition.[8] Workers
in Third World countries are more likely to be
exploited because market structures are more
imperfect in these countries. The Cambridge School,
following Joan Robinson and others, believes a
worker is exploited because a portion of his/her
total product is deducted and goes to the
capitalist as profit, which is solely a return
for ownership of capital.[9] The proportion
deducted varies inversely with the bargaining

power of workers. This is less in Third World
countries because of the weakness of workers'
unions and political power. For Marxists, exploitation consists of the surplus value (in excess
of the value of the wage) produced by the worker
and expropriated by the capitalist.[10] The rate of
surplus value or exploitation is greater for
workers in Third World countries because they can
be paid less and worked harder.

Thus exploitation is a *relative* concept,
bearing no direct relation to the *absolute* levels
of wages paid: so long as a worker does not
receive the full value of his/her product, however
defined, he/she is exploited. A higher wage may
also entail a higher rate of exploitation if
greater intensity of work, longer working hours,
and better equipment and organization of production
mean that labor productivity and hence the value of
the worker's output is proportionally greater in
the higher-wage than in the lower-wage sector.

In addition to being exploited in this
conventional economic sense in capitalist enterprises, women workers are additionally exploited
as women in certain industries where a higher
productivity is extracted from them at lower wages
than if men were employed. In patriarchal cultures
women are seen as secondary income earners whose
jobs and incomes are supplementary to total family
income. Thus it is considered justified to pay
them lower wages than men at equivalent jobs, and
to give them low-skilled jobs and jobs with insecure
tenure. Furthermore, socialization of women in such
societies causes them to exhibit characteristics,
such as patience and deference to male authority
in the workplace, which make them more productive
and manageable in certain jobs.

In addition to their exploitation as workers
and as women, female employees of multinational
corporations in developing countries are exploited
in a third sense: they are paid much lower wages
than female workers in the home countries of
the multinationals for the same work and level of
productivity. This is the result of the weaker
national economies of Third World nations, where
high unemployment, poor bargaining power vis-a-vis
foreign investors, lack of worker organization and
representation, and the repression of workers'
movements all combine to depress wage levels.

The empirical data for this paper are based
on the operations of electronics multinationals
in Malaysia and Singapore. The data were collected

from a survey of 70 electronics firms in these
countries, employing some 55,000 workers in 1976,
more than 90 percent women. This sample
represents about half of the electronics firms
in both countries and about 70 percent of the
workers in the industry.

The paper is organized as follows: Section I
examines the demand and supply factors leading
to the development of offshore sourcing industries
with particular reference to their present and
future activities in Malaysia and Singapore.
Section II analyzes the labor practices of these
multinationals and how they exploit certain
characteristics of women workers for profit
maximization. It also discusses the interaction
between multinational activities and culture.
Finally in Section III, I discuss some of the
theoretical issues and implications arising from the
empirical study of women's labor in offshore
sourcing industries.

I.   OFFSHORE SOURCING IN THE ELECTRONICS INDUSTRY

In industrial countries such as the U.S., the
major reason for offshore sourcing, the location
by parent multinationals of their plants in
Third World countries to manufacture consumer goods
or components which are then reexported to their
home countries, is the search for cheap labor to
produce goods that will be competitive in the home
and world markets. Other reasons include special
tariff provisions, technological changes,
absorption of cyclical fluctuations in offshore
plants, and proximity to overseas markets.[11]
But the most salient characteristic of products
sourced overseas is that they are "labor-intensive,"
that is, they have a high ratio of labor costs to
total costs of production.

Many such industries in the U.S. were
adversely affected by labor shortages and unrest
in the late 1960s and by the unwillingness of U.S.
workers to take on precise, monotonous, semi-
skilled assembly work even at higher wages. In
their attempts to escape rising wage costs and
increasingly intractable labor, American companies
which in the previous decade had moved from high
to low labor cost areas in the U.S. began expanding
overseas to Central America and more recently to
Asia.

Because of their mobility and impermanence, these companies are often termed "footloose" or "runaway" firms. Since low labor costs are vital to them, such firms employ "secondary" or "marginal" segments of the labor force--those workers with low skills who are willing to work for low pay and are not unionized. Furthermore, work in such industries is tedious, requires great patience, care, industry, and dexterity. It is no surprise that the recruits for such jobs tend to be predominantly female, and disproportionately nonwhite. Thus, female-intensive industries have the greatest propensity to move offshore. In these offshore plants, the ability of the firm to move to other locations is an effective threat used by management to hold down wage demands and unionization efforts of workers.

The electronics industry is perhaps the classic example of an industry which has used offshore sourcing extensively. Today, well over 90 percent of all assembly operations of U.S. electronics firms are conducted overseas, employing cheap female labor in Third World countries.

The electronics industry combines high technology with unskilled labor-intensive processes. Many assemblies are so complex that they are difficult to mechanize. While one process--often the assembly or finishing stage--may be labor-intensive, others are capital-intensive. The high rate of technological obsolescence in this industry further reduces the attractiveness of capital-intensive automation. At the same time, wage rates for unskilled labor in Asian countries are only a fraction of those in developed countries for workers performing the same operations. In 1969, for example, the wage of an unskilled worker in Singapore (the offshore location with the *highest* wage rates in Asia) was only one-eleventh that of an equivalent worker in the same industry in the U.S. and the wage differential gap has actually been widening.[12]

The record of multinational electronics firms in Asia in employment is quite remarkable: estimated total employment in offshore manufacturing of electronic components alone rose in the three years between 1971 and 1974 from 7,750 to 24,000 in Singapore; from 5,300 to 23,000 in South Korea; from 5,000 to 9,000 in Hong Kong; from 350 to 2,600 in Indonesia; and from zero to 18,000 in Malaysia and to 2,000

each in the Philippines and Thailand. U.S.
industry alone is estimated to have over
100,000 offshore workers in about a dozen
countries. There are also increasing numbers of
offshore electronics plants in Caribbean and
Central American countries, such as Barbados, the
Dominican Republic, El Salvador, and Haiti. The
vast majority of electronics workers in all these
countries are women, for which two main reasons
have been suggested: first, wage rates for female
workers are normally lower than for male workers
of similar grade and skills; second, it seems that
much of this work--e.g., in semiconductor
assembly--is "carried out with a higher degree
of efficiency by female than by male workers,"
most likely because of their greater tractability
and manual dexterity.

While labor-intensive industries in the
industrial nations are forced by domestic labor
problems and international competition to look
for offshore sourcing locations, governments of
developing Asian countries are engaged in
promotional efforts to attract foreign investment.

Like other developing countries, Malaysia
and Singapore experienced a phase of import-
substituting manufacturing ("second stage"
investment) in the 1950s and 1960s in which
foreign capital again played an important role.
It is import-substituting industrialization which
has been the main target of criticisms by dependency
theorists.[13] Such industries tend to be capital-
intensive, inefficient (especially when protected
by tariff barriers), and have limited growth
potential (because of the small domestic market
with unequal income distribution). This type of
industrialization is responsible for the limited
participation of women in the industrial wage
labor force.[14]

Offshore sourcing ("third stage" investment),
however, provides a different type of
industrialization which seems to escape many of
the criticisms usually leveled at multinational
corporations. Since it is export-oriented, it
has greater growth potential; being subject to
world competitive pressures it is likely to be
technically efficient. This has made such
industries particularly welcomed by host governments
as a potential solution to the growing problem
of unemployment, and because of the contribution
they are expected to make to foreign exchange
earnings. Thus, host governments in Southeast

Asia, including Malaysia and Singapore, offer the multinationals an array of investment incentives-- tariff exemptions, tax holidays, industrial estates, etc. In addition, they have instituted labor legislation to "stabilize" the industrial work force by severely limiting or banning the right to organize and to strike. "Protective" legislation prohibiting night work for female workers has been removed.

In Malaysia, high unemployment and the lack of jobs for males, the traditional "breadwinners," have forced many women to take on wage labor in order to partially or totally support their families, or at least themselves.[15] Unemployment of males in the family, ironically in some cases due to the displacement of farmers and fishermen from sites requisitioned for the construction of industrial estates and airports for Free Trade Zones, is one reason which has caused rural women, especially, to respond to the demand of multi- nationals for wage labor. Low wages in the agricultural and informal sector is another reason. Today, women form slightly over half of the total manufacturing labor force and one-third of the total labor force in Malaysia; 36 percent of all women are employed.[16]

In summary, manufacturing for export by multinational corporations in labor-intensive manufacturing industries has, by increasing both the demand for and supply of female labor, greatly contributed to a rapid increase in female participation in the industrial wage labor force in Malaysia and Singapore. Today, after ten years in Singapore and seven years in Malaysia, the electronics industry alone employs close to 50,000 workers in each country, over 90 percent of them female, engaged predominantly in assembly operations. However, limitations to the continued expansion of offshore electronics production in these countries have begun to appear.

Between 1971 and 1974, employment in multina- tional electronics corporations increased from 7,750 to 24,000 in Singapore and from zero to 18,000 in Malaysia. The success of labor- intensive export industries in creating employment for young women has quickly led to a shortage of young female labor. As early as 1974, U.S. multinationals were beginning to find the Singapore- Malaysia area "a bit claustrophobic," with an overpopulation of offshore electronics firms leading to tight labor supply and increasing labor costs.

This has prompted many companies to scout for new
offshore locations elsewhere in Asia and Latin
America. In Singapore, and to a lesser extent
in Malaysia, electronics firms have "upgraded"
their operations to become more capital-intensive,
involving more sophisticated production processes,
but still employing mostly women. The extent to
which such upgrading is possible depends in part
on the level of local skills. Further, within
the vertically integrated production structure of
the international firm, economies of scale in
higher-skill operations restrict their transfer
to only the few offshore locations that were
established earlier. Thus Malaysia is finding
difficulty in securing technological upgrading in
its electronics industry because the multinationals
have already established such facilities elsewhere,
such as in Singapore.

The attitude of the host governments to
foreign investment also affects the availability
of such investments. In recent years the Malaysian
government has attempted to increase its control
over foreign enterprise. These "nationalistic"
policies "go against the grain" of multinationals,
who have threatened to "withdraw if they [the
government] get touchy." The future of offshore
sourcing depends on other factors outside the
control of host countries such as technological
and market changes, protectionist measures such
as the withdrawal of tariff preferences for
developing countries' manufactured exports to
developed countries' markets, the rise in freight
rates because of rising fuel costs, and exchange
rate changes, especially the continuing decline
of the U.S. dollar vis-a-vis other currencies,
including the currencies of offshore locations in
developing countries.

Thus while offshore sourcing industries in
electronics create large-scale employment for
women, the competitive position of any one host
country depends very much on its labor costs and
government policies. After hitting an initial
peak within a few years, employment creation stops
or even declines, even though output may increase
as labor costs rise. Further investment in new
plants in the same industry is unlikely because of
the emerging labor shortage and because the risk-
minimizing global strategy of multinationals
dictates that they spread their offshore plants
to a number of different locations.[17] The
continuation of offshore sourcing is therefore

uncertain in the long run. Hence the jobs created
for women in these industries, though numerous,
are limited both in number and in duration.

II. MULTINATIONALS' LABOR PRACTICES AND WOMEN LABOR

     This section examines in detail the particular
labor practices which enable the multinationals to
extract a higher output at lower wages from women
workers in Third World countries than is possible
from men in these countries, or from women workers
in the industrial countries.

Hiring Practices

     Multinationals electronics firms in Malaysia
and Singapore prefer to hire women between the
ages of 16 and 23. Young workers are preferred
because they are malleable, obedient, and easily
disciplined. They are also less likely to get
married soon and burden the firm with maternity
benefits. Most workers have no previous wage
labor experience. They either are fresh from
school, or have only been involved with domestic
chores, small family businesses, or farming. In
Singapore they are overwhelmingly of urban origin,
while in Malaysia electronics workers come from
both urban and rural areas.
     Because of the labor shortage in Singapore,
firms are required by the government to employ
married women, but at the time of my survey,
firms in Malaysia often would not hire married
women partly because of their reluctance to pay
married women the maternity benefits required by
law. Several multinationals in Singapore prefer
to hire married women on midnight shifts (from
11 p.m. to 7 a.m). Another factor taken into
consideration is the educational achievements of
the workers. Aside from basic literacy and
arithmetic skills, there is no need for a high
level of education in electronics assembly work.
But most multinationals prefer workers with some
or even a full secondary school education. They
feel that workers who have "stuck it out" through
long years of schooling were more likely to be
conscientious and "disciplined" and better able to
bear the long hours of meticulous, tedious, and
monotonous work on the assembly bench. Sometimes,
however, workers with higher than necessary
educational qualifications were rejected because

it was felt that they would become bored and
dissatisfied with the work, and would be on the
lookout for better job opportunities elsewhere.
English education is preferred, especially by
American multinationals who consider the widespread
use of English to be one of the major advantages
for locating operations in Malaysia and Singapore.
     In addition to education, successful
applicants are expected to be healthy, have perfect
eyesight, and to pass tests for manual dexterity
and spatial visualization. At the interviews with
the personnel manager, attempts are made to
screen out potential "troublemakers."
     In summary, to ensure labor discipline in the
factory, multinationals prefer to employ female
workers who are young, formally educated, and have
passive, "cooperative" personalities. Young men
were not considered as employees because "they
cannot sit still for eight hours at a stretch"
and are "too impatient." One of the only two firms
I interviewed which had experimented with male
assembly workers in Malaysia experienced great
"discipline problems" with its 300 male workers out
of a total of 4,000 employees. There were many
incidents of insubordination, refusal to obey
female supervisors, and "nuisance" problems such
as graffiti on the walls. The greater docility
of female workers makes them easier to organize
and more productive workers. It also reduces the
risk of labor disruptions in factory work.

Wages

     In Malaysia and Singapore, women are legally
entitled to receive equal pay for equal work.
Nevertheless, male wage rates are often higher than
female wage rates. Differential wage rates are
not obvious because of job segregation by sex;
that is, men and women are found in different
jobs and different industries. Electronics and
other labor-intensive manufacturing industries
are typed as "female" industries because women are
said to have "innate" assets which suit them
to such work. The result is that women workers
are consequently trapped in low-wage female
industries. In Singapore wages in electronics are
about a third below the average wages for the
manufacturing sector.
     In 1976, wages in the electronics industry
in Singapore began at about U.S. $2 per eight-hour
day and those in Malaysia at about U.S. $1.20 to

$1.60, depending on location (being highest in
Kuala Lumpur, followed by Penang, Malacca, and
rural areas). After a three-month probation
period, workers who are confirmed receive a raise.
Thereafter, individual workers receive periodic
increments: the most common is an automatic
increment, granted to all but a few who do not
measure up to some minimum standard, plus
additional or "accelerated" increments based on
individual performance, which is assessed periodically. In 1976, Singapore wages were still one-
ninth of U.S. wages, one-fourth of European wages,
and one-half of Japanese wages.

Multinationals tend to "cooperate" or collude
with one another with respect to labor market
practices. In both Malaysia and Singapore,
personnel managers of the different factories keep
in close touch with each other, monitoring labor
market changes and making tacit if not explicit
agreements to keep wages low, or roughly "in
line" with one another, even during periods of
labor shortage. The advantage of such collusion
is to minimize wage competition. To control
"job hopping," firms in some areas agreed not to
hire experienced workers who move from one
company to another.

Unions

One of the attractions of Asian manufacturing
locations to offshore sourcing multinationals is
the absence of "labor problems" which confront
them in their home countries. To accommodate
multinationals' desires, host governments take
political action to control, undermine, or prevent
the formation of local unions. In Singapore, unions
are encouraged by the government as an institution
designed to ensure accommodation and cooperation
between management and labor. This makes them
a stable institution whose presence reduces
uncertainty and ensures uniformity and control in
the workplace, and is therefore welcomed even by
firms which in their own home countries have
consistently refused to allow their workers to
unionize. More than one of the multinationals in
my sample said, "The union leaders understand us
and are very cooperative," though the rank-and-file
are acknowledged to be sometimes more "radical."

In contrast to the situation in Singapore,
multinationals in Malaysia are very opposed to
unions, and American companies in particular

have put pressure on the government to curtail
the spread of unionization.

> Several American companies, including National
> Semiconductor, Motorola, Monsanto, Texas
> Instruments, and RCA, recently met with
> Federal Industrial Development Authority
> leaders to make known their concern with
> unions. "Not much agitation has appeared
> yet," said one executive here, "but we wanted
> them to realize that if there is a possibility
> of that, we'd like them to discourage it."18

Consequently, as one government official put it,
"Over the last five years we have negotiated to
forestall the extension of unions to the electronics
industry."19 The government has been known to
refuse recognition of representative unions voted
in by workers--like the Electrical Workers Union--
on the grounds that "electrical is not the same as
electronics" though by international definition
electrical includes electronics.

In addition to relying on the government to
curb unions, firms themselves discourage them in
their plants. According to one factory worker,

> If there's a union, we could ask for a pay
> increase more easily, but there's only a few
> of us who want to complain about the poor pay.
> We're scared. If the management finds out and
> the rest of the girls are not behind us, then
> we'll be sacked.

In both Malaysia and Singapore, as in
developed countries like the U.S., women are less
likely to organize in unions than men, and thus
more easily exploited. Conversely, where unions
exist, they are often directly or indirectly tools
of the host governments and companies rather than
of the workers they are supposed to represent, a
situation not uncommon in developing countries in
both male and female industries.

Employment Stability

Offshore manufacturing industries which
cater to foreign export markets where consumer
and industrial demands fluctuate with the business
cycle tend to be highly unstable. In some cases
offshore plants are established to fulfill
boomtime orders, bearing the brunt of world market

slack in slumps. In addition, the electronics
industry is also subject to the variability induced
by an "innovation and competition cycle" which
affects the semiconductor sector more seriously
than other sectors.[20] Downturns are experienced
every two or three years. Furthermore, multinationals with multiple offshore plants readily
switch production around to maximize global
profits. For these and other reasons, export-
oriented industries in developing countries do not
provide stable employment for women workers, and
layoffs are common. During the 1974-75 world
recession, about 15,000 electronics workers were
laid off in Singapore, nearly a third of the
industry's labor force.[21] Thousands of workers
in electronics and other labor-intensive industries
in Malaysia were also laid off.[22] Some firms
attributed the profits they make, even during
periods of recession, to their ability to
immediately retrench labor in response to business
slumps. However, not all layoffs in electronics
are due only to the cyclical output downswing.
Many firms said that even without the recession,
they were planning to increase efficiency and
reduce the size of the labor force. The recession
provided them with the "excuse" to lay off workers
who would have been made redundant with the
introduction of automation, and the shifting of
labor-intensive operations from Singapore to
cheaper neighboring countries. Several firms
reported using the "opportunity" of the slowdown
in production to improve the productivity--
introducing new machines and training workers to
use them. Part of the layoffs thus represented a
"shedding" or "shake-out" (words used by my
industry respondents) of obsolete or redundant
labor. The personnel manager of a multinational
I interviewed had this to say:

> It is good to have turnover because of the
> uncertainty of the industry, which makes it
> unwise to keep too much labor. Wage rates may
> rise, new products may be developed
> requiring either more or less skills. Turn-
> over helps to change the composition of the
> labor force--to higher or lower skill levels--
> as production changes.

Another reason for periodic layoffs is to
reduce the wage bill. The retrenchment of
relatively expensive longer-term workers provides

a welcome relief to the wage bill, since seniority
and annual wage increases for these workers cost
the firms more than the wages they pay for new
workers with almost the same productivity. Since
training periods for new workers and learning
curves are both short (one to two weeks, and
three to six months respectively), firms lose little
when they rehire cheaper new workers after the
"recession." Some firms also said that they could
rehire (their own or other firms') experienced
laid-off labor but pay a starting wage.

While layoffs are functional to the multinational firm, they are politically unpopular in
the host country. But in patriarchal societies
where women have secondary status in the labor
force, it is more "acceptable" for an industry
which "needs" to lay off workers periodically to
lay off women rather than men.

Another reason given by firms for preferring
to hire women is the "natural" way labor is shed,
i.e., by women leaving to get married or have
children. The average length of employment of
a rural woman in one particular electronics
factory in Malaysia is about one to two years,
after which she leaves the firm and is replaced
by a cheaper new worker.

In summary, export-oriented manufacturing
industries like electronics have a chronically
unstable pattern of unemployment, high labor
turnover, and periodic layoffs, all of which
serve to keep the average wage levels low.
Patriarchal attitudes on women's work justify
both the payment of low wages and the allocation
of jobs with short tenure to women.

Job Mobility

In offshore electronics manufacturing,
virtually 100 percent of production operatives,
or well over 90 percent of total labor force,
are female. Although initially most supervisors,
and almost all technical and managerial
personnel were male in Singapore, and still are
to a large extent in Malaysia, there has been
increased participation of women in the more
skilled jobs.

For most of the operatives, however, vertical
mobility within the firm is severely restricted,
simply because there are so few skilled and higher-
level jobs available in the offshore manufacturing
plants. These plants are designed only for

low-skill assembly operations. The vertically integrated multinationals that operate them usually retain higher-skill, higher-wage operations in the parent company and home country. A recent survey in Singapore showed that operatives still form 87 percent of the labor force in a typical electronics plant, supervisors 3 percent, technicians 5 percent, and "tradesmen" (white-collar workers) 5 percent.[23]

If worker mobility is restricted vertically within the firm, it is also restricted horizontally, both within the electronics industry itself and to other sectors of the economy. It was mentioned earlier that the collusive labor practices of multinational firms which discourage "factory hopping" by workers, or its corollary, the "poaching" of individual workers among firms, tend to prevent a competitive labor market from developing, hold down wages, and reduce labor mobility. Thus, an experienced worker who might try to improve her position by applying to another firm in the same area would be turned down, or would be hired only at the normal starting wage, irrespective of experience and productivity.

As for mobility from electronics to other manufacturing industries, the simple but exacting skills which the female assemblers acquire in a short period are not transferable to other occupations. Work experience gained in electronics assembly does not ensure a worker easier access to other jobs in the manufacturing sector, except where employers value the experience of disciplined factory work itself. Indeed, because of her age, the worker who leaves or is cast off from an electronics multinational may be disadvantaged in the job market.

Fringe Benefits

In Malaysia and Singapore where wage competition among multinational employers for female labor is ruled out by firm collusion, competition often centers on fringe benefits. Variation among firms involves the type rather than the level of fringes provided. Minimum benefits are legislated by the government in both countries and negotiated by unions in Singapore. Benefits are provided only to "confirmed" workers (those who have passed the probation period) and include annual leave, sick leave, medical benefits, accident insurance, social security, and collective

pension plan contributions. In addition to these
benefits, many electronics firms also provide a
food allowance or subsidized canteen facilities,
free or subsidized bus transport, free uniforms,
and free coffee and tea. In the rare cases where
factories provide housing nearby, this is seldom
subsidized. Such income in kind costs less to
the firm than if it paid higher wages to workers
directly.

Other fringe benefits selectively provided
by firms in Malaysia include annual dinners and
department functions, Western film shows, sports
facilities, beach outings and picnics, Christmas
parties, outstation trips, educational and library
facilities, workers' counseling and a variety
of extracurricular classes. Many of these fringe
benefits are geared to "feminine" interest and
include events such as cooking classes, fashion
classes, and even beauty contests. American
multinationals tend to favor the more "modern"
social and recreational activities for their
workers, like ballroom dances and beauty culture
lessons, while Japanese firms favor what they
consider to be more "healthy" cultural activities
like sports and group singing sessions.

This section has discussed some of the ways
in which employers in the electronics industry
take advantage of status and characteristics of
women workers to sometimes increase firm profits.
Multinationals selectively employ workers who are
young, female, with some formal education but no
previous wage experience, and passive. As women,
they are paid lower wages, especially because they
hold a secondary status in the labor force. These
wages are kept below the competitive rates by
collusive labor practices among the firms. Women
are generally less likely to organize as workers
than men are, and unions which may protect or
further the interests of electronics factory
workers are severely restrained. Employment in
export-oriented electronics is chronically unstable,
but patriarchal attitudes of both employers and
the host society justify the job insecurity, the
high labor turnover, and periodic lay-offs
that women workers experience in the industry.
Job mobility is restricted both vertically within
the firm and horizontally within the industry.
Fringe benefits enable the employers to compete
for labor without raising wages. Workers are also
vulnerable to the productivity improvement schemes
which raise their work effort and output without

offering commensurate monetary compensation. Both
fringe benefits and productivity schemes utilize
workers' feminine interests to get them to work
more for less pay.

Effects On Women Workers

At the same time, employment in multinational
electronics assembly factories imposes a
considerable welfare cost on workers. The work is
intense and meticulous, involving looking through
a highly magnified microscope for eight hours a
day, in a rigidly regulated environment. The
nature and pace of work lead to many widespread
problems--of which eye strain and eyesight
deterioration, persistent headaches, stomach
ailments, fatigue, and nervousness are the most
commonly reported. Shifts which rotate every
one or two weeks are damaging to workers' physical
and psychological health in Third World countries
no less than they are in industrialized countries
like the U.S., and mass hysteria is a frequent
occurrence on the late-night shifts, especially
in Malaysia.

Outside the factory, living conditions are
often poor, especially where most of the workers
are migrants and have to rent "deplorable"
housing facilities at exorbitant prices around the
industrial estates where housing shortages are
acute. The women are often crowded into dormitory-
like facilities, and rotation of bedspace among
women who work different shifts is sometimes
practiced. Others may live as far as thirty
miles away, and transportation is both scarce and
expensive. Given their low wages, heavy family
contributions, and monopoly pricing of basic
commodities around the industrial estates, many
workers can barely survive. At the same time, the
cultural impact of the multinational work
environment can cause strained relations between
the women workers and the local communities where
their factories are located.

The Interactions of Multinationals
and Local Cultural Systems

The cultural interactions between multinationals and the host society occur in a number of
ways. First, those cultural and social traits
of traditional societies in general, and of women
in these societies in particular, are reinforced

if they tend to increase productivity. For example, the traditional values of obedience, deferrence, discipline, etc., are encouraged. Women's social and physical aptitudes such as small and nimble fingers, patience, attention to details, experience with needlework, and docility are exploited for greater productivity.

Second, traditional values such as the premium placed on leisure and cooperative social interactions are discouraged while habits of punctuality, self-discipline, diligence, individual competitiveness, and response to material incentives are promoted.

A variety of incentive and punitive schemes have been enacted in the factory for increasing productivity. Individual responsiveness to pecuniary incentives, which may be absent or weak in the traditional society, are encouraged via exhortations, propaganda, and "industrial indoctrination" (really "cultural indoctrination") programs, as well as by a variety of competitive schemes.

The ethic of individual and group competitiveness for rewards is perhaps the major cultural value of modern capitalist society which most multinationals attempt to transmit to their workers. Competitions to increase output in work as well as outside work are instituted. These include competition in sports events and beauty contests, which may be alien to their traditional culture. In some cases workers are encouraged to compete with one another for increased productivity for the sake of competition alone; that is, they are not commensurately rewarded in monetary terms for their increases in effort and output. This is one way by which multinationals take advantage of workers' naiveté.

Sometimes the multinationals face cultural resistance to the competitive and meritocratic schemes they introduce. An American firm in Singapore told me it took a long time for it to get the supervisors to report accurately on individual workers' performance: several supervisors refused to report differentials in productivity, reporting instead average increases for each worker, because they did not want individual workers to "lose face" by being unequally rewarded.

Finally, the values that the multinationals introduce and the effects these have on the lifestyles of their workers cause friction with the

local communities. Beauty and fashion classes,
pop music and dancing lessons, parties, Western
movies, etc., which the girls are exposed to in the
factories as part of management's efforts to
raise workers morale, influence their consumption
patterns, life styles, and habits in ways which
are antithetical to those of the traditional
societies where they come from and where they live.
"Worker's morality" thus becomes an issue of
concern to local community leaders.   For example,

> As factory girls we already have a bad
> reputation. You're tempted to go to parties
> because everybody's going and you don't want
> to stay at home alone...Sundays are party-
> time for those girls who are "kaki enjoy"...
> some girls hang around hotels and nightclubs
> and discotheques to have a good time. They
> come back and brag to those of us who don't
> do all that. Because of a few straying
> girls, all factory girls get a bad name.

The antagonisms of the host community and the
bad publicity the firms receive (which can
adversely affect their hiring success) have led
them to respond to the criticisms in various ways.
Two opposite responses from two American firms in
Malaysia are cited here.
Company A, in an industrial estate outside of
Kuala Lumpur, believes in preserving traditional
mores in order to ingratiate itself with the local
community and the government. It follows a
paternalistic capitalist mode of operation, and had
"adopted" the Malay village nearby which is its
"catchment area" for workers. The firm has a
program to supply the elementary school in the
village with all the books it needs. To assure
the parents that their daughters will be well
looked after by the company and not subjected to any
corrupting influences, the company has installed
prayer rooms in the factory itself, does not
require uniforms, allows the girls to wear their
traditional attire, and enforces a strict and rigid
discipline in the workplace. The American manager
who had previously operated offshore factories
in Mexico believes that it is religion which makes
a good worker, since it guarantees "hard work and
honesty." In Mexico he emphasized Catholicism in
his factories; in Malaysia he emphasizes Islam.
He has established a good relationship with the
imam of the village mosque and gets him to announce

job vacancies after Friday prayers. "Open day" is
held for parents to visit the factory. The policy
seems to be successful. Despite the rigid
discipline and the lower wages which the firm pays,
it is highly regarded by the village community and
is able to attract and keep workers without any
difficulty.

Company B operates three different plants in
Malaysia and is the largest employer in the country
(after the government). Instead of emphasizing
tradition, it stresses modernity; instead of social
and parental authority, a kind of independence for
the women. I was told, with pride, of a fancy
annual dinner organized and paid for by the workers
themselves which was held in the ballroom of the
Kuala Lumpur Hilton Hotel, and to which American
Embassy personnel were invited. There were two
pop music dance bands. The women were dressed in
long formal Western gowns and had brought their
boyfriends along. This company encourages its
workers to learn English (it holds English classes)
and adopt Western customs, whereas the manager of
Company A is learning Malay himself and reinforces
the practice of traditional customs.

In sum, while some people in the host
community benefit from the employment generated
by the multinational electronics factories, there
exist conflicts between the multinationals and
their workers on the one side, and the indigenous
community on the other. These sometimes break out
into open hostility. Part of it is a result of
cultural conflicts between the traditional local
communities and the workers who have been
influenced by some of the firms' labor practices,
as well as the larger modern society.

III. MULTINATIONAL EMPLOYMENT AND THE
POSITION OF WOMEN IN DEVELOPING COUNTRIES

This paper has dealt with two major issues
related to the position of women in developing
countries. The first is whether foreign
capitalist industrialization in these countries
increases the participation of women in the
industrial wage labor force. While the "classic"
Marxist position, also held by some liberal
feminists, holds that it does, dependency theorists
and many feminist researchers argue otherwise.[24]
The latter argue that foreign capitalist industrialization both constrains the national

economic development of Third World countries, and
restricts women's employment opportunities in
these countries.[25] This conclusion follows from
their concern with import-substitution industrialization, which is mostly capital-intensive, tends
to disproportionately employ males, and has
limited growth and labor absorption possibilities.
My paper, however, focuses on a different type
of foreign capitalist industrialization, one
which has been dramatically successful in increasing
the participation of women in the industrial wage
labor force in export-oriented, labor-intensive
industries established by offshore sourcing
multinationals. While the dependency theorists
are correct in rejecting a naive classical Marxist
and liberal feminist view that foreign investment
in general,by promoting industrial growth,will
increase the labor force participation of women,
their view is limited to the extent that it does
not take into consideration new forms of foreign
industrial investment which may be female-
intensive.[26]

The second issue is whether the increase in
women's participation in the wage labor force is
beneficial or detrimental to the position of women
in developing countries? Classical Marxists and
liberal feminists believe that women's subordination
arises because they are confined to the domestic
(and traditional) economy and are denied
opportunities to participate in the growing
modern industrial and commercial sectors. The
increasing participation of women in industrial
wage labor is thus seen as a "progressive"
phenomenon, bringing women out of the homes and
into factories where they are proletarianized
along with men. This could enhance their
economic and political position.

International policy to improve the position
of women in development also concentrates on
measures to increase women's participation in
the developing modern rural, urban, and industrial
sectors.[27] On the other hand, there exists
opposition to the participation of women in modern
wage labor sector. This comes from both
conservative traditionalists and more radical
nationalists including dependency theorists in
the Third World, who abhor the potentially
disruptive cultural impact on host societies of
women's industrial employment in multinational
corporations.

The arguments of these different schools may

be summarized as follows. Those who believe that
multinational employment is "good" for the position
of women argue that: (1) it reduces the precapitalist exploitation of women by breaking down
traditional and feudal barriers to the emancipation
of women (a view held by classical Marxists and
liberal feminists); (2) it builds a basis for a
strong proletariat among women and the emergence
of class consciousness which will enable them to
collectively organize and fight for their rights
within the factory and within society itself (a
view held mainly by classical Marxists); (3) it
prepares women for better job opportunities, which
is a desirable end in itself (liberal feminists).

Those who believe that multinational employment
is "bad" for women argue that: (1) it leads to
new forms of exploitation of women (feminists and
radical nationalists); (2) it threatens to disrupt
traditional values and culture which have an
intrinsic worth (traditionalists), thereby
inhibiting class consciousness which would unite
all workers, regardless of sex, against the
foreign capitalists (radical nationalists); (3) it
promises much but gives little in the way of
economic gains to women, which are small, unstable,
and temporary (feminists and radical nationalists).

With respect to point (1) on the position of
women in precapitalist societies and its transformation in the capitalist economy, it should be
noted that women workers in Malaysia and Singapore
are ethnically and culturally Chinese, Malay, and
Indian. Confucianism, Islam, and Hinduism are
cultures which have conservative traditional
attitudes towards women, who are generally
confined to domestic economy and nonmonetized
productive activities such as subsistence
farming. It would seem then that the provision
of wage employment for women, under the modern
cultural influences of the multinational factory
and general urban environment, should "liberate"
women from the semifeudal and conservative
strictures of traditional society. They are
granted a measure of economic independence,
personal freedom, access to a wider range of life
experiences and activities, and an expression of
individual identity--all of which they never had
before.[28]

On the other hand, some multinationals
reinforce certain elements of the traditional
patriarchy where these help to increase their
exploitation of women workers. All multinationals

encourage traditional attitudes towards women
which justify giving women lower wages and which
induce deference to authority and diligent work
from them. Even the "modern" labor practices and
cultural influences introduced by multinationals
are often tools for the exploitation of women
in the factory. Any "liberation" of women workers
from precapitalist oppression is negated by
the new forms of exploitation to which they are
subjected in the multinational capitalist factory.

With respect to point (2) on class consciousness, the only evidence I have is inferential,
based on instances of what might be termed "class
action" by women factory workers. Such
initiatives are few in number.

Generally, however, worker tensions tend to be
expressed internationally--in mass hysteria, for
example--rather than externally in labor agitation
and unrest or work stoppages. There are many
obstacles to worker organization, in addition to
government restrictions on and control of unions.
Multinationals in their hiring practices tend to
screen out potentially active worker leaders or
"troublemakers." The recentness of the industry,
lack of previous industrial wage labor experience
of workers, lack of cohesion among workers because
of racial (mainly linguistic) differences, high
turnover, and short duration of employment for
individual workers all militate against workers'
organization. At the same time, new values and
attitudes which are introduced to the labor force--
competitive work ethic, response to individual
monetary gain, consumption ideology--may have the
effect of preempting the development of a working
class consciousness. Furthermore, the consumption
patterns and social behavior of some workers
antagonize members of the host community. The
conflicts between workers and the community over
this cultural disruption divide the local population and inhibit the development of a broader
class consciousness.

With respect to point (3) on the creation of
better job opportunities for women, this is not
as positive as it might appear. The jobs created
for young women in the electronics industry offer
low pay, little job mobility, virtually no
prospects for job improvement, insecurity of job
tenure, and constant threat of layoffs. Far from
contributing to women's economic advancement in
the long run, they offer at best temporary "dead-
end" jobs in segregated female-intensive

industries. Women are not integrated permanently
into the main stream of the economy; rather,
they are temporarily confined to an export manufacturing sector whose long-run viability itself
is in doubt.

In short, while the classical Marxist and
liberal feminist are correct in claiming that multinational investment does increase female employment
in developing countries, this has so far occurred
only in labor-intensive, export-oriented offshore
manufacturing sector which is not integrated into
the host economy.

An improvement in the position of women
should include the following. First, the economic
position of women is enhanced by multinational
employment if it increases their incomes and
standards of living, measured by the consumption
of goods and services; grants them economic
independence and security; and generally increases
their relative contribution to the economic position
and levels of living of their families and home
communities. Second, the social position of women
is enhanced if, as a consequence of their greater
economic participation in society, their self-image
and images of them held by the larger society
improve, in particular, where patriarchal attitudes
are changed and women are fully accepted and
respected as equal participants with men in every
aspect of the society they share.

In conclusion, neither women workers nor
the developing countries can expect to benefit
much from the large-scale female employment
generated by foreign investments in labor-intensive,
export-oriented offshore industries like electronics. However, more research remains to be done,
in view of the fact that this type of female
industrial employment is rapidly spreading to other
parts of the Third World.

NOTES

1. The major work advancing this thesis is
Ester Boserup, *Women's Role in Economic Development*
(London: Allen and Unwin, 1970). See also the
articles by Arizpe and Chincilla in *Women and
National Development*, Special Issue of *SIGNS,
Journal of Women in Culture and Society* (University
of Chicago), Vol. 3, No. 1, Autumn 1977.
2. For example, in Brazil, as cited by
Glaura Vasques de Miranda, "Women's Labor Force

Participation in a Developing Society: the Case of Brazil," *Ibid.*, pp. 261-274.

3. For example, in Puerto Rico. See Helen I Safa, "Class Consciousness Among Working-Class Women in Latin America: Puerto Rico," in June Nash and Helen I. Safa (eds.) *Sex and Class in Latin America* (New York: Praeger, 1976), pp. 69-85.

4. Norma S. Chincilla, "Industrialization, Monopoly Capitalism and Women's Work in Guatemala," in *Women and National Development*, pp. 38-56.

5. Thus in Chincilla's study of Guatemala, "Women have not been pushed into manufacturing industries in large numbers and have even declined proportionally in industries considered 'female'" such as textiles and tobacco. *Ibid.*

6. Some examples are: Robert T. Snow, "Dependent Development and the New Industrial Worker: The Export Processing Zone in the Philippines," Ph.D. dissertation, Department of Sociology, Harvard University, 1977; Janet Salaff, "Working Daughters in the Hong Kong Chinese Family"; Lydia Kung, "Factory Work and Women in Taiwan: Changes in Self-Image and Status," in *SIGNS: Journal of Women in Culture and Society*, Vol. 2, No. 1, pp. 35-58.

7. For example, see James Leontiades, "International Sourcing in the Less Developed Countries," *Columbia Journal of World Business*, Vol. VI, No. 6 (Nov.-Dec. 1971); Thomas K. Morrison, "International Subcontracting: Improved Prospects in Manufactured Exports for Small and Very Poor Less-Developed Countries," *World Development*, Vol. 4, pp. 327-332 (1976).

8. An exposition of this concept can be found in any introductory economics text, such as Richard G. Lipsey and Peter O. Steiner, *Economics* 4th edition (New York: Harper and Row, 1975).

9. See, for example, Joan Robinson and John Eatwell, *An Introduction to Modern Economics* (New York: McGraw-Hill, 1973).

10. The Marxist concept is expounded in several works, the classic being Karl Marx, *Capital*, Vol. 1 (New York: International Publishers).

11. Lee Ann Reynis, "The Proliferation of U.S. Firm Third World Sourcing in the Mid-to-Late 1960's: A Historical and Empirical Study of the Factors Which Occassioned the Location of Production for the U.S. Market Abroad," Ph.D. dissertation, Department of Economics, University

of Michigan, 1976; and Richard W. Moxon, "Offshore Production in the Less-Developed Countries--A Case Study of Multinationality in the Electronics Industry," *The Bulletin*, No. 98-99, July 1974, New York University Graduate School of Business Administration, Institute of Finance.

12. UNCTAD, "International Subcontracting Arrangements in Electronics Between Developed Market-Economy Countries and Developing Countries," (New York: United Nations, 1975), p. 20.

13. See, for example, Ronald Müller, "The Multinational Corporation and the Underdeveloped of the Third World," in Charles Wilber (ed.), *The Political Economy of Development and Underdevelopment* (New York: Random House, 1973), pp. 124-151.

14. As argued in Chincilla, "Industrialization, Monopoly Capitalism and Women's Work," for example.

15. One survey of workers in Penang, Malaysia, found that most of them were employed for the first time, and were new members of the wage labor force. Most of them took the factory jobs because they were the only ones available. One-third of the workers surveyed had at least one member of the immediate family seeking employment of whom two-thirds were males and 60 percent had been out of work for a year or longer. See Fred R. Von der Mehden, "Industrial Policy in Malaysia, a Penang Micro-Study," Occasional Paper of the Program for Development Studies, Rice University, Houston, Texas, June 1973.

16. Monthly Statistical Bulletins, Department of Statistics, Kuala Lumpur. It should be noted, however, that 60 percent of employed women are in situations of "underemployment." See *Women Today in Peninsular Malaysia*, Federation of Family Planning Associations in Malaysia, 1976.

17. For example, Intel Corporation, with plants in Malaysia and the Philippines, had this to say while planning a new plant in Latin America: "The idea is to have three plants operating at two-thirds capacity, rather than two at full capacity. If something happens, we can transfer production without a whole lot of risk." Richard Leger, "Semiconductor Concerns Put New Money into Capital Improvements as Sales Boom," *Wall Street Journal*, July 26, 1976, p. 22.

18. Quote in Andy McCue, "Electronics Industry in Malaysia Runs Into Some Hard Realities," in *Asian Wall Street Journal*, December 30, 1977.

19. *Ibid.*
20. See Chang, "Economics of Offshore Assembly?" for a discussion of the cyclical nature of the semiconductor industry.
21. "17,000 laid off in 1974," *New Nation*, Singapore, January 24, 1975.
22. After a strong recovery in 1976, layoffs occurred again in early 1977. See "Workers Axed at Short Notice Without Reason," *Business Times*, Singapore, January 21, 1977, referring to the retrenchment of more than 1,000 electronics workers in Penang, and rumors that "several factories were closing down and thousands of workers would be retrenched."
23. "Singapore's Electric Industry: Need for more skilled workers," *Business Times*, Singapore, November 21, 1977.
24. The summary discussion of these and other theories of women and development is to be found in "Theories of Development: An Assessment" by Carolyn M. Elliott in *SIGNS* Vol. 3, No. 1, pp. 1-8. For the original articulation of the Marxian perspective, see Frederick Engel's *Origin of the Family, State and Private Property* (New York: International Publishers, 1972), and V. I. Lenin, *On the Emancipation of Women*. For examples of the dependency theorist and related feminist position, see the works cited in Footnote 1.
25. See Chincilla, "Industrialization and Monopoly Capitalism," *op. cit.*
26. Chincilla, *op. cit.*, cautions that there is no universal homogeneous consequence of industrialization; rather there is "a cluster of consequences that are conditioned by the mode of production and by the function of the economy in an international economic system."
27. For example, the many efforts within development agencies of the United Nations to integrate women into national development follow this approach.
28. This is also the conclusion of other studies which have been done on women workers in labor-intensive factories in Taiwan (Kung, "Factory Work and Women in Taiwan"), Hong Kong (Salaff, "Working Daughters in Hong Kong"), and the Philippines (Snow, "Dependent Development and the New Industrial Worker"), cited in footnote 6. Snow, for example, found that "The fact that many of (the workers) were living away from home and earning an independent income for the first time

gave them a new degree of social freedom which
they valued highly. They had chances to meet new
friends and participate in new activities; they
purchased small personal items; they gained
satisfaction by supporting themselves and helping
their families. A zone job gave women workers
the possibility to prolong their independence by
delaying marriage and child-bearing."
R. T. Snow, dissertation abstract, *op. cit.*
pp. 4-5.

5
The Multinational Corporations and Inequality of Development

Arghiri Emmanuel

AN INCOMPLETE RECORD

One of the few points on which the Group of Eminent Persons appointed by the Secretary-General of the United Nations to examine the problem of multinational corporations (MNC) agreed was the penury of "useful and reliable" information. The majority of members emphasized this in their reports.[1]

Such a situation regarding a subject which has held pride of place in political and economic literature over the past decade is surprising in itself. It ceases to be so when considered in relation to the eminently ideological nature of this discussion which, as such, tends to overlook and even elude the data in favor of the deductions.

Not being a specialist on the subject myself, I could, in writing this article, assess the discrepancy between the inflated nature of the discussion and the meagerness of the facts. For example, the most recent figure I could find for the total "stock" of foreign investments in the developing countries dates from 1967 and was published in 1973.[2] Moreover, since the majority of the statistics dealing with the activities of the multinational corporations are mere estimates, very considerable discrepancies, which reflect the subjectivity of their authors, are commonplace. Thus, as regards the effects of the expatriation of American capital on employment in the United States, two United Nations estimates give a loss of 400,000 and 1,300,000 jobs respectively, while a similar estimate by the Harvard Business School reports a gain of 600,000!

The Champions of the Cause

In this speculative field it is as well first of all to distinguish the apologists from the detractors. The former's argument is simple. The multinationals merely eliminate the distortions caused by the discontinuity of political frontiers. They tend to render the economic space of the world as homogeneous and as unadulterated as that of the neoclassical free-trade models. They tend, therefore, to rationalize the system and maximize its yield.

Since this represents no specific argument in favor of the multinationals, it may be said that there is no mystification either. The multinationals do no more than restore, as well as they can, an ideal state of affairs which has been upset by the interventionism of national bureaucracies. They illustrate the original superiority of private enterprise over the management of governments. What is good for General Motors is good for the United States and, *a fortiori*, for Brazil.[3]

In so far as this approach is coherent and adds nothing whatsoever to the neoclassical traditional argument that the profit motive results in the optimal allocation of factors, there is nothing to add to its equally traditional refutation either.

The Right-Wing Adversaries

With the adversaries things are less simple. First, they must be divided into two major groups. The criticisms of the first spring from a defence of the existing economic system, those of the second from questioning it.

Objectively, the circles constituting the first group form an integral part of the system or even occupy dominant positions in it. As such, they enter either directly or indirectly into conflict with the rival power of the MNCs.

Ideologically, they see in the MNCs a misuse of the system. They put forward the same ideal of competition as the upholders, but unlike them find that the multinationals, owing to their oligopolistic nature, cause even more serious distortions and discontinuities than do the interventions of the nationalist state.

This group includes both international organizations, such as the Organisation for Economic Cooperation and Development (OECD), the

World Bank, and even the North Atlantic Treaty
Organization (NATO), and national states.[4] The
major trade union organizations of the advanced
countries also fall under this category.

Special mention should be made of the AFL-CIO,
which has carried on the most virulent and systematic campaign against the multinationals. Its
attitude is the least "ideological" of all in the
sense that it does not encumber itself with any
reference to the common good of mankind. It openly
concerns itself with the exclusive interests of one
section of the "labor aristocracy" of the world--
the workers of the United States. Here, its
analysts find themselves on solid ground.

Any attempt to show them that they are making
a technical error is vain. It consists of changing
standards upon transition from the initial period,
during which the outlay of funds exceeds income, to
the subsequent period when income exceeds new
investments. In speaking of the former, the positive effect on the balance of trade is invoked; in
speaking of the latter, it is the positive effect
on the balance of payments that is put forward.

The artful trick here is isolating the
operations of the multinationals from the rest of
the economy. It is true enough that exports of
capital are nothing but exports of unpaid goods,
compensated for by the acquisition of foreign
assets. Consequently, when in the first stage a
multinational corporation sets up in business
outside the frontiers of the United States and sends
dollars there, it is obvious that, assuming the
monetary reserves in the remainder of the world
remain unchanged, these dollars will be used to
purchase the means of production, failing which,
incidentally, it is difficult to see how the multinational corporation in question could establish
itself abroad. It is therefore true that, at the
time when it leaves American territory, the
multinational corporation creates additional
employment in order to produce the additional
exports which are the material form its "export of
capital" will take.

But, still assuming that reserves remain
unchanged, the subsequent reentry of dollars by way
of dividends and interest payments can only take
place by means of imports of goods not compensated
for by exports from the receiving country. Consequently, when during the second period--that of the
maturing of the investments--reentries begin to
exceed outgoings, the effect on the balance of

trade (which alone affects the level of employment)
will be negative by that amount although positive
where the balance of payments is concerned. Paradoxical though it may appear, the period detrimental
to the working class is not that when capital is
exported but that when its fruits begin to flow
back into the investing country.

These imports, which are the counterpart of
dividends, are not necessarily made by the multinational corporations themselves. They do not,
therefore, appear on their balance sheets, with the
result that figures as divergent as 1.3 million jobs
less and 600,000 more are obtained. But it is easy
enough to understand the process if we imagine it
taken to its logical conclusion, where American
capitalists will have sent all branches of industry
abroad (except those whose products are not
transportable), at which point, having become
"coupon clippers," they will be able to import any
consumer goods they want and pay for them with their
dividends.

The external balance will then merely show
imports of goods on one side and receipts of funds
on the other. The proprietors of General Motors
will be no worse off. Their works will be located
in Mexico or Brazil where wages are lower. From
these countries and others they will be able to
import their private cars and other consumer goods,
plus, perhaps, the ingredients of the soup for
distribution to the destitute, which they will have
to organize for their former workers. The external
accounts of the nation will be balanced, and so will
the budget. The dollar will be in a strong position. The workers will, so to speak, be "marginalized." They will then be free either to follow
General Motors abroad and join the other "emigrant
workers" or take jobs as domestic servants, the
employment of whom by the rentier capitalists
concerned will increase in proportion as their
remunerations fall.[5]

The AFL-CIO, therefore, sees things clearly
from its own point of view. Exports of capital are
prejudicial to the American working class. Whether,
from the point of view of the 2,000 million
inhabitants of the developing countries and of the
1,000 million who are hungry and from that of human
progress generally, this possible reproletarian-
ization of some of the American wage earners is a
negative or positive feature is quite another
question.

And Those on the Left

We now have to consider the second group of adversaries, who are much more numerous. To the extent that, in contradiction with their revolutionary projects, they slide irresistibly towards the attitudes inherent in the system of capitalist relations and end up by perceiving the MNCs as the constituent element of a variant of the system and criticizing it as such for the same reasons and in the same terms as its detractors to the right, they become the most "ideological" and the most productive of mythology of all. At worst, the issue is not one of after the MNCs what? but of no MNCs at all, not of the destruction of the system with or without the MNCs but of the destruction of the MNC *within* the system. At the best, the system would have to be destroyed all the same but the only reason for doing so is the impossibility of getting rid of its MNCs. This attitude is not unrelated to the historical constant of a *petit-bourgeois* opposition to the capitalist system which proceeds from a confused, subconscious basis in the "Paradise Lost" of precapitalist trading relations and periodically breaks out into reactionary campaigns against machinery, urban living, trusts, cosmopolitanism, and so on and whose "national roads" to socialism are today one of the variables of life's political hazards.

And yet it needs to be said that, so far as the MNC is concerned, it is not the theoretical attitudes of communist parties which are the most mystifying. On the contrary, by refusing to recognize that the MNC has a specific character and by considering it merely as a geographical extension of state monopoly capitalism, they do not in the least contradict their frankly reformist position towards this type of society, already considered as a variant of the capitalist mode of production. Moreover, since this position is chiefly adopted by the theorists of certain European parties who are increasingly turning aside from the problems of the developing countries and are only concerning themselves with the minor aspects of the problem, so to speak--or in other words the aspects directly affecting their respective countries: American penetration on the one hand and drain on national capital on the other--their arguments are of only secondary interest here.[6]

This applies even more to the social-democrat

parties, which are openly reformist, and to the
liberal theorists, progressives, and non-engaged
Marxists.

We can also leave aside the attitudes adopted
by certain theorists of the East European countries
who reconcile scientific abstraction with the
judicious pragmatism of their respective governments, in something like the following manner:
(a) first, they contribute to the universal
pillorying with the routine arguments; (b) next,
they declare outright that the MNCs (which, having
been proscribed in the capitalist world, have
probably become more accommodating) will find
opportunities for joint and mutually advantageous
operations in socialist countries and, in addition,
will enjoy these countries' well-known respect for
agreements and the stability of their governments;
(c) they explain the contradiction between (a) and
(b) by the fact that, in their case, the strategic
"heights" of the economy are well in hand and run
no risks. Foreign investors can make money but
never dominate them.[7] Since everyone knows that
foreign investors only want to make money and have
no particular ambitions to dominate the "heights,"
this is a perfectly safe statement which reassures
one side without worrying the other.

"Ideological" occultation is mainly to be
found on the left, in the multitude of small groups
claiming to preach revolutionary Marxism which, as
always happens in periods when, on account of
material circumstances, social movement is slowing
down, miss their target and resort to verbiage. In
particular I am referring to that infinity of shades
of opinion concerning the "internationalization of
capital."

To top it all, the very fact that the detractors of the MNCs are recruited in all camps confers
on their argument an outstanding respectability,
with the result that dissertations proliferate,
thus making quite a contribution to the general
confusion.[8]

Space does not allow me to examine these
innumerable doctrines one by one. Nor does it seem
to me to be necessary. Both the specific arguments
against the MNCs and the myths overlap with the
most widely divergent views of the world. I shall
therefore discuss the problem thematically, giving
priority to those concerned with development.

EXPORTS OF CAPITAL GENERALLY

A distinction should perhaps have been made
between the MNC problem and that of exports of
capital generally. The former are merely one
vehicle for the latter. However, in the case of
the least-developed countries, private foreign
investments are nearly always direct investments in
practice, since such countries have no extensive
undertakings of their own, and a portfolio investment can only take the form of minority participation or the acquisition of bonds in an existing
foreign undertaking which has, consequently, been
the result of previous direct investments.

As for direct investments themselves, except
for settlers' undertakings which are only a marginal
phenomenon today, the present trend towards widening
the definition of the MNC makes any distinction
regarding the status of the investor pointless. On
the other hand, the distinction between exports of
capital from developed countries to others on the
one hand and movements of capital between the
developed countries themselves, on the other, is
still very important. On this basis attempts have
been made to interpret the present "internationalization" of capital as a movement new in quality and
much superior in quantity to similar movements in
the past. So far as quality is concerned, that is
a matter of appreciation, and I shall put forward
my own analysis later. But quantity is a matter of
figures and, as such, the statement is false and
even grossly misleading.

In 1914 the "stock" of United Kingdom's
accumulated assets abroad came to 4,000 million gold
sovereigns. Whether one converts this figure on
the basis of the value of gold or on that of
purchasing power, it comes to about 130,000 million
1974 paper dollars. In 1974 total United States
public and private assets of all categories
(including short-term export credits) amounted to
$265,000 million, or in other words just about
double in absolute figures. But a comparison in
absolute figures between a United Kingdom with
45 million inhabitants in 1914 and a United States
of more than 210 million in 1974 has little significance, and in relative terms it turns out that
British external assets in 1914 accounted for about
double annual national revenue of the period,

whereas those of the United States today account
for only one-fifth.

If we took into account the economic "surface"
of the countries invested in at these same two
dates, the results would be about the same.[9]
Whether, therefore, from the point of view of
"overaccumulation of capital" and its need for
outlets beyond the frontiers of the "center" or
from that of the aggression to which the "periphery"
is subjected, whether focusing on departure or on
the arrival of capital, we find that the present
figure of $265,000 million which gives rise to such
emotion is laughable, since the United Kingdom was
doing ten times better sixty years ago.

If we add the other OECD countries we arrive at
a total which bears about the same relation to the
1974 American assets alone as did the assets of the
only four investing countries in 1914 (United
Kingdom, France, Germany, and the United States) to
the British assets of that time alone, i.e. about
double.

But this would give rise to a consolidation
problem, since these countries invest in each other.
This consolidation would have the effect of changing
the results in favor of my position. Thus, while
the United States had 265,000 million dollars' worth
of assets in the rest of the world in 1974, the rest
of the world (in effect, the rest of the OECD
countries) had $187,000 millions' worth of assets in
the United States at the same time. This reduces
the net assets of the United States from $265,000
million to $78,000 million.[10] This was not the case
with the United Kingdom in 1914 when investments
in the other direction were negligible.

If we leave aside total assets and deal with
direct investments in the developing countries only,
which is the true purpose of this article, we shall
find that in 1974, out of a total "stock" of
$118,600 million of American direct investments,
those which had been made in the periphery amounted
to only $28,500 million, including $19,600 million
in Latin America, which is not exactly the least-
developed region, by a long shot. Only $8,900
million remained, therefore, for the really underdeveloped countries--that is, more than 1,500
million people.[11]

But that is not all, for out of this amount
$4,700 million is invested in oil which, from every
point of view, is a special case and which, incidentally, concerns only a small proportion of the
populations of this group of countries. For all

other industrial activities, such as mining,
manufacturing, etc., therefore, only $4,200 million
remains for this group (this is 3.6 percent of the
total and represents less than $3 per inhabitant or
$7 per worker, just enough to equip each of them
with a good screwdriver).[12]
    So far as the direct investments of the OECD
countries as a whole are concerned, all that is
available is the 1967 figure, as I said earlier.
This is $8,200 million for countries other than
those of Latin America, not including oil.[13] If we
apply to this figure the same coefficient as that
represented by the increase in total foreign direct
investments between 1967 and 1974, we arrive at an
approximate figure of $16,000 million. (Here again
I am speaking of accumulated assets and not of
flow.)
    This is an extremely generous estimate in view
of the fact that, over the same period, the share
accounted for by investments in developed countries
was increasing, whereas withdrawals of investments
from developing countries were increasing as a
result of nationalization. However, it will suffice
to compare this figure with American investments in
Canada alone, which came to $28,300 million in 1974,
to see immediately that the Third World countries,
far from having been invaded by foreign capital,
have been starved of it.
    If we list the countries of the world, first
in decreasing order of capital received, from Canada
to India via Europe, Latin America, and the
developing countries of Africa and Asia, and
secondly in decreasing order of their GNP per head
of the population, we shall find that, apart from
a few exceptions, the two lists coincide exactly.
So either there is no causal link between foreign
capital and underdevelopment, in which case the
multinationals cannot be accused of having caused
a deadlock at the periphery, or the deadlock
occurred not because international capital flowed
in but because it has stayed out.

Exports of Capital and Marxism

    Although, in the present climate of intoxica-
tion, this latter conclusion appears paradoxical,
it fits in perfectly well not only with the most
traditional view of affairs but also with the most
orthodox Marxist teaching. Lenin did not feel that
he was innovating when he wrote in his *Imperialism,
the Highest Stage of Capitalism* that the effect of

exporting capital was to accelerate the development
of the countries to which it was sent and slow down
the development of the countries from which it
came.[14] Before him, Marx had already written in the
"Preface" to the first German edition of *Das Kapital*
that "the most industrially developed country
merely shows to those which follow it on the industrial ladder the picture of their own future," and
in his article in the *New York Daily Tribune* dated
8 August 1853 he explained how the building of the
railroad in India would inevitably result in the
development of India, whether the British wanted it
or not.

By a sort of communicating vessel process, the
backward region drained off the surplus from the
advanced region. As Rosa Luxemburg pointed out, the
cities of northern Italy sent their surplus capital
to finance the development of Holland during the
sixteenth century. During the seventeenth and
eighteenth centuries, Dutch capital contributed to
England's takeoff. British capital, in turn, took
the road to North America and Australia during the
eighteenth and nineteenth centuries. Local saturation discharged the surplus of nutritive substances
from the top to the lower slopes.

When Britain had already completed her industrial revolution at the beginning of the nineteenth
century, continental Europe had not even begun.
This did not make it the "periphery" of Britain:
it became a "Britain" in turn. Marx was not wrong
in considering that there was only a time lag
between development and underdevelopment.

What was it that caused such a rapid saturation
at the top and the cessation of internal accumulation, causing capital and technology to be poured
out on to the external valleys? It was the lack
of elasticity in the internal market which, beyond
a certain point, discouraged investments. This
lack of flexibility was due to the relative
stagnation of wages at a level close to the cost
of the biological reproduction of labor. The system
provisionally avoided grinding to a halt by
expatriating its surplus capital. But this was only
putting off the evil day, for there was not an
inexhaustible number of Indias. And when all the
Indias of the world had become Britains, the system
would have exhausted the margins of development of
the "productive forces which it is wide enough to
contain."[15]

Something happened towards the end of the
nineteenth century and this conventional Marxist

picture ceased to reflect reality. This was a
radical change in the distribution of power among
the classes within the bourgeois parliamentary
system in the industrialized countries, which had
the effect of finally lifting the price of manpower out of the swamp of the mere physiological
survival of the worker. In order to appreciate
the effect of this event it suffices to remember
that, for thousands of years, the worker's wage was
the most stable economic magnitude which existed.
The purchasing power of the average European worker
round about 1830 differed very little from that of
the worker in Byzantium, Rome, or the Egypt of the
pharaohs. In the following century and a half it
was multiplied by ten.

There followed a reversal of the conditions
for accumulation at the international level. In
the central countries, the domestic market under-
went expansion at breakneck speed. Moreover, since
the mechanism of unequal exchange enabled the over-
paid workers of the center to take greater advantage
of the consumers of the Third World than of the
capitalists of the country which paid them, all
barriers to the capitalization of profit broke down.
The trade union struggle in a way extricated the
system from the dead end against its will, at least
temporarily, by settling the argument between the
two prerequisites of investments: widening the
market without reducing profits.

That being so, capital no longer needs to run
off to the antipodes; it finds means of accumulation
at home, or at least in the region of the
"center."16 Its movement to less-developed countries, far from being a continuous, regulating flow,
has become merely casual. Perhaps Marxist theorists
were right when they believed that exports of
capital had a leveling effect. The only thing is
that such exports have just not taken place towards
a certain category of countries, except in insufficient quantities.

Those who speak of deadlocks apparently have
good reason to suppose that these quantities are
still excessive. In that case, if they cannot
explain why, they should at least tell us how these
countries could develop *without* these quantities.
The United Kingdom took 200 years about it. During
the century preceding the First World War, her
national revenue increased at a rate of 1-3/8
percent a year.17 In the absence of the "shortcut"
involving foreign resources of capital and technology, is there any reason why the countries in

question should advance within the capitalist
system any quicker than Britain did in former times?
If not, do they find acceptable a rate which causes
the GNP to double every fifty years and will ensure
that the average developing country of today will
reach the present level of France in the year
2176?[18]

But perhaps those in favor of "self-centered"
development do not mean development "within the
capitalist system," and here arises the major
misunderstanding in the controversy. As
Bill Warren points out, there is a constant shift
from the conception of development to that of
socially satisfactory development.[19] We simply
forget to make the distinction Marx made between
"the development of productive forces" and "their
appropriation by the people."

It is forgotten that capitalism is not a bad
dream but a social system which has a historical
part to play; a system which, as it developed,
gave not only gadgets and pollution but also
widespread literacy and an average life expectancy
of seventy years instead of forty. And that,
consequently while awaiting the social revolution,
it is by no means a matter of indifference for
people whether they live in India or the United
States, no matter what similarity may be recognized
between the production relations in these two
countries.[20]

THE CONCRETE POSSIBILITIES OF DEVELOPMENT

That does not mean to say that, in present
historical circumstances, India can become the
United States by accelerating her development
through foreign financial aid. The reasons why
such financing is falling off have already been
explained, but the author would go even further.
He thinks that in no circumstances can "Indias"
ever become "United States," even if they wanted
to. The United States are the United States only
because the others are not. The level of development reached there considerably surpasses the overall potentialities of the capitalist system on a
world scale. In the capitalist sense, they are
overdeveloped. Quite naturally, they can only be
so because all around them there are sufficient
developing countries which are exploitable.

It may perhaps still be possible to generate
this extraverted accelerated development in some

small country if the little international capital
available is concentrated there. This will be
because the others do not follow it along the same
road. For the developing countries generally, such
an attempt would be futile, quite apart from any
normative considerations. The only road open to
them then is to skip the capitalist stage. It may
then be hoped that, if only from the strictly
economic point of view, the mobilization of domestic
resources and the rationalization of production will
advantageously replace the few and increasingly
problematic crumbs available to them by way of
foreign finance.

All this, however, arises from calling into
question the system and not of the MNCs. If it
were a matter of socialist development, it would be
frankly ridiculous to reproach the MNCs for not
acting as the vehicle. And if it is a matter of
capitalist development, the only valid criticism
would be one making a distinction between the MNC
and the national capitalist corporation.

Such a distinction has never been made. In
particular, it has never been clearly explained how
the nationality of the owner can change the nature
of the capital. When people speak of centers of
decision they forget to tell us in what way the
location of the centers affects the nature of the
decisions and why. Two-thirds of all the capital
in Canada belongs to foreigners, 80 percent of
whom are Americans. On the other hand, India is the
country *par excellence* where industrialization was
carried out almost exclusively by the local
bourgeoisie. It is not very clear what the
Canadian people--who are among the richest in the
world--would stand to win if the "centers of
decision" moved from the skyscrapers of Manhattan
to the office blocks of Montreal, or what the
people of India--among the most poverty-stricken
of the world--would stand to lose further if her
capitalists handed over their factories to others
holding a Japanese or German passport.

Very much to the contrary, for whenever we
find, rightly or wrongly, that in any particular
aspect the behavior of the MNC differs from that
of the traditional capitalist undertaking, the
specific character of the MNC is generally to its
advantage.

Transfer of Technology

One of these alleged deviations, and perhaps

the most important, is that concerning the notorious problem of "appropriate" technology. From time immemorial, the entrepreneur has been blamed for wasting human labor by selecting his technology on the basis of the "paid labor time" and not the "total labor time" devoted to production. Market forces gave "to each his due," to the Ghanaian worker his hoe and to the American worker his tractor. Cheap muscles drove out gray matter and machinery from the low-wage countries, while gray matter and machinery took the place of expensive muscle power in the developed countries. The situation reached deadlock precisely because the rarefaction of gray matter and machinery maintained productivity at a low level, thus forcing the cost of muscle power even lower. This lowering of cost in turn rendered gray matter and machinery less profitable. We then thought that only deliberate intervention by the state, apart from capitalist rationalism, was capable of breaking the vicious circle and putting the "inappropriate" tractor into the African plantation; otherwise it was difficult to see how development could ever occur.

Now we are told that the MNCs--the most capitalistic-minded of all capitalist undertakings-- have discovered the dodge of locating heavy technology in regions where labor is cheap, or in other words exactly what the Soviet Union did during the early five-year plan and what any social- ist planner is supposed to do. And instead of rejoicing at the good news, we are supposed to meditate on the diabolical strategy of the multi- national corporations which waste capital (their own) exclusively in order to cause underemployment in the receiving countries.

In order to support the "appropriate" technology argument (which basically is just a euphemism for "intermediate" technology), reference is sometimes made to Chinese practice. But, in fact, the basic Chinese principle is the plurality of technologies which is just about the opposite of the "intermediate" technology suggested by critics, such as E. F. Schumacher. The latter dilutes the available capital among all the production units involved. The former introduces straight away the pioneer technology entailing the highest organic composition in as many units as possible, regardless of the fact that the shortage of capital prevents its immediate spread over the rest of the branch. Macroeconomic calculations show that this is the method giving maximum long-term output. However,

it is an impossible method in a market economy
where competition forbids any disparity between the
conditions of production in different undertakings.
It is only possible in a planned economy.[21]
The following passage from a text by Mao is
very explicit on this point.[22]

> The fact that we are developing small and
> medium-size industries on a large scale,
> although accepting that the large undertakings
> constitute the guiding force, and that we are
> using traditional technologies everywhere,
> although accepting that foreign technologies
> constitute the guiding power, is essentially
> due to our desire to achieve rapid indus-
> trialization.

It appears to me that the "appropriate" technology
is the very thing to be outlawed. An appropriate
technology for poor countries can only be a poor
technology; an appropriate technology made to
measure for underdeveloped countries can only be
an anti-development technology.[23]
Rehabilitating the neoclassical theory which
had been previously pilloried, certain people
complain that the technology introduced into
developing countries by the MNCs does not correspond to the resources available there. Nor should
it. If it did, the mix of factors would be frozen
and the deficiencies reproduced *ad infinitum*. If
"transfer" is seen as a vehicle of domination, it
is forgotten that, if there were no transfer at all,
the technological domination of the center would
be even more decisive.

"Autonomous" Technology

Sometimes it is not an "appropriate" technology
but a national, so-called "autonomous" one that is
called for. Without going into details on this
particular point, it may be said that, apart from
questions of political prestige, an "autonomous"
technology is the most disadvantageous product
that can exist, since technology is the most
undervalued commodity on the international market.
Although it is the product of the industrialized
countries, it is offered at abnormally low prices.
This is due to the fact that the direct or indirect
assumption by the state of part of the R & D
expenditure overcompensates by a wide margin both
the high remuneration of the technology production

factors and profits in all forms, even if excessive, of the seller.[24]

"Imitative" technology, particularly in Japan and Italy, has undoubtedly been good business for these countries. Italy, by importing the majority of her technology during the 1950s and devoting only 0.6 percent of her GNP to R & D, as against 3.09 percent in the United States and 1.51 percent in France, achieved a remarkable increase in productivity, and it is estimated that 72 percent of economic growth between 1954 and 1959 was due to technological progress.

Sometimes, moreover, a qualitative dimension is attached to this argument, and a certain impoverishment of culture arising from the standardization of consumer goods throughout the world is deplored.[25] Undoubtedly, in addition to the problem of means, there is also trade-off regarding ends. And it may be thought that social revolution will not be content with organizing the production and distribution of the automobile and television set more rationally but will profoundly modify them so as to adapt them to a less individualized and more human environment and way of life. But it would be utterly absurd to increase, in the meantime, the number of makes of cars and color television processes, with all the wastage and duplication involved, under the pretext of escaping from the domination of General Motors and the SECAM, just as it would be childish to keep the wooden plow in order to safeguard the authentic traditions of the people.

The cost of imported technology is another favorite subject for MNC myths. UNCTAD puts forward the figure of $1,500 million as the total annual cost for the Third World as a whole.

Even if this figure is correct, it would only account for about 0.4 percent of the GNP, whereas expenditure on R & D in the most advanced OECD countries came to about $50,000 million, that is 2 percent of the GNP of the same year.[26]

But the UNCTAD figure covers a composite statistical category. It includes not only the cost of patents, licenses, and know-how but also trade marks, royalties, the leasing of films and television programs, and all the revenue of intellectual property generally. It is obvious that a considerable part of this expenditure forms part of the balance of services rather than that of technological transfers.

The Local Outlet Prerequisite

Another specific feature of the MNC which is
vaguely considered to generate prejudice but which,
if it really exists, is eminently advantageous, is
its independence of the domestic market of the
receiving country. Since the main problem of
capitalism is not to produce but to sell, less
traditional capital was attracted by the low wage
rates of certain countries than was discouraged by
the narrowness of the local market associated with
such wages. This lack of capital in turn prevented
growth and hence wage increases. The result was
deadlock.[27]
In theory the solution was production for
exports alone. But except for standardized
primary products, such an operation appeared to
transcend the fief of the traditional capitalist.
In any case, it has never occurred.[28] The MNC, with
its own sales network abroad and, even more, its
own consumption in the case of a conglomerate,
would not be put off by the lack of "preexisting"
local outlets. It would, according to G. Adam,
take advantage of both the low wages of the periphery and the high wages of the center. I have no
idea of the relative importance of the phenomenon.
Here, as elsewhere, statistical information is
lacking. Albert Michalet considers that it is very
extensive in quantity and very important from the
point of view of quality.[29] All I can say is that,
if this is so, this gives us for the first time the
possibility of breaking the most pernicious vicious
circle which was holding up the development of the
Third World. It is rather a matter for rejoicing.

Enclaves and Profit Repatriation

It is somewhat contradictory to accuse the MNC
of being an enclave and a nuisance at the same time.
If the MNC becomes a real enclave, it ceases to be
a nuisance, since its relations--whether good or
bad--with the national economic space are
restricted, and if its effects on the environmental
economy increase it ceases *ipso facto* to be an
enclave.
Let us take the extreme case of an enclave--a
free zone. In exchange for authorization to close
off a few acres of beaches and allow goods to
transit, the foreigner pays certain dues. This is
a net profit, and there is no problem about it.

Now let us suppose that the foreigner asks
authorization to set up, in the perimeter covered
by the authorization and with his own resources, a
workshop for repairing his equipment or even a
factory to produce something of no concern to the
surrounding power. He offers extra payments in the
form of corporation tax, say 50 percent of the
profits. Can there be any good reason for refusing?
Would one be concerned with what he was going to do
with the other 50 percent? Next, he asks if he
can employ some nationals as workers. I would not
mind betting that, not only would one agree, but one
would be opposed to his bringing his own workers
from the other side of the ocean if some jobs
could be entrusted to the local population.

Naturally, this is the point where the unilat-
eral flow of advantages from the enclave to the
receiving country ceases. The wages paid are no
longer a "net profit." Labor power is provided from
which the enclave extracts a value higher than its
price--a surplus value. But one is an underdeveloped capitalist country, and, like all underdeveloped capitalist countries, has an
underemployment situation. So rather than send
workers to the multinational's factory on the other
side of the sea, it is much better if the factory
is set up on the other side of the road.[30] Lastly,
one will obviously be pleased if the enclave
purchases from local traders and producers as much
as possible of the supplies it needs and pays for
them, as it does for the wages, in foreign
currency.

The situation becomes more involved if the
enclave overlaps with the national economy to a
greater extent, i.e. when it ceases to be a real
enclave, particularly (a) if it sells part of its
production on the domestic market at prices higher
than world prices by taking advantage of protective
tariffs; (b) if it raises funds locally and
appropriates the difference between the interest
rate and the profits;[31] or (c) if it exploits
natural resources, mineral or other, inside the
enclave and exhausts them, paying only an abnormally
low ground rent, which is itself determined by the
fact that the country is underdeveloped and
insufficiently urbanized.

All the above is a matter of calculation--a
calculation which makes sense only if, as
W. M. Corden suggests, we neglect the relations of
the enclave with the outside world and confine

ourselves to those with the country containing it.
From this point of view, the much-debated question
of the repatriation of profits assumes quite another
meaning. Under conditions of underemployment which
are the common lot of capitalist countries both of
the center and of the periphery, capital, no matter
where it is invested, produces "value added,"
i.e. the gross total of wages, rents, profits, and
taxes. The profits and some of the rents can be
repatriated; the remainder accrues to the local
economy. Except in specific cases such as those
mentioned above, it is obvious that the center
suffers a loss of income as compared with the
situation where the same capital is invested within
its own frontiers, but it is difficult to see what
the receiving country loses as compared with a
situation where this capital had not come at all.[32]

Complaints about the repatriation of profits
are merely a reminder that the total value added is
more than the value added minus the profit. This
is not only trite; it is contradictory. For one
cannot regard the MNC as the supreme evil, while at
the same time hoping it will grow and multiply by
investing its profits locally. Moreover, there is
absolutely no difference either in practice or in
theory between repatriation of profits by a
foreigner and the expatriation of capital by a
citizen, and we have already shown that such
expatriation is indeed prejudicial to the country
of origin. The fact that, in this case, it is not
the center but the periphery which is exporting
makes no difference. It is not as an importer but
as an exporter of capital that the peripheral
country suffers when the profits of foreign capital
are repatriated.

Capital, whether multinational or national, is
governed by opportunities for its investment. Since
there is a sharp difference between wages in
industrialized and developing countries, these
opportunities are no longer a decreasing but an
increasing function of development. The same
capital reinvests its profits in Canada *ad infinitum*
and becomes Canadian; it withdraws them as quickly
as possible from Zaire and becomes an enclave there.
This has a cumulative effect on the development gap
to the very extent that the MNC does not thwart this
process; despite its alleged possibilities of
"delocalizing" production in relation to markets,
it is less specific than is claimed.

Accommodation Invoicing

As has already been noted, criticism of the
MNC often deals with possible abuses. This, from
the pen of Marxists, is heartrending. Marx always
emphasized that exploitation is not cheating but
the inevitable effect of the mechanics of the
system. This is what separates revolution from
reform. Fraud can always be eliminated by reform,
but the system can only be changed by revolution.
However, it may be supposed that there would not
have been such an outburst regarding "fictitious
prices" if the spirit of the former had not in fact
today overcome the spirit of the latter.

In concrete terms the problem is rather more
complex than is thought. There are two chief
reasons which may induce an MNC to under- or
overinvoice the goods dispatched from one establishment to another: taking advantage of differences
in taxation or evading exchange controls.

The second reason may, in fact, be prejudicial
to the developing countries since that is where
exchange controls are most widespread. But the
first generally acts in their favor, since their
levels of taxation are much lower than those of
the industrialized countries. There is a tendency,
therefore, for the one to cancel out the other.
Possible abuses are not necessarily actual abuses.

The MNC an Instrument of Domination

Another feature which is criticized is that the
MNC constitutes a one-way conveyor belt for political behests. Since the legal framework of the
corporation's hierarchy is based on the laws of
property, certain legal prohibitions may be
conveyed from the parent company to the subsidiary,
but not vice versa. Thus, the laws of the United
States may require the headquarters of General
Motors to forbid its subsidiary in Brazil to export
certain equipment to China, whereas Brazilian law
cannot require the local subsidiary to forbid the
parent company in the United States to do anything.

First, we are here concerned with the direct
intervention of a noneconomic factor, and the main
loser is the MNC itself. It also presupposes that
the MNC is centralized and loyal to its country of
origin to an extent that is not proven. On the
other hand, there is a multitude of concrete
examples to the contrary, the most spectacular of
which was the refusal of Exxon-Philippines to

refuel the United States Fleet at Subic Bay in 1973
out of respect for the Arab embargo.[33]

But quite apart from that, a prohibition of
this sort can only affect the receiving country if
there are no national undertakings capable of
fulfilling the contract which the MNC has been
forbidden to undertake. There is no reason to
believe that such undertakings would exist if the
MNC were not there. On the contrary, there is no
doubt that if General Motors Brazil did not exist,
the American government would not have on its
hands the additional problem of stopping the
Brazilian loophole in its embargo.

Lastly, so far as the balance of power between
the MNC and the local government is concerned, it
is simply not true that the former is in a
stronger position than a national undertaking
would be. It seems obvious to me, for example,
that, whatever the foreign interferences, Allende
would still be alive and in power if he had been
content to nationalize Anaconda and had not
touched national capital. In the same way I am
quite certain that Saudi Arabia would not have
been able to nationalize Aramco so easily if its
capital had been Arab.[34]

CONCLUSIONS

The majority of critics who take an interest
in Third World problems do not represent the MNC
as a factor contributing to increased tension--
with which, probably, nobody would quarrel--but as
a primary, structural force, a factor determining
the "freezing" of the periphery on the one hand
and contributing to a corresponding increase in the
development of the dominant countries on the other.
This is unacceptable.

The attitude of writers who base their opinions on revolutionary Marxism is particularly
interesting. Having first isolated the MNC as the
characteristic evil of the century, they study
it concretely as an excrescence of the system.
Nevertheless, they continue to see salvation outside the system in planned local development. This
contradiction between the analysis and the conclusions makes it possible to agree with the latter
while at the same time disagreeing with the former.

For it is either one or the other. Either the
economic calculations of the MNC are essentially
the same and conducted in the same way as those of

158

any other capitalist undertaking, in which case in
order to explain the deadlock in certain countries,
it is enough to show how the capitalist optimum
differs from the social optimum, even though the
very existence of the MNC has a certain amplifying
effect; or the MNCs calculations are basically
(and not just circumstantially) in contradiction
with those of the independent firm, in which case
the conclusion cannot be avoided that a simple
anti-MNC policy and a return to a free market
economy would liberate centrifugal forces.

[*Translated from French*]

NOTES

1. "The Impact of Multinational Corporations
on Development," United Nations, 1974, E/5500/
Rev. 1 ST/ESA/6.
2. "Multinational Corporations in World
Development," United Nations, 1973, ST/ECA/190.
3. This is the viewpoint sometimes expressed
by *Business Week*. It is also more or less that of
Harvard. Lastly, it is also roughly the one
expressed by some members of the Group of Eminent
Persons who insisted on submitting remarks and
expressing reservations individually on the 1975
report.
4. Particularly those of the industrialized
countries. Those of the others are content to
maneuver in such a way as to profit from the guilt
complexes of the multinationals to increase their
bargaining power, without ever calling into
question the principle of foreign investments. On
the contrary, they make a virtue of attracting as
much as possible by means of increasingly
generous "investment codes."
5. Certain features of this imaginary
situation are already appearing today in some of
the oil-exporting countries, where disproportionately high "external" revenues exist side by side
with a very low domestic level of employment.
Nineteeth-century Great Britain, moreover, bore
the distinctive signs of the process outlined
above. At the beginning of the nineteenth century
the balance of trade was positive and revealed a
net export of capital. Subsequently, there was a
radical change in the situation. There were net
imports of capital, particularly from 1870 onwards,
which went on increasing till 1914, with a negative

balance of trade and, as a corollary, a trend towards a parasitical economy, the stagnation of domestic industry, and an increase in the number of unemployed or people in unproductive employment. As recently as 1934, domestic servants accounted for 11.8 percent of the working population.

In the United States, since the Second World War, the cycle has, to be sure, been less pronounced, since not only is the volume of operations concerned, in spite of all the talk about it, much smaller in relative terms than that of Great Britain in former times but also, as a result of public international aid of all sorts combined with a partial accumulation of dollars in the reserves of the other countries, investment operations are diluted within a greater volume of other financial movements. However, a reversal of the trend was already perceptible in 1971, when the formerly regular balance of trade surplus ceased to exist, while on the other hand the balance of payments, which had formerly shown a clear deficit, began to move towards a surplus.

6. Cf. P. Herzog and G. Kebabdjian, *Économie et Politique*, April-May 1974: "The export of capital is today still not the constitution of a national capital but the external effect of over-accumulation on national bases."

The theory of oversaturation is more or less shared by Rowthorn, Hymer, Baran, Sweezy, etc. Albert Michalet asks why, if that is so, the corporations move the productive process instead of merely exporting the produce, and the SIFI Group asks why capital moves from one central country to another when both are equally afflicted by overaccumulation.

7. Cf. G. Adam, "New Trends in International Business," *Acta Oeconomica*, Vol. 7, 1971, and "The Big International Firm and the Socialist Countries," International Colloquy, CNRS. Typical in this connection was the naive disappointment of participants in the 1974 Europe-Third World Seminar in the Netherlands at the following statement of the Rumanian position: "Romania is not prepared to boycott the MNCs or reduce her relations with them because: (a) such relations are already at a minimum; (b) the MNCs are a reality of the capitalist system; (c) such relations are founded on principles of reciprocity and mutual advantage; (d) Romania is still a developing country."

Lastly, Richard Barnet points out that

"China...has already begun to allow foreign corporations to use its huge labor pool to manufacture exports," *Global Reach*, p. 67, New York, 1974.

8. In the most conservative universities throughout the world, a doctoral thesis criticizing the MNCs does not raise any objection on principle. A revolutionary student can thus remain "pure" without endangering his chances of getting a degree. The result is that recently the proportion of social science students who choose this subject has become frightening.

9. Resulting in negligible quantities at both dates so far as the periphery is concerned. But no matter how small the share of the periphery at all times, it is obvious that, in domestic relative terms, the share was much greater in 1914 than today. For, apart from a few exceptional cases such as India and Japan, there was not a shop, a chimney, or a mile of railroad in the nowadays developing countries which, in 1914, was not owned by foreign capital. We are a long way from that situation today, if only as a result of the various nationalizations which have occurred.

10. Cf. *Survey of Current Business*, October 1975.

11. Cf. *Survey of Current Business*, September-October 1975. I differ from current doctrine in considering that the difference, from every point of view, between Argentina and even Mexico and Chile on the one hand and India and Central Africa on the other, is infinitely greater than between the former group of countries and those of the OECD generally. I even consider that difference in the extent to which foreign capital has penetrated is not unrelated to differences in the level of development between the two groups. But the figures given here show that, even in the case of Latin America, the favorite target of multinational capital, the penetration is much less than is generally thought.

12. It should be emphasized that this is the value of the accumulated assets and not of the annual flow.

13. Cf. Table 14 in *Multinational Corporations in World Development*, New York, N.Y., United Nations, 1973.

14. *Complete Works*, Vol. 22, p. 263, Paris, Éditions Sociales, 1960.

15. K. Marx, *Avant-Propos au Manuscrit de 1859*, Pléiade, Vol. I, p. 273 (literal translation).

16. This is something which was lost sight of
by those who find the "investment codes" too
generous and consider it advisable to give the
governments of developing countries practical advice
on how to avoid overbidding and come to an agreement
on dictating their conditions. They forget that
capital has not only a choice between one developing
country and another but also the choice between
expatriating itself and staying put.

They also forget the first "investment code"
ever was the "Law on Concessions" adopted by the
USSR in 1922 and promulgated by Lenin himself; this
not only granted to foreign capital a maximum of
the usual advantages (fiscal privileges, repatriation of principal and dividends, etc.) but also
granted something which the developing countries of
today are particularly unwilling to accept--
international arbitration in the case of disputes
between the investor and the Soviet government.

However, in adopting Resolution No. 2626 on
24 October 1970, the United Nations General
Assembly was farsighted enough to recommend the
developing countries to adopt "the appropriate
measures to attract, encourage and use effectively
foreign private capital...and propose conditions
which would encourage continued investments."

17. According to Schumpeter, who is not very
far from the results of calculations by Bairoch
and others.

18. However, in an ad hoc report of the United
Nations experts dated 1951, the situation was
described with remarkable simplicity. The
developing countries lacked capital and technicians.
To provide both, they needed an enormous amount of
time, which was not available. The only solution,
therefore, was to import them.

19. Cf. "Imperialism and Capitalist Industrialization," *New Left Review* (London), No. 81,
September-October 1973. Also A. Emmanuel, "Myths
of Development versus Myths of Underdevelopment,"
op. cit., No. 85, May-June 1974.

20. This does not mean that development of
the productive forces is an end in itself. The end
is man. Granting, however, that the development of
the productive forces is neither the same thing as,
nor the sufficient condition of, social and human
progress, it nevertheless remains its necessary
condition. Moreover, indirectly and whatever the
time lags, development as such does generate social
progress, if only because it makes the existing
system ripe for overthrow and replacement by a new

162

one. It is, therefore, unscientific to try to
assess development in terms of its direct social
effects and deny the existence of the former merely
on account of the momentary absence or even negative
features of the latter. One cannot dissociate
development from its social content, we are told.
Very well! Are we then to say that the United
States is undeveloped, if it so happens that its
social structure appears to us as unsatisfactory?
And what about those who suggest that Cuban society
is more human, or less inhuman than that of the
United States? Are they supposed to claim that
Cuba is also more developed than the United States?
Yet, it seems to me that in the everyday intercourse
nobody, whatever his social philosophy, has ever had
a communication problem, when people at large say
that the United States is more developed than
Cuba. Is that not the proof that the dissociation
between "development of the productive forces"
and their "appropriation by the people" is already
being made implicitly, even by those who oppose
it explicitly?

21. Cf. C. Bettelheim, *Le Problème de l'Emploi*,
p. 106, Paris, 1952 (literal translation).

22. Hu Chi-Hsi, *Mao-Tse-Tung et la
Construction du Socialisme*, p. 85, Paris, Le Seuil,
1975.

23. "There cannot be," says Boumediène, "one
industry for the under-developed and another
industry for the developed."

24. In the United States, for example, the
Federal Government finances between a half and
two-thirds of R & D directly.

25. Though much more subtly and avoiding
carefully any normative statements,
Albert Michalet also refers to this "homogenization." Cf. "Transfert des Technologies," *Tiers
Monde*, January-March 1976.

26. But this is only direct expenditure. If
indirect expenditure, particularly the entire
educational and cultural infrastructure, libraries,
universities, and so on which the private producer
of technology enjoys, were included, the cost to
society would amount to more than double the sum
acknowledged by the statistics.

27. This is what Rosenstein-Rodan calls the
difference between the private and social
marginal products, which constitute a decisive
barrier to the installation of new industries in a
developing region.

28. Except, they say, in the case of plastic
Christmas trees manufactured in non-Christian
Japan.
29. Michalet considers that this is the real
syndrome of the internationalization of the
capital cycle, and here he is right. No matter what
the quantitative extent of the phenomenon, it is
an unusual novelty, since it is the work process
itself which is affected by it. On the other hand,
the circulation stage, internationalized according
to Christian Palloix, has in fact to do with
trade, and international trade has always existed.
It existed even before national trade.

As for the internationalization of money-
capital, either this is a phrase devoid of meaning
or it means merely the convertibility of currency.
But what the MNCs may be doing in this field
today, with difficulty, laboriously and skating
on the thin ice of the law and exchange control
regulations, was done a century ago quite openly
and without formalities by the man in the street
simply by going to his money changer or banker.
So if it is considered that overcoming obstacles
is a more internationalist situation than one in
which there are no obstacles, this is a problem
of terminology which is quite beyond me.
30.   It would certainly make no sense to
have boats bringing metropolitan workers into the
"enclave" and carrying back on their return trip
the *"Gastarbeiter"* of the host country. One should
certainly be able to persuade the MNC's subsidiary
that everybody would be better off if this
absurd coming and going ceased and everybody worked
where he lived.
31.   There is little chance of this happening
in the least developed countries, such as those
of Africa south of the Sahara, or if it did the
funds would not be for investment but would be
squandered on luxuries or find their way to
Switzerland, if the MNC did not make use of them.
32.   Cf. Robert Gilpin, *United States Power
and the Multinational Corporation*, London, 1975.
33.   For the conflicts between the American
MNCs and the State Department, see an interesting
article in *Politique Aujourd'hui* by
Joseph D. Collins, January-February 1975.
T. Dos Santos notes astutely that "...the very
interests of national economies...determine an
objective determination which places pressure
on subsidiary undertakings which are obliged to

conform if they do not want to be marginalized."
"Les Sociétés Multinationales, une Mise au Point
Marxiste," "L'Homme et la Société," July-
September 1974.

34. Ambassador William Eberle, in his
statement to the National Executive Conference in
Washington on 7 February 1974, recalled that there
had never been a case where an MNC had won a
conflict against a sovereign government of any
sort or size. (True enough, but we should add:
after the failure of Mossadegh in 1952 and since
the fiasco of the Suez gunboat operation in 1956.)

PART 2
IMPACT ON KNOWLEDGE SYSTEMS

Editorial Note

The four chapters in this section indicate
the several ways in which the operations of TNEs
affect knowledge systems. Keith Smith in the
sixth chapter examines the role of book publishing
TNEs in the diffusion of intellectual knowledge
to developing nations. According to him, there is
little doubt that book publishing TNEs facilitate
the flow of intellectual knowledge to these
countries by establishing their subsidiaries or
through direct exports. This diffusion, he points
out, is not necessarily unidirectional. These
firms also solicit manuscripts from local authors
and market them internationally. However, only
those authors who write in international languages
or can get their works translated in them, can
profit from the presence of book publishing TNEs.
Thus from a broader point of view, both the readers
and authors in developing countries benefit from
them. Smith, however, notes some undesirable
consequences of their operations. He points out,
for example, that their very presence can have some
disincentive effects on local publishers who are
unable to compete with them. Moreover, as most
book publishing TNEs are based in metropoles, they
have a "metropolitan orientation." Smith therefore
concludes that while book publishing TNEs are
instrumental in diffusing intellectual knowledge,
their activities, in the context of contemporary
economic and political relationships among nations,
can reinforce the "intellectual dependence" of
developing nations.

Fernando Reyes Matta in the next chapter
focuses on the effects of the transnational news
agencies on the dissemination of information in
Latin America. He presents the findings of his
study about the news coverage of international

events in sixteen newspapers from fourteen Latin American countries. His findings confirm the general impression that despite the technological and scientific advances, Latin American countries continue to be dependent on transnational news agencies for international news. For example, about 60 percent of the news about international events comes from UPI and AP, the two giant TNEs based in the United States. This undue reliance on news agencies, according to Reyes Matta, contributes to imbalances in the coverage of news from different geographical regions. The events and personalities relating to North America, Western Europe, and their allies receive better coverage than those from developing nations. Reyes Matta finds that there is not even an adequate coverage of events about Latin America in the regions' own newspapers. He therefore suggests that the widespread dependence on transnational news agencies in developing nations serves the existing "dominant interests" in the international arena.

Ali A. Mazrui's chapter deals with the impact of TNEs on educational and cultural processes in African nations. His analysis indicates that historically TNEs and educational systems have established a symbiotic relationship; the two have profoundly affected and reinforced each other. TNEs contributed to the secularization of education, freeing it from the influence of missionaries. Moreover, they helped to stress its "practical component." Both of these efforts, according to Mazrui, have been functional in the growth of the modern educational system, which has in turn facilitated the functioning of the TNEs by creating what he calls "culturally relevant manpower" and "culturally relevant markets for Western goods." He also points out that TNEs also affect educational processes and output by the diffusion of technical know-how relating to the overall organization of the modern productive processes that have been critical for the commercialization and industrialization of the African continent. And it is this aspect, Mazrui suggests, that has distorted "certain directions of both cultural and educational change" in Africa.

Dmitri Germidis in the ninth chapter discusses the role of transnational enterprises in vocational training. He distinguishes two kinds of vocational activities: the first concerning training of employees within TNEs, and the second concerning impartation of certain skills to the suppliers and customers, and research and development (R & D). He mentions that TNEs in developing nations undertake a wide variety of training programs for their employees and even depute them to other educational institutions for this purpose. They often send their middle level technical and management personnel to their headquarters and sister firms for necessary training. However, Germidis believes that the educational value of these programs is limited to the host country because the skills created remain confined to TNEs themselves. The training which TNEs provide to their local suppliers, subcontractors, and buyers of capital goods can have some multiplier effects. The skills created can be utilized in various other fields. Germidis also points out that with the exception of those industries where environmental or market conditions necessitate R & D in host developing nations, TNEs prefer to have R & D close to their head-quarters. Therefore they do not contribute to the building of what he calls "national innovation capacity." Thus Germidis suggests that the overall educational value of the various kinds of vocational training programs undertaken by TNEs is indeed limited.

6
The Impact of Transnational Book Publishing on Knowledge in Less-Developed Countries

Keith B. Smith

Books are frequently a central feature of intellectual activity and intellectual communications. They are vehicles for transferring knowledge internationally and within countries. Along with other media they capture and carry the knowledge, culture, information, and entertainment of societies. Although books are one of the oldest media products, book publishing is the least-researched communications industry. It has never received the attention given to the newer media such as broadcasting and newspapers. In most countries publishing remains shrouded in a fascinating blend of trade folklore and mystique, breached only by publishers' memoirs and company histories. Yet it is known that books are influential. They have provided resources for religions, inspiration for revolutions; they have taught, destroyed, guided, humored, and in hundreds of ways influenced peoples' lives.

Writers, publishers, educationalists, librarians, and book distributors determine what books people can read. Publishers also appear to decide the fate of authors and their manuscripts, when they select from the vast number of manuscripts they receive. What real control do publishers have over manuscripts and what guides their choice? In particular what results from publishing being transnational rather than local or national? In what way are the intellectual activities and structures of societies affected by publishers acting as agents of knowledge?

No particular category of book has exclusive influence on the development of intellectual knowledge. The division of books into intellectual and cultural categories is itself a cultural

distinction dependent on how functionally a society
views art and culture. Nevertheless this paper
focuses primarily on non-fiction publishing rather
than fiction publishing and within non-fiction on
the areas of publishing variously termed scholarly,
academic, tertiary, educational, and reference. To
widen the focus would be to overgeneralize. These
categories cover the books most likely to be found
in use by university and college personnel, in
schools and non-formal and informal education, in
reference libraries and being read by individuals
wanting to learn and inform themselves. I will
generalize so widely over the continents of Africa,
Asia, and Latin America that the exceptions may
sometimes prove as instructive as the generaliza-
tions. Part of the fascination of looking at the
international aspects of publishing is that it is
largely this very trade in books that distributes
theories on the transnational system. Yet this
book trade may be a part of that very system.

TRANSNATIONAL BOOK PUBLISHING

The recent United Nations definition of transnational corporations covers publishing enterprises
that vary in the degree of their transnationalism.
In the slightest form a transnational publisher can
merely sell books to export markets. Most of the
companies now referred to as transnationals started
their foreign operations in this way but are now
distinguished from national enterprises by owning
or controlling branch offices or subsidiaries
outside their home country. In some areas of the
developing world, particularly South America, the
transnationals operate through agents rather than
by opening their own offices.
Educational systems followed the British and
French imperial expansion throughout the world.
Colonial schools taught the same curriculum as that
used in schools in the imperial country. Standard
British and French textbooks were imported to
accompany the imported syllabuses.
At the turn of this century British firms began
the growth to transnationalism when companies such
as Longman, Macmillan, and Oxford University Press
opened offices in India. Shortly afterwards the
French publishing company Hachette began expanding
into countries in the French sphere of influence,
starting with Turkey and Egypt. Publishers based
in the United States of America did not start

exporting beyond North America until the 1940s.
They are now major exporters of college and
scientific books to some developing countries.

Following Christian mission publishing and the
colonial education systems, the growth of transnational publishing has resulted in a large net
inflow of books from the United Kingdom, France, and
the United States to less-developed countries
(LDCs). In most LDCs with market or mixed economies, the transnational publishers dominate the
areas of book publishing which have the greatest
impact on intellectual knowledge, except where
governments have reserved primary-school and sometimes secondary-school publishing for state
publishers.

METROPOLITAN ORIENTATION

Initially the transnationals confined themselves to exporting their metropolitan titles to
the developed countries, where they were read by
the expatriate colonialists and used in the schools
set up to educate a local middle class. In some
Asian countries, following the lead of the
missionaries, these publishers started issuing
books in local languages and at least one publisher
was reporting this a profitable line by 1909. By
1925 the colonial governments of some areas felt it
necessary to encourage the writing and publication
of schoolbooks that were more suited to local
conditions; slowly this change occurred, with the
first titles for anglophone Africa appearing in
the 1930s.

Because of the acknowledged role played by
books in the cause of peace and international
understanding and the prominence given to education
in national planning, books have remained largely
free from tariff barriers. This allows the transnational subsidiaries in LDCs to concentrate on
distributing their parent company's titles. This
is particularly true of United States tertiary and
scholarly publishers. Where subsidiaries also
engage in import-replacement publishing it is
largely because the national school system, through
its syllabuses, demands localized books. These
books have only marginal sales outside that
particular country. Such local lists have grown
during the 1970s, so that in some cases they
account for up to 80 percent of the transnational
publisher's turnover from that geographical region.

The peripheral offices of the transnationals have
a third function, that of referring manuscripts to
the editors in their head office, who decide
whether they will constitute books with an international or continental market. It is these three
functions that locate transnational publishers in
the wider international pattern.

The world book pattern contains a set of
imbalances and a pervading metropolitan orientation.
In 1950 the LDCs of the world contained 37 percent
of the world's literate adults and 42 percent of
the school population for whom they produced 24
percent of the world's books. By around 1970 their
share of book production had dropped to 19 percent
while their share of the school population had
increased from 42 percent to 63 percent and of
literate adults from 37 percent to 50 percent.[1]

Less-developed countries import most of their
academic books. This is not surprising since the
major exporters, Europe and the United States, have
been the major generators of scientific knowledge
and intellectual literature over the last few
centuries. Most LDCs are signatories of one or
both of the international copyright conventions
and therefore import from the West the books containing this new knowledge. That transnational
publishers (TNPs) and metropolitan authors benefit
from this trade is evident from the distress copyright piracy causes them and from the vigor with
which they reinforce the conventions in spite of
the demands for relaxation coming from groups of
LDCs.

The predominance of metropolitan books combined with other transnational forces has led to
the polarization of intellectuals in LDCs into a
larger metropolitan-oriented transnational class
and a smaller fervently nationalist protest class.
Book publishing is just one agent in the creation
of this transnational intelligentsia. Other agents
are overseas study schemes sited in metropolitan
centers, the "brain-drain," and the growth of
metropolitan-oriented colleges. Wealth plays a
direct role too, for the central countries can
positively select which research programs to fund
and thereby influence the resultant publications.
This wealth also funds agencies exporting culture,
such as the United States Information Services, the
British Council, and various French and USSR
government agencies. Intelligence agencies will
sometimes subvert academic institutes and publishers
in the cause of furthering metropolitan interests.

Transnational book publishing, international
languages, and transnational intelligentsias are
closely linked together. Imperial expansion
imposed the English and French languages on large
areas of the world and brought in its wake transnational publishing. International languages of
metropolitan origin are still commonly used for
intellectual writing and reading in Asia and Africa.
The situation is somewhat different in South America
where, rather than relying entirely on Spanish,
academic intellectuals give much attention to books
written in English, French, German, and Russian.
They find that Spanish-language publishing does not
link them sufficiently to the metropolitan-linking
international languages. Of all the international-
language publishing industries, Spanish-language
publishing is the least metropolitan centered.
Spanish publishers have to compete with Argentinian
and Mexican publishers.

Publishers in other European countries have
become aware of the advantages of publishing in
international languages. The Scandinavian countries, the Netherlands, Federal Republic of Germany,
and some East European countries have publishers who
are expanding their English-language publishing,
and may thus begin to challenge the traditional
book exporters to LDCs. The activities of the
transnational publishers, as I will show later,
tend to entrench the metropolitan-focused international languages in LDCs.

Within LDCs where international language books
predominate, they reinforce the intellectual
division between the formally educated who have
access to them and the poorer literates who are
confined to the more parochial books in their own
local language. There are, of course, many historical precedents of an imported language providing
a barrier between elites and others in societies.[2]

National book policies in some LDCs have
modified this divisive metropolitan transnationalism. In Cuba the extensive literacy campaign,
the rejection of international copyright, and the
creation of a state publishing monopoly under the
Instituto del Libro have ensured that books do not
become instruments of transnational dependency.
The United Republic of Tanzania's less centralized
program of using the Swahili language and insisting
on local content, local orientation, and local
manufacture but using some of the resources of
transnational publishers in their schoolbook
publishing, is a milder policy. On the other hand,

Indonesia's policy of switching to Bahasa Indonesia
as the medium of learning, without either insti-
tuting sufficient state book publishing or
encouraging commercial book activity, has led to
acute shortages, instead of a break with dependency.

THE IMPACT ON READERS

Transnational publishing has transferred much
knowledge from the advanced centers of the world
to the peripheries and has helped build up the
intellectual resources of many LDCs. This trade and
the development of a transnational intelligentsia
has led to the transfering of metropolitan
influences on to the local production and consumption of intellectual knowledge. The next two
sections will explain those transfers that take
place within transnational publishing and through
it on to reading publics. A later section will
investigate how these transfers affect national
publishing in LDCs.

The TNPs that dominate schoolbook publishing
in so many of LDCs transfer aspects of metropolitan
education to the LDC. One aspect of LDC education
that is affected is pedagogic methodology. In
this case the transfer often occurs through the
adoption of a course of books that has been
developed in the metropolitan center. This
procedure has been a feature of schoolbook
publishing ever since British schoolbooks were
superficially adapted for African schools; a
process captured in the adage "potatoes to yams."
The TNPs vary in the extent of their adapting
activities in relation to their United Kingdom
publishing. The most common background for
adaptation is large involvement by parent
companies in a new development in secondary school
math or science in the United Kingdom, such as
new math or the Nuffield pupil-centered discovery-
method science of the 1960s. These teaching trends
have been transferred to African education through
professional educational channels with the help
of aid and publishers' adaptations. Whether this
modernizing influence on African education is
developmental is a moot point. From the publishing
viewpoint it depends mainly on the degree of
adaptation. Changes made to a math series to
incorporate the local environment of the pupils
are insufficient if they ignore such features as
cultural variations in perception and cultural

attitudes to and relative familiarity with abstraction, ordering, and measuring.

The degree of adaptation in major courses depends largely on the size of the potential market and on the adapting team, who are now usually an official or ministry-approved group. For example the School Mathematics Project originally published by Cambridge University Press for United Kingdom schools was partially adapted for Botswana, Lesotho, and Swaziland but more extensively rewritten for the larger East African market. Three new features of this adaptation trade are appearing. Two of these indicate that the trade, though benefiting the metropolitan publishers, is not entirely confined to an intra-transnational circuit. First, many of the requests for adaptations are official and, second, some of the originating publishers such as Blackie/Chambers and John Murray, though British, are not trans-national and a few of the adapting publishers are quasi-indigenous firms such as the East African Publishing House.

The third new feature is a small flow of adapted geography and ecology material to metropoles and between Third World markets.

The transfer of new pedagogic methodologies is rarely initiated by transnational schoolbook publishers. More often they provide support for the transfer which is taking place as a result of direct international contact between educationalists or as a result of professional writing.

Another aspect of educational transfers from metropole to periphery results from the colonial transposition of metropolitan educational systems already mentioned. The books that followed this transposition were a major instrument of trans-ferring metropolitan culture. For decades African and Asian pupils were learning Western history, geography, constitution, and temperate science. This package of knowledge has formed much of the formal intellectual base of the transnational intelligentsia found in most LDCs. As exam boards have been localized and national cultural regener-ation brought into the school curricula, metro-politan schoolbooks have become less acceptable and TNPs have had to respond to local demand or the guidelines laid down by Ministries of Education. Ministries of Education in countries with small school enrollments of not have the same influence over TNPs and on occasion may decide that curricula reform is impossible unless the new textbooks are published by state houses.

At tertiary level LDCs have little power to influence transnational publishing, except when they have large tertiary educational sectors as in India. Except for basic textbooks the LDC market is usually too small to exert much influence on the publishing program of TNPs.

The basic ideology of transnational publishers like that of all capitalist enterprises is focused on making a profit. Among the projects launched by the commercial companies there are, of course, some series and titles which are not planned to return a profit but to embellish the company's image. More interestingly though, there is an occupational ideology prevalent among groups of metropolitan editors which diminishes the profit orientation; this ideology is particularly influential in British and United States university publishers: with the partial exception of school textbooks, conditions of high market uncertainty and a high rate of new product initiation generally prevail in the publishing industry. This makes it difficult to judge a manuscript's sales appeal and easier to justify other selection criteria such as intellectual importance or literary worth. The nature and operation of these criteria will be determined by such factors as the structure and tradition of the company, the self-image and reference group of the editor, and whether the editor takes a largely prescriptive or largely interpretative view of the editorial function.3

The different TNPs' head offices distribute various degrees of editorial power to the subsidiaries. Editorial ideologies, operating through these structural variations within TNPs, determine the nature of TNP influence on intellectual knowledge. The larger TNPs appoint a local editorial manager who is granted a considerable degree of autonomy to publish schoolbooks and titles in local languages but has to refer back to head office nonfiction and literary manuscripts written in international languages. In these situations the local editor's apparent power is far greater than his or her real influence, for schoolbooks are more closely tied to visible market forces than any other category of book. Textbooks in LDCs are usually addressed directly to the syllabus, and the large commercial schoolbook TNPs are the least disposed to waver from the pursuit of profit.

There are, though, types of manuscripts that

are less tightly bound to the local market forces
and allow the selecting editor a greater chance to
exercise creative judgment. Adult nonfiction,
academic, and literary books in international
languages are such. But most of the decision-making
power in these cases lies with editors who are
metropolitan-based and are therefore most aware of
the tastes and interests of readerships in the
metropolitan countries.[4] Some power may lie with
subsidiary offices, but where it does, it is
usually only the authority to report back whether
the local readers and institutes are likely to buy
the book. This amounts mainly to interpreting the
taste of a local but metropolitanized transnational
intelligentsia. Thus, even when the transnationals
are publishing manuscripts by authors from LDCs,
the selection process and therefore the publishers'
lists tend to reinforce LDC intellectual dependence
on the metropolitan countries.

This dependency would not be so extreme if
there were a larger and wider reading public in
LDCs; it is not an aim of metropolitan publishers
to extend their market through long-term support
of literacy schemes or of an extended rural library
service. The main occupational ideology outside
profit seeking is a search for high-quality
manuscripts rather than for breadth of readership.
The extension function is usually adopted by the
state, using libraries and sometimes literature
bureaus which publish commercially unattractive
manuscripts. In spite of such state action it is
probable that the dominant book distribution pattern
leads to an even more marked version of the communications effect gap among book readers than among
users of the mass media. That is, as the book
industry increases, segments of the population with
higher socio-economic status tend to acquire
information at a faster rate than the lower status
segments, so that the gap in knowledge tends to
increase rather than decrease.

So in spite of TNPs pluralist ideology the
major influences determining the distribution of
intellectual knowledge outside schoolbooks are
metropolitan editorial decisions and the
metropolitan-dominated international market.

It is interesting to note in passing that
politically critical and sensitive manuscripts on
specific LDCs sometimes find a metropolitan
publisher when no local or truly transnational
publisher could issue them.

THE IMPACT ON AUTHORS

The activities of book publishers affect not only intellectual consumption but also intellectual production. This impact is located in the relationship between writers and publishing.

In spite of recent agglomeration in metropolitan book publishing the industry's ideology is essentially pluralistic. Even when they have become part of a conglomerate companies often retain a large degree of independence. The TNPs have carried this attitude into LDCs, where the extension of state publishing monopoly is greatly feared. This fear sometimes becomes one factor in motivating transnationals to assist the development of a local commercial publishing industry as a force against state publishing. The pluralism allows authors a wider choice of opportunity channels than in countries with more centralized industries. But the range of titles published is not merely a product of pluralist attitudes, it is also determined by publishers' interpretation of the market and by the pervading editorial ideology.

As we have seen, when a writer submits a manuscript to a transnational, it is judged against an international market unless it is a schoolbook, basic textbook, or written in a local language. Because TNPs have access to many markets around the world they can often accept a manuscript and publish it as a commercial venture, when a nationally limited publisher would not have been able to do so. This can be of great benefit, particularly in the more internationally transferable disciplines such as science and technology where, for instance, a book on some aspect of tropical forestry might become viable by reaching a tropical market rather than a merely national market. This international reach is most important to very small countries. It has also been of increasing importance in the academic market where the global expansion in scholarship has led to greater specialization and smaller markets for the resultant highly specialized publications. This same advantage to the extension of knowledge could be gained if LDC publishers reached a worldwide market, but they do not. Very often they do not even reach their own continental market, though there are some new and promising ventures which may extend their markets.

It is in the more closely culture-bound fields of social science, literary, general, and children's books that transnational publishing distorts

intellectual production. Many writers, particularly
those based in universities, write from two
motives--to communicate and to gain status and/or
money. When metropolitan editors receive the
manuscripts of these writers they will usually pass
them to an external reader for an opinion on their
merit. Unfortunately no research has examined the
interaction between editors and these advisers but
it is probable that the decision on whether to
publish is made in the light of metropolitan
opinion, international taste, and the standing of
the author in the transnational elite. It is
therefore a metropolitan-based or metropolitan-
oriented authority that is acting through the TNPs
as the main gatekeeper to intellectual knowledge
in the LDCs. It is within this framework that the
legitimacy of work can be conferred or withheld,
for it is only very rarely that unpublished ideas
gain authority. For the university writer in some
academic systems, publishers also hold the key to
personal promotion. The need to satisfy these
authorities must influence LDC writers in their
work. Many will be writing with an eye on what
they think is wanted by the metropolitan-oriented
transnational nexus. In some regions with particularly small readerships for certain types of books,
such as academic books in the West Indies, authors
must almost inevitably concentrate on the international readership.[5]
     In some LDCs writers have the alternative of
submitting manuscripts to local commercial
publishers or local non-commercial publishers.
Except in India, there is very little academic
commercial publishing. Although the number of
subsidized university presses is growing in both
Asia and West Africa, the number of titles they
publish is still small. It usually carries less
prestige for authors to be published by these
local publishers than by transnationals. A few
esteemed African literary authors are reacting to
the TNP dominance by consciously placing some of
their manuscripts with local publishers.[6] This is
part of the small antithetical protest movement I
referred to earlier.
     So, on the one hand TNPs' access to the
international market confers commercial viability
on a variety of titles. On the other hand TNP
metropolitan orientation operates along with LDC
transnationalism as a powerful control on the
legitimizing of LDC intellectual writing.
     Some forms of book-aid have a disincentive

effect on local writing, in particular those schemes
by which TNPs attract subsidies for their titles.
This lowers the retail price and enables buyers to
purchase a book which, without the subsidy, they
might not be able to do. At the same time the
subsidy allows the TNPs' title to undercut
equivalent local books and, by the same token,
render some unpublishable. This acts as a disincentive to local authors. That is not to say that
book-aid schemes are, on balance, harmful, but
they do require more thorough evaluation than they
have received.[7]

NATIONAL AND LOCAL PUBLISHERS
IN LESS-DEVELOPED COUNTRIES

Transnational publishers also have an
indirect impact on intellectual knowledge by means
of their impact on national publishing in LDCs.
To examine this we must first distinguish between
the importantly different types of national
publishing.
The patterns of local and national publishing
in less-developed countries are products of a
wide variety of factors which include: the extent
of literacy and education; the governments'
political policies on state educational publishing;
the development of library services and purchasing
power; the availability of inputs and infrastructure, from manuscripts through printing to
bookshops; access to capital and know-how;
government policy towards capitalist, foreign, and
state publishing; and the power and influence of
transnational publishers compared to that of
national and local publishing. Out of these factors
come two basic types of book publishing organizations operating in LDCs, the commercial and
noncommercial. The noncommercial are usually
either state organizations publishing schoolbooks,
or academic publishing operations subsidized by
universities or institutes. The state publishers
are nearly always given a monopoly on primary
textbooks. These state houses usually come some-
where between being a reflection of national
political ideology, such as the Instituto del Libro
in Cuba, and an interventionist organ set up to
conserve foreign reserves, produce cheaper books,
and ensure that schoolbooks are in accordance with
government thinking, such as the Educational
Publications Bureau in Singapore. The resultant
monopoly consists of the government's curriculum

development department and the state publishing house controlling the intellectual content of schoolbooks. In the case of the subsidized non-commercial publishers it is usually the academic staff of a university or institute that make the publishing decisions.

Commercial profit-oriented local publishers tend to originate in three types of situations. Some are entrepreneurs, possibly starting as self-publishers such as the Onitsha publishers of Nigeria. Others have developed publishing as an offshoot from a bookshop; several Indian importers developed in this way. Yet others are the outcome of political or cultural movements or are intellectuals keen to publish certain types of books. Very little LDC publishing has followed the pattern, common in metropolitan countries, of editors leaving established publishing houses to set up their own small companies.

All these types of commercial publishers at some time or other encounter the dominance that TNPs exercise over the most profitable areas of the market open to commercial publishers. Advantages allow the TNPs to retain this position, thereby largely confining the local publishers to marginal areas of a fairly marginal industry. Resentment of this dominance has also shown itself in Canada and Australia during the 1970s.[8] Australian publishers have suffered as a result of the British Traditional Market Agreement which has been attacked by the United States Justice Department in a cartel-busting action. This agreement prevented the signatory British publishers from trading in rights with United States publishers unless the British publisher is offered the title in the whole "traditional market," which consists of almost all the old British Empire. This mechanism has allowed British publishers to retain control on their markets and limit United States incursion. British publishers argue that if their market fragments, their print-runs will fall and book prices will increase. While this may happen, it would not come about if publishers in all countries had access to the international market and thereby could print in the longer runs and achieve the wider distribution which are still largely the preserve of TNPs.

Two extensive exceptions to the confinement of LDC publishers are the fields of popular and light local fiction, books of social and personal advice, and cram books for school students. The

major TNPs have concentrated on their areas of
metropolitan expertise which have not included
light fiction. Light fiction is therefore open
to local publishers and to the importers who bring
in books and magazines from other metropolitan
publishers. The editorial ideology of transnational
publishers and their urban marketing orientation
have accounted for their espousal of respectable
and educational schoolbooks and their avoidance of
cram books designed merely to help students through
exams. LDC publishers find it difficult to compete
in the schoolbook field. A few have been able to
use cram books to give themselves a secure base
from which to extend into more serious intellectual
publishing.

As a result of this historical imbalance, an
unplanned schism has grown up in most of those LDCs
which do not have a large academic market. This
leads readers to expect the more intellectual work
in the commercial field to appear from the TNPs and
tends to lower the credibility of the few intellectual works produced by local commercial publishers.[9] In many LDCs where it is found, the
imbalance is at least partly redressed by the
publishing activity of local subsidized publishers,
such as university presses. Recently a trend has
appeared for transnational publishers to start
issuing both cram books and light fiction but it
is not yet clear whether this will reduce the
schism or threaten local publishers' staple markets.
One of the historical benefits enjoyed by metropolitan TNPs is that their metropolitan head
offices are at the center of African and Asian
transport and communications systems. The local
LDC publishers are at the peripheries and the
interperipheral sending of books and of information
about books is constrained by this radial
pattern.[10] These restraints on LDC publishers tend
to route inter-LDC intellectual communications
through the metropolitan centers, rather than
allowing them to flow directly from country to
country. The pattern is less marked in East Asia
where books flow between countries like Hong Kong,
Singapore, and Malaysia. It is also less marked
in South and Central America where books published
in Argentina and Mexico are sold elsewhere on the
continent.

Among the more intellectual African and Latin
American publishers there is a tendency to try to
match metropolitan styles and standards in book
design and production. Sometimes it is in the

quality of the paper or the binding, other times it
may be the illustrations. The distinction between
functional design features such as legibility and
durability and opulent design such as high-quality
paper and full-color covers has been eroded. Some
local publishers feel forced into this position
by the taste transfer that has occurred in the
market as a result of book-buyers' acculturation
to metropolitan styles of book design.[11] These
publishers quote occasions on which the staff of
ministries of education have rejected their books
as unsuitable because, although cheaper, they did
not look as attractive as books published by TNPs.
On other occasions it seems more a psychological
dependence on the part of the LDC publishers, who
wish to achieve the standards of metropolitan
publishers without much regard for appropriateness.
This always increases the price of books and therefore restricts the distribution of their contents.

THE THREE MAJOR IMPACTS OF TRANSNATIONAL PUBLISHING

The most evident feature which emerges from
the above is the international range that transnational publishers give to intellectual knowledge,
the spreading of learning, knowledge, ideas,
creative work, etc., to those literate in international languages and occasionally to readers
using local languages. This has an international
distributive effect and acts as a force for
international intellectual appreciation and understanding. This transfer is not totally one way;
TNPs take on the manuscripts of LDC authors and
market them internationally. From this point of
view the internationalism of transnational
publishing benefits readers and writers alike.
I have also pointed to a less-recognized
feature of transnational publishing which results
not from its internationalism so much as from its
metropolitan base. Almost all TNPs are based in
the metropolitan countries or if not then in the
dominant country of the area. This leads to a
metropolitan orientation, which combines with other
forces to reinforce intellectual dependency in
LDCs. This syndrome is the outcome of patterns of
knowledge generation and colonial history and is
now reinforced by elements of world capitalism and
intellectual, linguistic, and academic transnationalism.
This debilitating impact is encouraged by a

somewhat symbiotic relationship between the elites of LDCs and the transnational corporations, tending to retain the benefits of transnational publishing for the elites. Unfortunately some instruments of the beneficial internationalism entrench the one-way flow in books and therefore also retard the growth of intellectual independence. There are forces acting against this dependency, even within the transnational publishing system of metropolitan transnationalism. Probably the most interesting and unusual among these weaker counterforces is that the intermittent TNP distributes the LDC publisher's books in the metropolitan country. Outside the transnational system there are other counteracting forces ranging from writers tiring of the TNP domination, to publishing houses such as Quimantú in Chile, which are set up in full awareness of the weakening effects of dependency on the metropoles.

The third area of TNP impact is through LDC publishing. I have shown how LDC publishing is stymied by the power and global reach of the TNPs and how TNPs determine the market space open to LDC publishers, except when the state intervenes and declares a state monopoly. A large-scale study would be required to measure the impact of TNPs on LDC publishing and in particular to uncover the power and potential of small, independent publishers. Books and pamphlets have appeared from such sources and had enormous impact in the literary and intellectual fields and even on national history.

On the whole, therefore, while the internationalism of transnational publishing is an intellectual benefit, its metropolitan domination reinforces dependency.[12]

NOTES

1. *Unesco Statistical Year Book 1973*. Paris, Unesco, 1974. And Barker, Robert, and Escarpit, Robert (eds.), *The Book Hunger*. Paris and London, Unesco and Harrap, 1973, also a French edition published by Unesco.

2. The urban elitism of publishing is highlighted in Thapar, Romesh, *Book Development in National Communications and Planning*, Karachi, Unesco Regional Center for Book Development in Asia, 1975.

3. Recent work on editors has not yet been
published in full, but for the USA see
Coser, Lewis A., "Publishers as gatekeepers of
ideas" and for the UK, Lane, Michael, "Shapers
of culture: The editor in book publishing," both
in Altbach, Philip G., and McVey, Sheila (eds.),
Perspectives on Publishing, Part I.
Massachusetts, Lexington Books, 1976, xii + 283 pp.
4. During a survey of the head offices of
six large British TNPs in October 1974 there was
some indication that in one case the relevant
editors were more closely linked to overseas staff
than to the rest of their head-office staff. It
has not been possible to follow up these inconclusive indications.
5. "From Imitation to Innovation: the
Production and Distribution of Books in the
Caribbean: Report on the Seminar on Regional
Problems of Book Production and Distribution at
the University of the West Indies 1973," available
from The Library, University of the West Indies,
St. Augustine, Trinidad, p. 12. See also
Omotoso, Kole, "The Missing Apex: A Search for
the Audience," in Oluwasanmi, E., McLean, E., and
Zell, H. (eds.), *Publishing in Africa in the
Seventies*, pp. 251-261, Ile-Ife, University of
Ife Press, 1975.
6. Achebe, Chinua, "Publishing in Africa:
A Writer's View." In: Oluwasanmi et al.,
pp. 41-46. Also, interview with Kole Omotoso,
African book publishing record. Vol. II, No. 1,
January 1976, pp. 12-14.
7. Altbach, Philip G., *Publishing in India:
An Analysis*. Delhi, Oxford University Press,
1975, p. 67.
8. For Canada, see books detailing the Royal
Commission, *Canadian Publishers and Canadian
Publishing* and *Background Papers*. Toronto,
Queens Printer for Canada, 1973. For Australia,
see Ferguson, G. A., "The publisher and national
development." In: *The Book under Challenge*,
pp. 21-40, Canberra, Australian Government
Printing Service for the Australian National
Commission for Unesco, 1973. UNCTAD has recently
criticized the British Traditional Market Agreement.
9. McQuail, Denis, *Towards a Sociology of
Mass Communications*. London, Collier-Macmillan,
1969, p. 47.
10. Similar patterns in mass communications
are found. See Elliot, Philip, and Golding, Peter,

"Mass communication and social change: The
Imagery of Development and the Development of
Imagery." In: de Kadt, Emmanuel, and
Williams, Gavin, *Sociology and Development*,
pp. 229-254, London, Tavistock Publications, 1974.

11. Nottingham, John, "Establishing an African
Publishing Industry: A Study in Decolonisation."
African Affairs (London) No. 63, April 1969,
pp. 139-144. And *From Imitation to Innovations...*,
pp. 94-115. Compare Langdon, Steven, "Multinational Corporations, Taste Transfer and Underdevelopment: A Case Study of Kenya." *Review of
African Political Economy* (UK) No. 2, 1975,
pp. 12-35.

12. *Bibliographies:* The best bibliographies
in English to the author's knowledge are in
Philip G. Altbach, *Publishing in India: An
Analysis*, Delhi, Oxford University Press, 1975,
115 pp., which concentrates on Asia; and one by
Hans Zell which is confined to Africa, in *African
Book Publishing Record* (Oxford), Vol. II, No. 2,
April 1976. New writings are noted in the trade
press or in *Book Promotion News* issued by the
Division of Book Promotion and Development, Unesco,
or the *Tokyo Book Development Center News Letter*.

7
The Information Bedazzlement of Latin America

Fernando Reyes Matta

In spite of technological advances and research carried out in the theory of communication,
Latin America continues to be dependent in the
field of international information services.
Transnational press agencies--particularly UPI and
AP--set the trends of knowledge for public opinion
in the region. In addition, there continue to be
signs of *information inertia* in the presentation of
events. By this we mean that certain regions,
countries, and personalities assume the dominant
role in generating an information framework for
reports on international relations that determines
which information on foreign affairs shall be made
available to the public everywhere.
These conclusions emerge from the analysis of
a sample of sixteen Latin American newspapers from
fourteen countries published during a four-day
period in November 1975.* The research results are
still substantially the same as those obtained in
studies carried out in the 1960s. If some progress
has been made in the handling of international
information, it has been the result of using a
greater variety of sources and of the use of
articles from such internationally influential
newspapers as the *New York Times* or the *Washington
Post*. These are reproduced in either news of
editorial pages. In addition, some newspapers have
significantly increased the use of their own
correspondents.

*The author is indebted to the sociologists
Alicia Espinosa and Perla de la Parra for the
statistical calculations.

Two main approaches to the problem of international information may be said to characterize this study. The first is a quantitative and percentile analysis of activity by transnational press agencies and international media in Latin America, together with some assessments of the importance in the region of news from the Third World and from industrialized countries. The second is an evaluation of the information, analyzing its characteristics and drawing attention to the way in which some of the news is over-emphasized while other news is played down or simply not reported at all.

The criteria utilized in this analysis are based on a commitment to the positions of the Third World as developed over the last few years. That is why the conclusions of this paper could not remain exclusively quantitative. The paper also attempts to present a political interpretation of the context in which Latin American newspapers select and present the news. The actual consequences for Latin America of the practical application of the principle of "free flow of information," for example, has meant that, whereas the region is significantly ignorant of its own realities, it is flooded by information which either is irrelevant or has little bearing on its future. Similarly there is much ignorance about what is happening in other Third World regions, particularly about events, recorded in the industrialized world, that are of special importance to the struggle for self-reliant development in Third World countries.

THE CHARACTER OF THE PERIOD CHOSEN

The period studied was from 24 to 27 November 1975. Two events in Europe were the most note-worthy news during the week: the funeral of Franco and the accession to the throne and first acts of King Juan Carlos, including the amnesty decree that provoked opposition both inside and outside Spain; and the left-wing military revolt in Portugal which was crushed between Wednesday and Thursday of the week.

Both events can distort the overall analysis since the information, mainly that from Madrid, has an exaggerated importance when compared with the usual international news value of events in Spain. This has been taken into consideration in Table 7.2, in order to obtain percentages that in content and balance are nearer a normal news week.

In Latin America, the week is noteworthy for the birth of a new republic on the continent, Surinam. In addition, during this week there was the US decision not to apply to Venezuela and Ecuador the tariff preferences for Third World products. Among other external events were the international coffee agreement, reached in London, which affected Brazil, Colombia, Costa Rica, and other Latin American countries, and the announcement in Washington of some relaxation in the restrictions on trade with Cuba. In the region a number of events occurred which are reflected in the media in a cursory or minor way. Among them we find the ministerial contacts between Peru and Bolivia, and between Venezuela and Argentina, as well as the strong attitude taken in Panama by the Torrijo government to the negotiations with the USA about the future of the Panama canal.

News of the Third World was mostly about the Angola situation, the conflict over the Western Sahara, the crisis in Lebanon, and the Middle East conflict. But apart from these events, which were reported, events of direct interest to the Third World were recorded in New York, Geneva, and other capitals, that, though reported, received a *low-profile treatment* hardly matching their importance for the development of Latin American and Third World countries--which will be reverted to later.

SELECTING THE NEWSPAPERS

The basis of the study was a representative selection of South and Central American newspapers, along the lines of previous studies, and in the light of the personal experience of the author of the evolution of the Latin American press in its treatment of international news. This meant the inclusion of newspapers that retain a traditional attitude to the treatment of international information, as in the straight reproduction of news cables largely derived from the transnational agencies that have most influence in the region. In addition, newspapers are represented that have developed a more flexible treatment of international news by using a variety of sources, cables from different information agencies, material from various internationally influential newspapers or, more important, by printing the dispatches of their

own correspondents. This is the case with newspapers like the *Excelsior* in Mexico, the Brazilian
O Estado (São Paulo), and to some extent *El
Nacional* in Caracas and *Clarín* in Buenos Aires.
   To complement these, there are two newspapers
whose ideological posture could be expected to
reveal a different approach to the treatment of
international news, in their sources for it and in
the likelihood of a more careful processing of the
press material that comes into their offices.
These are Lima's *La Prensa*, whose ownership had
recently been transferred from the private to the
public sector, and *La Crítica* of Panama.
   Thus the final list of newspapers for the
study was as follows: *La Prensa* and *Clarín*,
Buenos Aires (Argentina); *El Diario*, La Paz
(Bolivia); *O Estado*, São Paulo (Brazil); *La Nación*,
San José (Costa Rica); *El Nacional*, Santo Domingo
(Dominican Republic); *El Comercio*, Quito (Ecuador);
El Imparcial, Guatemala City (Guatemala); *El Tiempo*,
Tegucigalpa (Honduras); *Excelsior* and *El Heraldo*,
Mexico City (Mexico); *La Prensa*, Managua
(Nicaragua); *La Crítica*, Panama City (Panama);
La Prensa, Lima (Peru); *El Día*, Montevideo
(Uruguay); *El Nacional*, Caracas (Venezuela).

SOURCES OF INTERNATIONAL NEWS

   The study shows that the international
information available to Latin American newspapers
today offers more possibilities of choice than was
the case in the 1960s. Nevertheless, the
predominance of certain news agencies, particularly
of North American origin, is still very clear.
   Out of 1,308 news items, we found that 506
came from UPI, 39 percent of the international news
in the study. In second place came AP, with 270
news items, some 21 percent of the total news
quantified. Thus the two agencies supplied 60 percent of all the world news published in the sixteen
Latin American journals during the period studied
(see Table 1).
   The figures show some progress since the
CIESPAL study was made in the 1960s, which revealed
a dependence on these agencies of nearly 80 percent.
However, there is no significant shift in the
preponderance of foreign criteria, as may be seen
from the way in which the UPI and AP operations
analyze, rate, and quantify the news. Next in
order comes Agence France-Presse (AFP) with 132

TABLE 7.1
Sources of News Items Studied

Agency, newspaper, etc.	Number of items	Percentage
UPI	506	39
AP	270	21
AFP	132	10
Reuter-Latin	123	9
EFE (Spain)	111	8
ANSA (Italy)	55	4
LATIN[a]	49	4
New York Times	31	2
Le Monde	12	1
Washington Post	7	0.5
Prensa Latina (Cuba)	4	0.3
Others	8	0.5
Total	1,308	

[a]An agency of large Latin American newspapers.

news items, 10 percent of the total. Reuter-Latin
follows with 123 news items (9 percent). Irrespective of the events in Spain during the period under
study it is worth noting that, compared with
previous studies, the Spanish agency EFE has gained
some weight in the total information studied. It
contributes 8 percent of the total recorded news
items, more than ANSA's 4 percent and the 4 percent
of LATIN.

Other agencies of more independent character
and showing a better understanding of Third World
problems are the Cuban agency Prensa Latina and
Inter-Press Service of Rome. They have very
little significant impact upon total international
news in spite of the fact that they have made big
efforts, for more than a decade, to enter the
Latin American market for information.

A new element on the Latin American international news scene, compared with earlier studies,
is the reproduction of material from newspapers
that are internationally influential. The *New York
Times* in particular has an important role among
those newspapers that are qualified as "big" in
Latin America. Although it is true that, of the
news studied, the *New York Times* contributed only
31 news items (2 percent), these were concerned
with important events and were given some
prominence in newspapers like *Excelsior* (Mexico),

La Prensa (Managua), *O Estado* (São Paulo), and
El Nacional (Caracas). For example, the Madrid
news concerning the coronation of Juan Carlos
and the circumstances of General Pinochet's visit
from Chile, with the lack of sympathy that the
Spanish monarchy showed for it, were published by
the *New York Times* and prominently reproduced in
O Estado (São Paulo) and *La Prensa* (Managua). In
the latter newspaper the news appeared on the first
page, supported by a wire-photo and a banner
headline.

The number of agency and other news items
published on 24 November 1975 on the front page of
the newspapers studied was as follows:

UPI	20
AP	14
Reuter-Latin	4
AFP	3
EFE	1
ANSA	1
New York Times	1

Among the variety of sources for international
information, *Le Monde* (Paris) should be noted, with
1 percent of the total news reproduced, and also
the *Washington Post*.

It is true, in spite of earlier qualifications,
that there has been some progress in the search for
greater *diversity* in world news sources. Dailies
like *O Estado* (São Paulo), print a note like the
following one on their front page: "The international news service of *O Estado* is produced
with cables from AFP, ANSA, AP, DPA, LATIN,
Reuter, and UPI." These agency sources are
complemented by material from newspapers and
magazines of international influence. Mexico City's
Excelsior also acknowledged seven sources in a
rather better balance of news agencies and newspapers for its news, from Madrid, of Wednesday,
26 November: "Information from the *New York Times*,
Le Monde, *Washington Post*, AFP, AP, ANSA, and
Reuter-Latin."

The analysis reveals the existence of certain
journalistic methods that provide a more rounded
and better balanced picture of the news, drawing
on the different perspectives of the various news
agencies at work in the region. This seems to be
the normal approach of newspapers like the
Excelsior and *El Heraldo* from Mexico, *Clarín*
from Buenos Aires, and occasionally Lima's

La Prensa and the Caracas daily, *El Nacional*.
There are two styles in this approach: (a) the
world news is rewritten by the newspaper in its own
perspective, drawing on the accounts of earlier
events, quotations, and figures provided by a
variety of news agencies; (b) the dispatches and
news bulletins are accumulated in sequence and
published without being reworked.

The difference in these two techniques can be
appreciated by comparing, for example, the editing
of international affairs by *Clarín* and *O Estado*.
In the latter all the material is clearly rewritten
using a wide range of techniques, giving it a
particular editorial and ideological tone; in
Clarín we find a tendency to accumulate the
dispatches, using in most cases two or three international agencies as sources.

In contrast to this picture of new techniques
and innovations for a broader view of international
events, we find *old shortcomings of dependence* still
persisting in the rest of the press. This is
almost the general rule throughout Latin America.
Newspapers that come into this category are of two
types: (a) those that simply reproduce news
bulletins from the agencies, selecting from the
output of two or more teletype machines; and
(b) those that reproduce cables sent by a single
agency, thus depending absolutely on that agency's
viewpoint on current international situations.

Examples of the first type are newspapers like
El Comercio (Quito), *El Día* (Montevideo), *La Nación*
(San José), *El Diario* (La Paz), *La Prensa* (Lima),
and, to a large extent, *El Nacional* (Caracas).
Newspapers of the second, even more dependent
type include the long-standing and influential
conservative newspaper *La Prensa* of Buenos Aires,
whose sole source of foreign news is UPI. (*La
Prensa* was the first link in the chain of penetration of UPI in Latin America, when the latter
managed to break the monopoly cartel of European
agencies in the 1920s, getting its first contract
in Buenos Aires.) Guatemala's *El Imparcial* and
El Tiempo of Honduras are also exclusively dependent on UPI. This sort of information dependence
is quite common in the news outlets of small towns
and cities in Latin America. There are hundreds
of examples of local newspapers that are the prime
source of news in their area. They paint a one-
sided picture of world affairs and they have a
powerful influence on the local community, which
they shape into an ideologically conformist mold.

It should also be noted that, even after changes
in ownership structure, information dependence
lingers on. *La Prensa*, the Lima daily, illustrates
this. Despite recent changes in control, as
mentioned above, and working within the ideological
framework developed in Peru, it is strongly
dependent on UPI, choosing UPI cables for its
main reports and selecting themes that reflect
the character that the transnational news agencies
give to reality.

Chile's experience during the Unidad Popular
period provided further confirmation of this. In
spite of the atmosphere of change prevailing in
the country and the efforts to break with economic
dependence, the old methods were continued. It is
surprising, and disappointing, that newspapers
which gave militant support to the movement led by
President Allende, like *Puro Chile*, *Clarín*, and
Ultima Hora, continued to draw most of their world
news material from the transnational agencies, UPI
in particular, without any processing or real
perspective. Both the choice of important news
themes and the focus on the facts have followed the
market-inspired criteria laid down by the agencies
that for decades have dominated information in the
region.

The journalists and cable editors, in spite
of their personal ideological commitment to the
process under way in the country, were unable to
escape from the behavioral enertia generated by
the information model imposed by the agencies.

THE GEOGRAPHICAL BEDAZZLEMENT

Years of news supply from the dominant
agencies have created a pattern in which certain
place names turn up in the news again and again.
What happens in these places determines the
importance and choice of news.

In the period studied, examples are provided
by New York's financial crisis, a big fire in
Los Angeles, and the transport strike in Tokyo,
which receive considerable attention in the Latin
American press. Such is the inertia created by
the dominant information system that New York
events--the launching of a balloon in a demonstration organized by municipal employees, for
example--are prominently featured. This draws the
Latin American reader and journalist away from
local news, about his own affairs, as well as away

from the major trends underlying international events.

The news classified in the study (items running to 10 or more column-centimeters) made reference to eighty-four different geographical locations. Eighty-three percent of the total news flow concerned twenty-one of these places (see Table 7.2).

TABLE 7.2
Places Receiving Most Attention in the News Studied
(Including and Excluding Madrid)

Name	Amount of news (in column-cm	Percentage of News		Number of news items printed	Average length of item (in column-cm
		Including Madrid	Excluding Madrid		
Madrid	4,182	18	...	103	40.6
Lisbon	2,538	11	14	54	47.0
Washington	2,462	11	13	89	27.6
New York	1,043	4.5	6	32	32.5
Beirut	1,028	4.5	5.5	34	30.2
London	879	4	5	33	26.6
Buenos Aires	816	3.5	4	29	28.0
Moscow	656	3	3.5	25	26.2
Paramaribo	629	3	3	23	27.3
Rome	505	2	3	19	26.5
Santiago, Chile	500	2	3	21	23.8
UN, Geneva	474	2	2.5	22	21.5
Detroit	472	2	2.5	16	29.5
Jerusalem-Tel Aviv	459	2	2.5	16	28.6
Bogota	431	2	2	20	21.5
Paris	429	2	2	16	26.8
Lima	369	1.5	2	14	26.3
La Paz	366	1.5	2	8	45.7
California	276	1	1.5	14	19.7
Hong Kong	185	1	1	8	23.1
Dallas	174	1	1	6	29.0
SUBTOTAL	18,873	82.5	79		
Others	3,958	17.5	21		
TOTAL	22,831	100	100		

Madrid plays an important part in this week, as mentioned earlier, because of the funeral of Franco and the coronation of Juan Carlos. Table 7.2 also includes the percentages of news obtained by omitting Madrid, in order to obtain a geographically "normal" distribution. The first twenty places account for 79 percent of the total news, in this adjustment.

The figures confirm the pattern of dependence revealed by other studies during the past decade. The importance of Madrid and Lisbon is understandable in view of the news originating there, which was typically good sales material in the information market. But the week in the USA was not any more or less newsworthy than any other. Nevertheless, out of the total news from eighty-four different places, over 20 percent was from the USA, chiefly from Washington, New York, Detroit, California, and Dallas.

The significance of Detroit resulted from the speech there in which the US Secretary of State admonished Cuba and the USSR for their participation in the Angola conflict. Dallas was present because of one saleable news item: it was twelve years since the assassination there of President Kennedy. This was accompanied by long news dispatches assessing the investigation, continuing the debate about the circumstances of the assassination and its authors, following up an affair that continues to be attractive news material for the Latin American press which, because of the influence of the dominant culture/information system continues to be fascinated by the Kennedys.

These main US news centers are representative of others habitually reported, making up an information whole in which events in the USA take priority, thus distorting what should be a balanced view of world affairs. Such distortion is not only present in the material coming over the teletype, but also in the total volume that the news media supply to their public, with the effect that the persistent journalistic bombardment has had on the behavior of those in charge of selecting and handling the international news in Latin American newspapers.

The situation is further exemplified by the fact that the 779 items under study, which add up to 22,831 column-centimeters, are geographically distributed as shown in Table 7.3

TABLE 7.3. Areas Receiving Most Attention in
the News Studied

Region reported	Column-centimeters of news	Percentage of total
Western Europe	9,264	40.5
USA	4,634	20.2
Latin America	4,479	19.6
Middle East	1,579	6.9
Asia	837	3.6
Africa	806	3.5
Eastern Europe	701	3.0
UNECLA	531	2.3

We need to recall that the news of Western Europe
is overweighted by the events of Madrid and
Lisbon. The table brings out clearly the weight
of news originating in the USA, the total flow of
which is even greater than that originating in
Latin America. The poor news standing of Eastern
Europe, Africa, and Asia is equally eloquent.
Asia is low down because Vietnam is "no longer
news."

SURINAM, A GLARING EXAMPLE

During the period under study, there was one
episode which dramatically exposed the distorted
character of internal information and the lack of
political awareness on the part of those in charge
of selecting what should be published in the
continent's newspapers: the birth of the Surinam
Republic on 25 November 1975.

How is it that the declaration of independence
of a country as large as Uruguay or Ecuador and the
world's third largest producer of bauxite, a
neighbor of Brazil and near neighbor of Venezuela,
received so little attention in the Latin American
press?

Why did none of the newspapers surveyed
consider it important enough to send a special
correspondent to cover the news and why did they
all limit themselves to the news-agency bulletins,
mostly UPI, once again?

Underlying such behavior is an information
model that needs to be totally changed. The Surinam
case exposes the continent's inability to look at
itself, and its failure at self-interpretation.

The easy option was taken, to reproduce a version
of the news whose political character was
obviously different from that which motivates the
Third World countries.

On 24 November, some newspapers published
cables giving background information on the new
country. Most bore the stamp of UPI, as shown in
Table 7.4. In the other newspapers studied, there
was *no information whatsoever* on the new country
about to be born in Latin America. Could this be
explained by the fact that according to the
dominant information practice there is little
interest in providing "advance news"? Let us see
what the picture was on the day after the event.
On Wednesday, 26 November, among the newspapers
studied, the picture, as far as Surinam was
concerned, was as follows:

Clarín (Argentina): The Surinam news was given
    relatively moderate importance; the same
    coverage as the news of cooling relations
    between Pinochet and Costa Rica.

La Prensa (Argentina): Two columns of UPI news,
    inside page.

El Diario (Bolivia): AP news, reduced to 6 cm
    although on the front page (at the bottom).
    Given the same importance as a disaster in
    Tijuana, Mexico, in which twenty houses were
    destroyed by fire.

TABLE 7.4.   Sources and Extent of Published News
               About Surinam

Newspaper	Agency used	Column-cm	Number of columns	page
La Prensa (Argentina)	UPI	56	3	2
El Imparcial (Guatemala)	UPI	38	2	1
La Prensa (Nicaragua)	Reuter-Latin	27	5	3
La Nacion (Costa Rica)	UPI	27	1	25
La Prensa (Peru)	UPI	24	4	15
El Dia (Uruguay)	UPI	20	1	2
La Critica (Panama)	UPI	15	3	2

O Estado (Brazil):   Rewritten news but with
   evident preponderance of Reuter and UPI; three
   columns on an inside page of minor importance.
   An item reprinted from the *New York Times*
   gives much more importance to programs in the
   USSR for developing its eastern territories.
   Similarly, news of a New York jewel robbery
   is given greater importance, as well as the
   Western Sahara situation.   Yet Brazil is one
   of the immediate neighbors of Surinam.
La Nacion (Costa Rica):   AP news on an inside
   page, over three columns.
El Comercio (Ecuador):   UPI news, front page,
   45 cm.
El Tiempo (Honduras):   News from UPI over five
   columns, but on page 16, an unimportant page
   in the newspaper.
El Heraldo (Mexico):   AP news cable over 2 columns
   (15 cm).   Obviously a low-tone item.   News
   about the murder of the Oregon chief of police
   is given more importance.   On another page, a
   wire-photo from The Hague, showing
   Queen Juliana signing the decree of independence.   The same photograph appeared in some of
   the other newspapers.
Excelsior (Mexico):   Publishes an AP wire-photo
   on page 1.   Inside is a good news summary,
   based on Reuter, AFP and AP.   The only
   newspaper to report the Third World content
   of Premier Henk Arron's speech.
La Prensa (Peru):   UPI and AFP news on inside
   pages.
El Día (Uruguay):   Two columns of UPI material with
   a picture, but of relatively less importance
   than e.g. a warning cable for Israel to Syria.
El Nacional (Venezuela):   The cable sent by
   President Carlos Andrés Pérez appears as home
   information on the first page.   Page 2 carries
   an average piece, with AP news and a UPI
   wire-photo.
El Nacional (Dominican Republic), *El Imparcial*
   (Guatemala), *La Prensa* (Nicaragua), and
   La Critica (Panama):   No news.
In these circumstances, we must ask ourselves how
long will it take for Latin American public
opinion to realize the importance and implications
of the existence of another sovereign country on
the continent.   Worse still, maybe those who have
been informed will understand the event in the
light of the views transmitted by the agencies.

200

On the one hand, in the search for conflict
as news, the European agencies, especially AFP,
stressed a "racial tension that clouds the future
of the new country." On the other hand, however,
an agreement between the government and opposition
regarding a political and electoral program
apparently did not have the same "news value" as
the theme of racial conflict on the doorstep. This
confirms the persistence of colonial stereotypes in
the treatment of the news.
For UPI, the racial question was a matter of
"some disquiet," but it put the accent on the
country's main natural resource: bauxite. The
stress was, of course, put on the interaction of
North American interests with the Latin American
reality. The result was the following text:

> Surinam's economy relies mainly on the exporta-
> tion of seven million tons of bauxite a
> year, which represents one-tenth of world
> supplies and provides the government with an
> estimated yearly income of US $30 million in
> taxes paid by Alcoa Aluminum Company and
> other producers. Arron's government has
> adopted a liberal attitude toward foreign
> investments in Surinam, mainly North American,
> which total some US $300 million. Nevertheless
> Arron has insisted that all new enterprises
> must obtain participation agreements.*

Again the classical stereotypes are reiterated.
The activities of the North American company--not
the work of the people of Surinam--constitute the
basis of the economy because they "provide the
government" with a large income. The government's
attitude towards foreign investments is described
as "liberal."
This use of language is now so common that it
is not rejected by the reader. It is taken as
normal. But UPI, in its main bulletin, which is
the most important, did not record the new premier's
statement that the new state would adopt a Third
World policy with more direct consequences for
Latin America and the Caribbean. Similarly, the
following declaration was not recorded:

---

*It should be noted that all quotations from news
agencies have been retranslated from Spanish.

We shall not let the riches of our land serve
to confer greater benefits on others and
leave us poor. Our natural resources and our
human energy, the capital we dispose of, will
be used exclusively for the economic growth
of the whole of the nation.

Paramaribo's place in the international geographical
list with 629 column-centimeters of news (3 percent
of the total--see Table 7.2) should be seen in this
light and also in terms of the content and form of
its news, not merely the figures. Furthermore,
since then Paramaribo has not appeared much in the
international news.
   This example serves to underline two elements
in the present analysis: (a) the preponderance of
the interpretation given by the transnational news
agencies, particularly from North America, to
current events; (b) a receptive and unreflecting
attitude by the media, in general, towards the
flow of news that the teletype pours out as international truth.

IGNORANCE OF THE THIRD WORLD

   In the circumstances, it is easy to understand
why little or nothing is known about the various
events, occurring during the four days, that were
the expression of the dominant themes and preoccupations of the Third World.
   Thus, for example, during the four days, the
following news was released from UN headquarters in
Europe:

   Geneva (AFP).--The majority of pharmaceutical
   products on sale in the world are useless or
   they imitate one another, according to a
   report published here by the United Nations
   Conference on Trade and Development (UNCTAD).
   The report, drawn up at the request of the
   UNCTAD Secretary-General, was made by
   Doctor Sanjaya Lall of the Oxford University
   Institute of Economics and Statistics.

This cable goes on to reveal that, although medical
needs in India can be met by 116 medicines, as
many as 15,000 are on sale there. It went on to
report that in Brazil, a basic list of 116 products

was made, of which only 52 were considered
essential, whereas 14,000 were on sale.
    The information is important. Besides AFP,
Prensa Latina and AP take up the data from the
document. AP presents the facts this way:

> Geneva (AP).--Developing countries should
> combine their resources in order to set up
> a pharmaceutical trade of their own that can
> adjust to the health needs--and purchasing
> power--of the Third World, proposes a report
> published by the United Nations Conference
> on Trade and Development.

Using the same basic document, the Cuban agency
Prensa Latina transmits this:

> Geneva (PL).--Transnational manufacturers of
> pharmaceutical products inundate capitalist
> markets with 25,000 medical products of which
> only one percent is really useful.

In different ways, the three news dispatches bring
out the essential elements characterizing the market
approach to health of the transnational laboratories. This is a subject of growing disquiet in
the Third World; scientific and technical dependence
is here coupled with a cultural dependence through
which consumption is stimulated by a strong
advertising system.
    What happened to this news in Latin American
newspapers?
    Except in Mexico, the statement went practi-
cally unnoticed. In Quito (Ecuador), *El Comercio*
printed it over two columns which reproduce part
of the AFP cable. In Lima, *La Prensa* gave it only
a modest 14-cm column, printing the Prensa Latina
cable in part.
    In this case, the news agencies covered the
story. The act of rejection came from the media,
from those in charge of selecting international
news. Possibly the story touched internal interests
very strongly and they preferred to ignore it.
This may explain why *O Estado* (São Paulo) did not
report it, although this journal does use the AFP
and AP services and the story referred directly to
Brazil. In the other cases, the explanation can
be commonplace: development themes are not "news"
and, therefore, they are not interesting. Because
of this stereotype, however, stories that are
directly linked to the situation of domination and

dependence of center and periphery are rejected
for lack of "color."

There were other cases of this type during
the week in question.

The agency EFE transmitted on 23 November
a cable, also from Geneva, about the negotiations
between oil-producing and Third World countries.
La Prensa (Nicaragua) published it on Monday the
24th. The text was as follows:

> Geneva (EFE).--The representatives of 48
> Third World nations are carrying out fruitful
> negotiations with oil-producing countries at
> the United Nations palace in Geneva. First,
> they have laid down the fundamental terms of
> cooperation with Third World countries which
> do not have oil resources, by which they will
> make interest-free loans for the acquisition
> of crude oil, to insure them from lack of
> supplies. In addition, developing countries
> will be helped to intensify their explorations
> in search of oil, and also in the refinery
> and fuel transportation sectors.

None of the other fifteen newspapers refers to this
event. Possibly no other agency transmitted it--
which is doubtful. Even if this were so, there are
six newspapers in the study which make considerable
use of EFE for their international pages. Once
more, we have to blame traditional news criteria
for this lack of information. With such criteria,
the agency and media wiremen do not hesitate to
give greater importance to the New York opening of
an exhibition of eighty photographs by
Caroline Kennedy than to the oil agreement.

The same news treatment is given to the meeting
of the Group of 77 at the United Nations, organized
as part of the preparations for UNCTAD IV. Among
other things, it is at this meeting of the Group of
77 that the idea is put forward, by Mexico, of
creating a Third World Economic System.

This is news of which Latin America remains
ignorant.

The news about the International Coffee
Agreement, signed in London during the week, finds
some echo in the newspapers of the coffee-producing
countries.

The news does not reach countries like Peru,
Bolivia, or Argentina, however, although the
agreement is in harmony with the efforts made by
other groups of raw-material-exporting countries

to define a common stand in the international
market. Because this dimension to the story is not
understood, the news is not published; such is
the effect of engrained attitudes.

The same thing happens upon the announcement
and signature of the general system of tariff
preferences made by the US President on 24 November.
This excludes Ecuador and Venezuela, countries
which, naturally, obtain a version of the fact
through a news decision of the agencies, chiefly AP
and UPI in New York. However, except for *Excelsior*,
not a single newspaper in the study has its own
correspondent's account of the matter.

IGNORANCE OF LATIN AMERICA

Examples of news dependence, like those
illustrated above, are innumerable. Latin American
countries, although territorial neighbors,
communicate the news between themselves according
to decisions made by international agencies outside
the region.

The uneasiness expressed in 1972 by the Andean
Pact countries, when pointing out their concern
because the greater volume of international information circulating in their countries was processed
outside the region, is still felt.

This is a problem which cannot be dealth with
at the level of action and decision of the agencies
that operate in Latin America. It has to be faced
at a political level, with a serious attempt to
break the atomization and dependence. For this
reason, the start that has been made within the
framework of the Latin American Common Market is
important, as a point of departure towards setting
up an information system that will provide the
content of "another news," in harmony with what
has been called "another development," independent
of the model that is imposed by the center on the
periphery.

To the examples given earlier, we may add
some more events of the week that were disregarded
in Latin America, receiving little or no coverage
in the newspapers studied:
Costa Rica (San José). Meeting and expert seminar
on problems of human rights, organized by the
United Nations, attended by high-level

judges, prosecutors, and magistrates from the
Third World and the USA.

Ecuador (Quito). Andean Group meeting on the
protection of the artistic heritage, under the
auspices of UNDP and Unesco, attended by
officials and experts concerned.

Guatemala. Fifth conference of ministers of labor.
On the agenda, a round table entitled:
"Transnational Enterprises and Their Impact
on Labor Relations and the Role of Ministries
of Labor."

Panama. General Torrijo's declaration, telling US
negotiator E. Bunker to bring a serious
proposal "or don't come back." This news
figured prominently in the Panamanian press.

Why was this news not reported in the Latin
American press? Wasn't it transmitted by the
agencies? This is doubtful, since much of it was
newsworthy and of more than limited interest.

Two interpretations are possible:

1. The agency transmissions--especially those
   from the major transnationals--do not give
   this sort of news the status or coverage
   that automatically indicates its importance
   to those who choose the cables: it has a
   "low profile"; it doesn't figure in the
   headline statements periodically transmitted by teletype.
2. To those who are responsible for deciding
   what is to be printed, this sort of
   information is not "news," as they know it,
   or else it contains material that they
   think they had better not make known, to
   avoid complications.

The conclusion is that there is an obvious manipulation of the international news made available
throughout the continent, that serves only to
perpetuate the dominant structure.

Professional shortcomings and distortions
persist in this area of journalism more than in
others, in spite of the importance that international news has for political attitudes which are
necessary to the search for a more independent
development. This external news domination is the
common experience of Latin American countries.

In all but a few newspapers there is no
capacity for an independent interpretation of
world or regional affairs.

Few newspapers have correspondents of their own in key capitals or send reporters to cover important events.

There is no capacity for relating the many regional or international events. The atomization of information that the agencies have instituted is not questioned.

There is subjection to dominant models in the overemphasis of events of little or no importance to Latin America.

In short, if we consider the extent to which the front page is dominated by agency material (see Table 7.1), or the monopoly of photographic news material by AP and UPI wirephotos, we must conclude that the pattern of information has changed very little.

There is a bedazzlement which conditions the practice of editors and wire-men. The old inertia makes them follow certain editorial patterns. The persistence of this stereotyped behavior confirms the news agencies in their belief that "this is what the media want." So the vicious circle of domination perpetuates itself, condemning Latin America to ignorance of its own affairs and cutting it off from the profound changes that are unfolding in the Third World.

[Translated from Spanish]

This article was originally published in *Development Dialogue*, the journal of the Dag Hammarskjöld Foundation, Uppsala, Sweden, 1976, Vol. 2, pp. 29-42. Reprinted by permission.

8
The Impact of Transnational Corporations on Educational Processes and Cultural Change: An African Perspective

Ali A. Mazrui

We should begin by simply noting that every society has both formal and informal processes of education. In literate societies, the formal aspects are preeminently realized in schools and colleges and in formal private lessons. But the informal processes of education are broader, sometimes omnipresent. They range from special educational programs on television and other media to the instructive experiences of life itself.

In preliterate societies, the distinction between formal and informal processes of education is less sharp, though it still exists. The ritual aspects of an initiation ceremony, for example, are clearly formal. But children are socialized and trained in informal ways as well, ranging from listening to the conversations of adults to observing the behavior of cattle in a tropical storm with thunder and lightning.

When we examine the impact of multinational corporations on educational processes, we should be careful not to limit ourselves to the effects on formal schooling and curriculum building. There are wider ramifications for society which should also be borne in mind.

Another point which needs to be made is that commercial firms are only one kind of multinational corporation. Some educational institutions are themselves multinational corporations. These latter are cultural rather than commercial or industrial corporations.

Many of the characteristics that have been attributed to *commercial* multinational corporations in Africa may apply also to *cultural* multinational corporations, of which university institutions are

preeminent examples. Almost all African
universities in the colonies started as overseas
"subsidiaries" of metropolitan institutions in
Europe. Decisions on priorities for development
had to respond to the orientations of the parent
cultural corporations in Britain, France, or
Belgium. The cultural goods sold to a new African
clientele did not necessarily bear relevance to the
real needs of the African market. Skills were
transferred without adequate consideration for
their value in Africa; other skills were withheld
because they did not conform to world criteria
of "excellence" as defined by the parent body.[1]
    In the cultural domain, the pinnacle of the
structure of dependency was the university, that
institution which produced overwhemingly the
first generation of bureaucratic and political
elites of postcolonial Africa, whose impact on the
fortunes and destinies of their countries seemed
at the time to be potentially incalculable. The
university, like the British Broadcasting
Corporation, was a cultural corporation with
political and economic consequences. The multinational commercial company was an economic
corporation with political and cultural consequences. There was a process of mutual
reinforcement in the functions served by these
corporate entities. What should be emphasized is
simply that the university lay at the pinnacle
of the structure of cultural dependency, and the
multinational commercial enterprise at the pinnacle
of the structure of economic dependency.
    But just as the African univeristy has its
genesis in European imperialism, so does the
commercial multinational corporation. Some of the
recent literature on these corporations seems to
assume that such international entities are a new
thing. But the East India Company was established
in the reign of Queen Elizabeth I, and for many
decades effectively ruled a substantial part of
India before the crown took over directly.[2]
    Elsewhere in the empire, companies in search
of natural resources and raw materials, were created
early.

> From about 1860 onwards manufacturing
> companies began to establish production
> facilities outside their own countries,
> and by 1914 many of today's giants were
> already operating in several countries.

...International companies are certainly
not a new phenomenon....In the past the main
impact of international companies, except in
banking, insurance and finance, was felt in
the colonial and semi-colonial territories.
The companies themselves were generally
involved in trade, the running of public
utilities, or the exploitation of raw
materials through mining, plantation and
ranching ventures.[3]

In Africa, mining--especially in the southern
third of the continent--was internationalized from
a very early period. The "gold rush" of South
Africa, the diamonds of Kimberley, the copper of
Katanga and Northern Rhodesia, though each was
dominated by one Western national enterprise, were
soon linked to related enterprises across national
frontiers.

Elsewhere in the continent, the Imperial
British East Africa Company held sway for a while.
Kenya and Uganda seemed to be on the verge of
actually being ruled by the company--in the old
tradition of the East India Company. If such
companies were not multinational, they were
certainly multiterritorial. They had operations
in two or three or more colonies, and their headquarters were in the European metropole. Because
communications with that metropole were not as
developed as they became in the second half of the
twentieth century, these old international
companies were not as centrally controlled as their
modern counterparts. The Imperial British East
Africa Company was establishing itself across the
seas more than two generations before the full
development of the International Telephone and
Telecommunications complex of the period following
World War II. In those older times, there were no
instant intercontinental telephone calls, no urgent
cables, not even air letters. Centralization of
commercial enterprises across continents was not
feasible. But these companies were certainly
precursors of such commercial octopuses of the
future as Unilever, Lonrho, and Anglo-American.

But while the commercial multinational
corporation as a phenomenon in Africa antedated the
full establishment of colonial control in large
parts of the continent, the African university as
a cultural corporation took longer to evolve. Few
policy makers in Europe doubted that the commercial

penetration of the "virgin lands of Africa" was
something "positive." Lord Lugard's[4] vision of
"the Dual Mandate" in Africa legitimized the
collective *exploitation* of Africa by Europe *as a
whole*.[5] He regarded the tropics as a "heritage of
mankind" and felt that "neither, on the one hand,
has the Suzerain Power a right to their exclusive
exploitation nor, on the other hand, have the races
which inhabit them a right to deny their bounties
to those who need them."

But the same Lugard who called for commercial
internationalization of Africa's resources was
profoundly distrustful of Western *cultural*
penetration into Africa. He sought to protect
northern Nigeria from Christian missionary education, and was disturbed by the influence of the
English language on "the natives." He argued that
"the premature teaching of English...inevitably
leads to utter disrespect for British and native
Ideals alike, and to a denationalised and disorgan-
ised population."

Although some of the institutions in Africa
which later became universities were established
in the first two decades of the twentieth century
or even earlier, actual elevation to university
standard mostly came after World War II. There
was also the anomaly that many of those among
imperial policy makers who wanted to ensure that
universities were relevant to African needs and
values were in other respects regarded among the
most conservative and least liberal of the time.
Here an important difference did arise in origins
between the movement for higher education in British
Africa and such a movement in French Africa.
British colonial policy had already been profoundly
influenced by the whole doctrine of indirect rule,
based substantially on Burkean principles of
cultural relativism. The colonial subjects were to
be ruled partly according to principles and partly
through institutions which had grown up in those
very societies themselves. What was at least
aspired to was the dictum of Edmund Burke: "Neither
entirely nor all at once depart from antiquity...
for people will never look forward to posterity
who never look backward to their ancestors."

This kind of reasoning affected some of the
initial ideas about the nature of all levels of
education in British colonies from the eighteenth
century onwards. And even when the movement for
African universities gathered momentum in this
century, it was possible for an official advisory

committee to the British government to emphasize in a statement which became a white paper in 1925: "Education should be adapted to the mentality, aptitudes, occupations and traditions of the various peoples, conserving as far as possible all sound and healthy elements in the fabric of their social life."[6]

The committee included among its members Lord Lugard, the architect of the British policy of indirect rule in Africa and perhaps the greatest British administrator in the history of the continent.

In French Africa, within the educational domain, the policy of assimilation continued to hold sway even after it had declined in effectiveness in other areas of policy. There were fewer concessions to indigenous cultures and indigenous institutions in countries ruled by France than in those ruled by Britain. While schools in the British colonies utilized African languages in at least the first three years of primary education, schools in the French colonies continued to be supremely indifferent to the pedagogical case for the utilization of "vernaculars." As for Belgian educational policy for the colonies at the preuniversity level, the emphasis on European culture was less than was evident in French policies, but the emphasis on *practical training* was greater than in either British or French visions.

Yet in the conception of a university, the differences among British, Belgian, and French policies narrowed considerably in the end. In spite of all the cultural relativism of people such as Lugard and James Currie (who had once been a director of education in the Sudan), the vision of an African university moved in the direction of creating an institution of higher education based overwhelmingly on metropolitan standards and metropolitan values. We use the term "metropolitan" here to denote the particular European countries which had empires. The Asquith Report, submitted to the British Government in 1945, provided a blueprint for higher education in the colonies. The basic assumption of the report was that a university system appropriate for Europeans could still be made to serve the needs of Nigerians, Ugandans, and Jamaicans without a major transformation. The stage was set for a significant new level of intellectual penetration by the West into African cultures.

Structurally, the new universities were for a while integrated with the metropolitan university system. On the whole they were overseas colleges, or official overseas subsidiaries of universities in Britain and France. Makerere College at Kampala in Uganda, the University College at Ibadan in Nigeria, and the University College at Legon in Ghana were all overseas extensions of the University of London. They admitted students on the basis of requirements specified by the University of London; they appointed lecturers and professors partly through the good services of the Inter-University Council for Higher Education in London. The syllabuses needed London approval, though there was a good deal of consultation with the African branches. The examination questions at the end of each year were first formulated in the colleges in Africa, then submitted to London for criticism and revision, then some consultation might continue, before London finally approved the questions. The questions themselves were then printed, put into envelopes, sealed, returned to their African campuses, and opened for the first time at the actual taking of examinations.

All the colonial university colleges were mere reflections of the parent bodies in Europe. Like the commercial multinational corporations, they showed a faithful response to external decision makers in the home countries. They responded to the local environment only within the boundaries permitted by the broader policies of the metropole. They had cultural goods to sell to a new African market--goods marked "made in Europe."

THE LINK BETWEEN CULTURAL AND ECONOMIC DEPENDENCY

What ought to be remembered is that a successful sale of cultural goods helps to expand the market for economic goods. This brings us to the direct links between cultural and economic dependency, and therefore between cultural and economic corporations.

During the colonial period, the most immediate goal for Western education in Africa was to produce *culturally relevant manpower*. But at least as important an enterprise was to expand a *culturally relevant market for Western consumer goods*, ranging from toothpaste to automobiles, from readymade Western shirts to canned tuna fish. The significance of an African university for

commercial multinationals lay precisely in these
two areas of producing manpower and of redefining
the market through acculturation.

In the earlier stages of the history of
Western education in Africa, it was the lower-level
manpower which was needed by the colonial
administration and the expatriate companies. By
the 1930s, in much of British Africa young Africans
with Cambridge School Certificates were in great
demand for jobs as bank clerks, junior customs
officials, assistants to managers in business firms,
government administrators, police cadets, teachers,
church novices, and the like.

By the 1940s, some of the companies with fore-
sight were already looking for Africans to take on
lower-level managerial roles, but the educational
structure was not always keeping pace with these
demands. The higher the position in the commercial
company for which an African was needed, the
higher the level of Western education normally
expected. Before long, the highest managerial
positions were to require the minimum of a
bachelor's degree from the local university. The
link between cultural and economic multinationals
had by then become direct.

The importance of Western education for
Western investment in Africa grew rather than
declined with the growth of African nationalism. On
one hand, Western education had itself helped to
stimulate local nationalism, as we shall indicate in
the next section. On the other hand, that same
nationalism demanded the "Africanization" of as
many jobs and roles as possible within each enterprise. The history of American investment in
Europe was being repeated in the third world.
American companies in Europe discovered early the
advantages of employing local managers who understood the needs and sensibilities of the local
market and who could serve as a protection against
local hostilities.

> The U.S. Westinghouse Airbrake was induced to
> establish manufacturing facilities in France
> because of stipulations in railway contracts
> that supplies had to be made locally. Edison
> built a plant in Germany because it found
> that "national feeling" resulted in local
> supplies receiving preference over imports.
> In addition governments could in effect force
> importers to set up local plants by insisting
> that patents should be worked in order to

maintain their validity.[7]

Tugendhat[8] has even gone as far as to suggest
that one of the important reasons for the growth
of multinationals in the last thirty years of the
nineteenth century was itself an aspect of the
growth of nationalism within the receiving
countries. Governments in different parts of the
capitalist world and its appendages introduced
tariffs to reduce imports of manufactured goods
from elsewhere and to foster the growth of their
own industries. There were times when the tariffs
were actually intended to encourage foreign
companies to invest locally, instead of simply
importing goods they had manufactured elsewhere.
Canada was a classical case in this regard. The
Canadian government wanted American companies to
establish plants locally instead of supplying the
Canadian market from across the border. An earlier
version of Canadian nationalism had thus encouraged
American investment in Canada--of which a later
version of Canadian nationalism became under-
standably resentful.[9]

With the establishment of local plants came an
increasing need for local manpower. Protectionism
and nationalism could compel the multinationals to
localize higher and higher levels of its staff. As
Lord Leverhulme, the founder of Lever Brothers,
once said, in a somewhat exaggerated but suggestive
manner:

> The question of erecting works in another
> country is dependent upon the tariff or duty.
> The amount of duties we pay on soap imported
> to Holland and Belgium is considerable, and
> it now only requires that these shall rise to
> such a point that we could afford to pay a
> separate staff of managers with a separate
> plant to make soap to enable us to see our way
> to erect works in those countries.[10]

But while local personnel recruited for
multinationals in Europe or North America are
themselves products of the same Western civilization (broadly defined), local personnel in Africa
need to be partially de-Africanized in advance
before they can become culturally relevant for the
multinationals. Hence, the same Western education
which helped to create the new nationalism in
Africa has to be called upon to meet the demands
of that nationalism. The economic interests of the

newly Westernized Africans become interlinked with those of the multinationals at some levels. More and more jobs within the multinationals become accessible to the locals. More and more decision-making roles are "Africanized." Increasingly, the faces behind the managerial desks are local. Increasingly, the boards of directors coopted Westernized locals to lend further legitimacy to their operations. What a Dutch company in Mombasa, Kenya, found hard to find as they scraped the cultural barrel in the 1940s, the same Dutch company now succeeds in obtaining more abundantly. The Western educational institutions of Africa have been doing part of their original work successfully--producing culturally relevant manpower to consolidate economic dependency.

The second major area of linkage between cultural and commercial corporations concerns the expansion of the market for Western consumer goods. Demand for such goods is, to some extent, culturally determined. The range includes toilet preparations, cosmetics, canned foodstuffs, furniture, wrist watches, soap, cassettes and tape recorders, readymade clothing, cigarettes, jam and marmalade, radio and television sets, detergents, lawn mowers, automobiles, linens, and the like. Some of these goods are an outcome of modernization, but modernization is itself defined in terms of Western culture.

Some of the consumer goods were locally produced, but many of the local products were themselves linked to wider multinational concerns. There were also African "middle countries" serving the role of "middlemen" in a regional context. Kenya has often attracted expatriate industries with an eye on the eastern African market as a whole. Goods produced and packed in Kenya have then been exported to, say, Tanzania, Uganda, and, more recently, Zambia.

The growth of this market for Western consumer goods partly depended on the spread of Western tastes and lifestyles. These tastes and lifestyles were disseminated by a variety of devices, from advertisements to the Western demonstration effect, as revealed through magazines, films, and direct example. But linked to all these other disseminative devices has been the solid core of educated and semieducated Africans, at once followers of the West and leaders of their own societies in many areas of life.

Some aspects of African culture have reinforced the temptation to emulate and imitate the West. Much of Western political and economic culture has been conditioned by the respect given to both political individualism and the profit motive. On the other hand, much of African political and economic culture has been influenced by social collectivism and the *prestige motive*. Precisely because traditional African society was so collective, the applause of kinsmen in the event of success assumed extra importance to balance the dreaded disapproval of those same kinsmen in case of failure. The conditions of a face-to-face traditional society, influenced by collectivist primordial solidarity, made conspicuous consumption a major method of acquiring prestige. This tendency was strengthened by the traditions of a society without the written word. Publicity as a way of acquiring social prestige could not be obtained through the gossip columns of mass-circulation newspapers and magazines. Fame needed to be spread by a combination of ostentation, large-scale patronage, and social hospitality.

This quest for prestige did increase personal consumption, but it also served as a distributive device. Those who prospered needed to share their good fortune if their name was to become widely known in the villages. The money which in the West would have gone to public relations firms and to the entertainment of editors of relevant columns is thus "diverted" in Africa and distributed more directly to neighbors.

As the "European" way of life became part of the measure of social prestige, Western consumer goods started to widen their culturally relevant market. To quote J. Clyde Mitchell and A. L. Epstein in their analysis of social status among working Africans in colonial Zambia (then northern Rhodesia): "Success in achieving this 'civilized' way of life is demonstrated conspicuously by the physical appurtenances of living. The most important of these is clothes, but personal jewelry (especially wrist-watches), furniture and European-type foodstuffs are also important."

Some of the more excessive luxuries now seen in Kenya, the Ivory Coast, and Senegal may be a declining phenomenon. But there are other aspects of Western styles of living which will not be relinquished too readily by the newly educated African elites. Those few leaders that are struggling to control the revolution in consumption

patterns risk their own survival in doing so unless
they combine these efforts with a revolution in
education. Tanzania has been trying to do
precisely that. The link between the nature of the
personal economic ambition of a Tanzanian and the
type of educational system the country has produced
was assessed. A struggle to control certain
aspirations of young people has therefore
necessitated changes in the structure of formal
socialization. And in order to reduce the widespread taste for Western consumer goods, the
educational system of Tanzania itself in the long
run has to be drastically modified.

It is not clear if Tanzania's efforts to
combine educational reform with economic reform
will succeed in the face of considerable domestic
and international difficulties. Tanzania has
succeeded in greatly reducing the role of commercial multinationals in the economic destiny of the
country. It is too early, however, to predict the
final outcome of Tanzania's experiments. What is
clear is that a diagnosis has already been undertaken, and the fact seems to have been grasped
that here is a link between educational dependency
and economic dependency.

THE MULTINATIONALS AND TECHNOLOGY TRANSFER

Closely interlinked with the process of
creating relevant manpower is the process of
technological transfer through multinational firms.
These firms have in fact become the major media
of technology transfer outside the military field.

The transfer takes place mainly in four forms.
The technology is embodied in, first, physical
goods and equipment; second, skilled labor; third,
know-how which is legally recognized in patents and
trademarks; and fourth, knowledge which is either
not patented or not patentable. All these four
types are relevant to educational processes, both
formal and informal. G. K. Helleiner[12] sees a
consensus emerging among analysts and some planners
that unpatentable know-how about the process of
production is of greater significance than
patented knowledge.

> Technology payments in licensing and
> collaboration agreements in which patent
> rights are not involved typically exceed those
> in agreements in which they are. Knowledge

embodied in the patent is, in any case,
normally insufficient by itself to permit its
efficient working. As Johnson has put it,
"In contemporary conditions, public tolerance
and legal protection of commercial secrecy
has become more important than the patent
system."13

Helleiner regards the effect of patents on
technology as *restrictive*, but a good deal depends
upon the options available in a given situation.
There are certainly occasions when commercial
secrecy is an inescapable de facto alternative to
patented knowledge--and the secrecy can be a worse
constraint on technology transfer than the patent.
But where the knowledge is indeed made available for
local use, an educative process may be under way.
A substantial part of the debate about technology transfer has concerned the issue of appropriateness. And within this issue the distinction between
labor-intensive and capital-intensive technology
has loomed large. Both forms of technology have
educational implications.
The bias in technology transfer by multinationals has on the whole been toward capital
intensity. There have been a number of reasons
for this bias. Helleiner has drawn our attention
to the following, among others:

1. Multinational firms have access to
   relatively cheap capital.
2. Unskilled labor is frequently of very low
   productivity; the wage rate may seem low
   "but it is not cheap in terms of efficiency
   wages."
3. The heavy protection which the multinationals enjoy reduces the incentive to change to
   the really efficient labor-intensive
   techniques.
4. The multinational firms have tended to
   operate in industries (such as mineral
   processing) in which technology is both
   capital intensive and fixed.
5. In the manufacturing sector their products--
   originally designed for richer markets--are
   standardized and subjected to strict quality
   control. (These controls over standard
   "imply relatively capital-intensive and
   inflexible techniques of production for
   these particular products although it might
   have been possible to meet consumer demand

for the same basic characteristics through
the provision of an alternative product with
a more appropriate production technology
and/or more flexible quality controls.")

6. Labor-intensive technologies tend to be
   associated with smaller-scale production--
   whereas the multinationals have on the whole
   preferred to produce on a large scale.
7. Shortages of skills in less developed
   countries make capital a more efficient
   functional alternative.
8. Labor relations in less developed countries
   are at least as uncertain as in the developed states. (Labor-intensive techniques
   increase the risks of disruptions and
   interruptions.)
9. Capital-intensive techniques sometimes
   provide better insurance against unexpected
   fluctuations in demand than do labor-
   intensive ones.
10. Governments and private purchasers of tech-
    nology in less developed countries often
    prefer "the latest" in technological devel-
    opment as a status of "modernity" even if
    the latest technique is less appropriate for
    the particular developing country than an
    older method or older model of equipment.[14]

From an educational point of view, what should
be borne in mind is that capital-intensive techniques also tend to be *skill intensive*. Initially,
the skilled personnel are imported into the developing country from outside, sometimes in response to
demands by the authorities for the establishment of
a local plant. The quest for import substitution
may indeed succeed in reducing the importation of
finished products, but sometimes in exchange for
increasing the importation of skilled manpower.

But then the pressures for greater indigenization of manpower gather momentum, as the Nigerian
experience illustrates. In the words of a high
Nigerian official:

Perhaps more important than ownership is the
effective participation of Nigerians in the
management of local enterprises. Even
considering various difficulties--shortage of
people with higher qualifications, obstacles
to mobility of higher manpower--the record of
local industry in training Nigerians and
appointing them to positions of responsibility

> has been very disappointing....A fund for
> industrial training...will establish targets
> of progressive Nigerianization....To speed the
> process the Government will mandatorily
> progressively reduce from year to year the
> expatriate quota allocations of all enter-
> prises making due allowance for expansion
> and diversification.[15]

In those enterprises which are capital
intensive and technologically complex, the training
required for the indigenization of personnel may
be substantial. This has implications for the
whole problem of the brain drain, especially in
situations where a country first adopts capital
intensity and then shifts from capital-intensive
to labor-intensive techniques. In Black Africa,
the problem is not as yet acute, but both India and
Nasser's Egypt had personnel who were well-trained
for certain roles in multinational firms and who
then left their own countries when those skilled
roles were no longer available in adequate numbers
at home.

A relatively sudden contraction of skill-
intensive enterprises in the country--either
because of the consequences of a change in
ideology or a change in techniques of production--
may result in the transfer of technology in the
reverse direction as well-trained engineers,
technicians, and accountants from the third world
seek the kind of employment in the industrial
countries which is more "appropriate" to their
new skills.

> As soon as it is granted that some technology
> is embodied in human capital, and that it can
> therefore be transferred internationally
> through the movement of engineers, scientists
> and managers, it follows that the "brain
> drain" can also be viewed as part of the
> international technology transfer question.
> While it is quite customary to consider the
> role of the multinational firms in transfer-
> ring technology through human capital from
> rich countries to poor, it has been less usual,
> though no less logical, to analyze their role
> in transferring it in the reverse direction.
> Their employment of indigenous talent for the
> pursuit of their own particular interests may
> deflect it from more socially profitable
> research and development activity, even if it

does not physically leave the country.[16]

On the other hand, there are occasions when the training and education imparted go beyond the particular job in a multinational firm and could make the recipient an innovator in his own right. In the words of Jack Baranson, "more important than the imparting of technical knowledge and manufacturing capabilities is the ability and willingness to implant indigenous engineering and design capability for continued technological transformation."[17] This is what Kenneth Boulding[18] would presumably describe as "knowledge which has the capacity of generating more knowledge in a single head."

Where the training transmitted by a multinational firm promotes such self-generating knowledge in a single head, it could indeed contribute to the innovative capacity of a particular sector of a developing economy. But what should continue to be borne in mind is that such a level of knowledge may as likely be diverted toward the brain drain. This particular dilemma of skill intensity continues to pose problems for the policy maker.

Does it therefore provide an additional argument for shifting to labor-intensive techniques which require lower levels of expertise? As indicated earlier, labor-intensive techniques which follow a period of sustained capital intensity could in any case aggravate the problem of the brain drain by aggravating the problem of skilled redundancy following the shift.

But a distinction does need to be made between modifying factor proportions in an industry already established and selecting new industries or new products on the basis of their being more labor intensive. Whether labor can be substituted for capital in a particular manufacturing process depends substantially on the product:

In continuous process industries (chemicals, pharmaceuticals, metal refining, oil refining) and in the production of many consumers' goods and intermediate goods on an assembly line the scope of such substitution is quite limited, except in certain ancillary operations, particularly materials handling and packaging. The main type of activity in which gain (measured in terms of social costs) may be achieved by the substitution of labour for capital are in road-building, irrigation, housing and construction generally, and in the production of woven fabrics, clothing, wood-working, leather, some foodstuffs (including foodstuffs for local consumption in local areas), bricks, tiles, and some of the simpler metal products.[19]

The level of training needed for the second category of employment is on the whole less complex than for the first category. Moreover, the less complex skills lend themselves better to in-service or in-plant training than the advanced technical skills. This is a gain if one agrees with the U.N. Economic Commission for Africa[20] that "in-plant training is more effective than formal technical training in an academic atmosphere."

There are times when an existing industry which is capital intensive can be scaled down and in the process be made more labor intensive, or research could be undertaken to develop unconventional indigenous raw materials. The development or utilization of raw materials could itself create new skills in the society. The scaling down of an industry to adjust to the smallness of the market may alter factor proportions in favor of labor.

One example of "scaling down" was the plant specially designed a few years ago by Philips N. V. of the Netherlands for the assembly of radios in certain less developed countries. "The main object of this design was to develop a low cost production unit for a smaller volume of output than is typical in Europe; in the process the unit also turned out to be somewhat more labor intensive. The firm also developed simpler types of equipment which can more readily be repaired or replaced from local stocks."[21]

From an educational point of view, the following propositions have therefore emerged from this analysis so far:

1. Capital-intensive technological processes tend also to be skill intensive.
2. The education required for capital-intensive projects is likely to be at least partly formal, acquired in an academic atmosphere.
3. Manpower trained for capital-intensive projects is subject to the temptations of the brain drain partly because the technical

skills involved have a market in the
advanced economies.
4. Labor-intensive processes lend themselves
more easily to informal training and
education, in-service or in-plant.
5. Labor-intensive processes, almost by
definition, spread skills more widely in the
society and help democratize education by
broadening its distribution.

To the extent that multinationals have had a
bias in favor of capital intensity, they have been a
constraint on educational democratization. The
skill intensity required has tended to aggravate the
elitist tendencies inherited from the patterns of
education under colonial rule.

MULTINATIONALS, SECULAR EDUCATION
AND PRACTICAL RELEVANCE

A more positive contribution of multinationals
in the field of education is related to two
processes in the third world--the *secularization of
education*, in the sense of reducing a religious
focus, and the *practicalization of education*, in the
sense of promoting greater relevance to concrete
social needs.
On the whole, the impact of the multinationals
on colonial schools was in the direction of both
reducing the focus on religion and increasing
interest in practical skills. The multinationals
contributed to these two trends in five main ways.

1. By helping to create a labor market in which
practical skills were needed
2. By becoming an additional secular lobby on
colonial policy makers to counterbalance the
influence of the missionaries
3. By the demonstration impact of some of their
own training programs, especially for lower-
level manpower
4. By helping to promote a "consumer culture"
in the colonies with its emphasis on
materialistic tastes as opposed to religious preoccupations
5. By helping to promote urbanization and
general labor migration

Tensions between multinationals and the

missionaries in the colonial territories were sometimes inevitable. Those colonies which had extractive (mining) industries experienced special types
of tensions. There were times when the missionaries
favored alternative forms of practical orientation
in education, especially those skills which would
help to keep young Africans in their own villages.
From the missionary's point of view, it seemed that
the African who remained in his farming community
was more likely to remain "faithful to spiritual
values" than the migrant to, say, the multinational
mining industries.

In 1933, for example, a Commission of Inquiry
was set up by the Department of Social and Industrial Research of the International Missionary
Council, and its terms of reference at the narrowest
were the "effects of the copper mines of Central
Africa upon Native Society and the work of the
Christian Missions."

Among the commission's recommendations was that
the "educational emphasis of Missions should be
directed towards preparing Bantu youth to serve the
needs of Bantu rather than European society." There
was indeed sincere anxiety that "Bantu labour" for
the copper mines could in certain circumstances be
at the expense of "native society." The commission
recommended: "...the missions' societies of the
Territories study together the goals towards which
their education is directed, define its purpose and
visualise the results which they are aiming to
achieve. If such study is to be of ultimate value
the cooperation of the Government must be secure."[22]

No less significant was the commission's
recommendation that for the sake of rural stabiliza-
tion "the syllabuses for the mission schools should
be drawn to dignify farming as a vocation...."[23]

In the Belgian Congo (now Zaïre), multinational
interests, missionaries, and the state gradually
evolved a working alliance, and much of the
emphasis in both missionary and state schools was
in time put on practical training. The very
readiness of the missionaries in the Belgian
colony to promote vocational training helped to
satisfy the need of multinational enterprises and
to consolidate a relative missionary monopoly of
education in the country until the last decade of
Belgian rule. A major reason was the more
successful relationship in the Belgian Congo
between the multinationals, the missionaries, and
the colonial authorities. The practicalization of

education could therefore take place without "excessive" secularization.

The multinational corporations played a major role in promoting the changes referred to already, not least because they were often the most important agencies for industrialization, mechanization, and commercialization in most of the colonies.

What should be borne in mind is the distinction between the multinational industries themselves and the facilities and servicing industries which grow up because of the multinational presence. The Belgian colonial authorities used to boast that the Belgian Congo had the best transport facilities in Africa. The claim was an exaggeration, but there was no doubt that impressive progress had been made in this field. The construction of an infrastructure is not always in itself a multinational enterprise, but the need for such an infrastructure is in part often defined in response to multinational pressure.

A garage in Lusaka or Nairobi with African mechanics may not in itself be part of a multinational firm, but the demand for garage services could have been initially escalated by the needs of personnel employed in multinational enterprises.

In assessing the impact of multinationals on the diffusion of skills in African societies, one must therefore consider both the direct and the indirect consequences of a multinational presence. The multinational firms may themselves be capital intensive, but their presence helps to promote labor-intensive infrastructural developments and servicing industries. And these in turn have educational and training implications.

But when all is said and done, it is important to remember that building transport facilities and producing semiskilled artisans is not the be-all and end-all of the task of meeting the "practical" needs of such societies. These developments create new problems of their own.

The multinationals have indeed substantially contributed to industrialization and commercialization; in the process they have also contributed to the secularization of education and to the trend toward giving education a greater practical component. But the precise nature of the industrialization and commercialization has itself distorted certain directions of both cultural and educational change. The need for a new adjustment is now becoming more urgent.

This chapter has been more an interpretation of what has happened than a recommendation of what ought to happen, more a diagnosis than a prescription. But certain prescriptions are perhaps implicit in the diagnosis. We should now proceed to recapitulate the main components of that diagnosis.

We have noted that multinationals as economic enterprises have to some extent been analogous to universities as cultural enterprises. Universities in Africa started as "cultural" subsidiaries of parent bodies in Europe. These colonial universities were therefore branches of cultural multinational corporations.

The lower (primary and secondary) levels of the educational pyramid in each colony were substantially shaped by what was expected for university admissions. A link was created between economic dependency as fostered by commercial multinationals and cultural dependency as promoted by universities.

The formal educational institutions operating in the colonies consolidated economic dependency in the following ways:

1. By creating culturally relevant manpower to help serve multinational commercial and industrial enterprises
2. By creating a culturally relevant market for Western or Western-style goods and equipment

But the multinational firms also helped to select which aspects of Western culture entered the whole stream of normative and educational change in the third world. Particularly significant was the impact of the multinational firms on:

1. The secularization of education
2. The trend toward practical relevance in education and training

But in some ways the most explicit role of multinational firms in the field of education and training concerns technology transfer. The nature of that transfer has on the whole been capital intensive, which in turn has also been skill intensive. But diffusion of technical knowledge more widely has also taken place in a variety of both formal and informal ways. Some of that distribution and diffusion of technical knowledge has been through the infrastructure and supportive industries rather than directly by the multinational firms themselves. But those infrastructural requirements have themselves been highlighted by the multinational presence.

There seems to be little doubt that the multinational commercial and industrial firms have been among the major carriers of knowledge from the industrial world to the less developed countries. The major tasks for the future revolve around the following questions:

1. How can the knowledge which is transferred to the third world, or disseminated among its people, be made the basis of self-generating additional knowledge? *This is the imperative of innovation.*
2. How can the knowledge so created or exchanged be mobilized to reduce the economic and cultural dependency of the third world upon the industrial nations? *This is the imperative of decolonization.*
3. How can all available and potential knowledge be mobilized to improve the living standards of the peoples in the third world, enrich their lives, and fulfill their creative potentialities? *This is the imperative of development.*

Both miltinational firms and domestic policy makers have to address themselves to the challenges posed by these three imperatives.

NOTES

This paper was presented at a meeting of experts on the study of the impact of transnational corporations on development and international relations within the fields of competence of UNESCO, held in Paris, June 1-5, 1976.

1. This theme is discussed more comprehensively in Ali A. Mazrui, "The African University as a Multinational Corporation: Problems of Penetration and Dependency," *Harvard Educational Review* 45:2 (May 1975): 191-210. The following few pages of this paper have been borrowed from that article.

2. Jonathan David Aronson of the Department of Political Science, Stanford University, has compiled a useful bibliography on multinationals in historical and comparative perspective. See J. D. Aronson, "The Multinational Corporation,

the Nation-State and the International System: A
Bibliography," mimeo.
    3. Tugendhat, Christopher, *The Multinationals*.
London: Penguin Books, 1971, pp. 30-32.
    4. Lugard, Sir F. D. *The Dual Mandate in
British Tropical Africa*. Edinburgh and London:
Blackwood and Sons, 1926, pp. 60-62.
    5. Lugard was perhaps the greatest British
administrator in Africa. He ruled Nigeria for a
while and helped to shape the destiny of Uganda.
    6. *Educational Policy in British Tropical
Africa: Memorandum...by the Advisory Committee on
Native Education in the British Tropical African
Dependencies*, 1924-1925, Cmd 2374, xxl, 27.
    7. Tugendhat, *op. cit.*, pp. 33-34.
    8. *Ibid.*
    9. For a brief discussion of the impact of
protectionism on the spread of multinationals,
see Tugendhat, *Multinationals*, pp. 34-35.
    10. Wilson, Charles, *The History of Unilever*.
Vol. 1. London: Cassell, 1954.
    11. Mazrui, Ali A., "The Monarchical Tendency
in African Political Culture." *British Journal of
Sociology*, Vol. 18, No. 3 (1967), p. 234.
    12. Helleiner, G. K., "The Role of Multina-
tional Corporations in the Less Developed Countries:
Trade in Technology." *World Development*, Vol. 3,
No. 4 (1975), p. 165.
    13. I am indebted to G. K. Helleiner for
stimulation and bibliographical guidance.
    14. Helleiner elaborates on some of these
arguments and mentions additional ones. See
Helleiner, "Multinational Corporations," pp. 169-
171.
    15. Asiodu, P. C., "Planning for Further
Industrial Development in Nigeria." Paper presented
at the Conference on National Reconstruction and
Development in Nigeria, Nigerian Institute of Social
and Economic Research, 1969. P. C. Asiodu was
then Permanent Secretary to the Federal Ministry
of Industries, Lagos.
    16. Helleiner, *op. cit.*, p. 165.
    17. Baranson, J., Comments on "Transfers of
United States Aerospace Technology to Japan," by
G. R. Half and R. E. Johnson. In *The Technology
Factor in International Trade*, ed. Raymond Vernon.
New York: National Bureau of Economic Research,
1970, p. 362.
    18. Boulding, K. E., "The Economics of
Knowledge and the Knowledge of Economics." *American
Economic Review*, Vol. 56, No. 2 (1966), p. 3.

19. *The Multinational Corporations in Africa.*
Document by U.N. Economic Commission for Africa.
London: Rex Collins, Africa Contemporary Record
Current Affairs Series, 1972, p. 13.
20. *Ibid.*, p. 19.
21. *Ibid.*, p. 15.
22. Davis, J. Merle, International Missionary
Council, *Modern Industry and the African.* London:
Macmillan, 1933, pp. 338-339.
23. *Ibid.*

ADDITIONAL REFERENCES

Aronson, Jonathan David, "The Multinational
Corporation, the Nation-State and the International
System: A Bibliography." Mimeo.

Lugard, Sir F. D., *Annual Reports, Northern
Nigeria, 1900-1911.* Cited in James S. Coleman,
Nigeria: Background to Nationalism. Berkeley
and Los Angeles: University of California Press,
1971.

Mazrui, Ali A., "The African University as a
Multinational Corporation: Problems of Penetration
and Dependency." *Harvard Educational Review,*
Vol. 45, No. 2 (1975), pp. 191-210.

Mitchell, J. Clyde and A. L. Epstein,
"Occupational Prestige and Social Status Among
Urban Africans in Northern Rhodesia," *Africa,*
Vol. 29 (1959), pp. 34-39.

This selection is reprinted from Krishna Kumar, ed.,
*Bonds Without Bondage: Explorations in Transcul-
tural Interactions.* Honolulu: University Press of
Hawaii, 1979, pp. 155-173. Reprinted by permission.

9
The Role of Multinationals in Vocational Training

Dmitiri Germidis

The role of the MNC in vocational training becomes apparent through a number of activities taking place either within the parent company or the subsidiary or outside the latter, mainly in connection with its environment in the host country.

What might be termed the more traditional part of these activities is connected with the management and production functions of the MNC and therefore concerns its personnel. Another, which is of growing importance, is closely connected with its vocation (actual and potential) as a channel for technological transfer, and is therefore manifested through its relationships with its local suppliers and its customers, and with the scientific and technical potential of the host country.

TRADITIONAL AREAS OF ACTIVITIES

Training Practices and Transfer of Technology

Recruitment and training of local personnel are considered to be one of the most important aspects of technological transfer by the MNC. This is more intensive as the subsidiary takes on more local staff at high levels of skill acquired largely in the MNC or with its help. There might be a multiplier effect through the mobility of labor: skilled workers leaving the subsidiary to work in national firms take scientific and technical knowledge with them to other sectors of the economy, thus helping to broaden the host country's capacity to absorb technology.

Recruiting of unskilled or other slightly skilled workers does not appear to raise any

problem. The surplus of supply over available
vacancies enables the subsidiaries to be selective
and then to exercise some control, which incidentally largely explains the high level of
productivity found in subsidiaries.

Training policy takes various forms depending
on the qualifications required for the job, the type
of industry, and the level of ability of the work
force available on the market.

Unskilled or only slightly skilled workers are
usually trained on the job.

The difficulties and genuine problems arise
over recruiting and vocational training from the
level of technicians upwards, and become greater
as the higher levels of the technical and administrative hierarchy are reached.

Scarcity is the most important factor in the
recruitment not only of top management but also of
foremen and certain specialists (maintenance staff,
electricians, etc.).[1]

This scarcity has an impact which varies
according to the structure and level of development
of the host country. It is most acute in countries
such as the Ivory Coast, Kenya, Morocco, and to a
lesser degree in Argentina, Greece, and Spain.

The reasons for this have to do not so much
with low standards of secondary and higher education
(which are not so low in several developing or
insufficiently developed countries such as the
Philippines, Greece, Spain, and some Latin American
countries) as with

1. the unsuitability of education to the
   requirements of national and multinational
   industry;
2. competition from national administrations
   in which the career prospects look more
   attractive--this is especially true of those
   African developing countries whose administrative system and, above all, scales of
   pay and other benefits, are modelled on the
   French;
3. the strength of demand either from other
   foreign investors or from domestic industry,
   whose needs rise with the level of
   industrialization in the country;
4. the lack of interest shown by local
   management, and still more by technical
   personnel in operational field duties
   often carried out at a great distance from
   the main urban centers.

This shortage of local management personnel has two consequences for the MNC: they have to rely heavily on expatriate workers, at least in the initial period of starting up a subsidiary, usually lasting between two and five years, and at the same time make a special effort to carry out vocational training to the extent that most firms appear to wish to replace their expatriate managers (at least so far as middle management and a high proportion of expatriate top management are concerned) by local recruits. There are three main reasons why the MNC should wish to act in this way:

1. the growing difficulties of recruiting, in the source country or elsewhere, qualified staff who are prepared to work abroad;
2. the high cost of expatriate staff, because of the better salary conditions offered them and the cost of moving them and their families;
3. the desire to meet the requirements (de facto or de jure) of the host countries that a proportion of the management personnel shall be native ("Africanization," "Morocconization," etc.).

It is therefore at this level of middle management and technicians that the firms' training activities are most intensive. They are mainly based on sending future foremen, technicians, and administrators to training courses at the head-quarters of the parent company where advanced training courses are regularly organized, or to other subsidiaries of the MNC.[2] Thus staff of a subsidiary specializing in the manufacture of transmission equipment in the Philippines is some-times sent to the Brazilian subsidiary of the group.[3]

This category of staff will later have a further opportunity to travel for shorter periods for the purpose of what may be called continuous training, namely the learning of new techniques (new manufacturing methods, marketing, etc.).

Journeys by middle management do not appear to take place as often as those of top management and engineers, who frequently go to the head office or other subsidiaries to get up-to-date with new techniques and products. Side by side with technical recycling there are also general meetings of highly qualified staff and those with management responsibilities.

So far as the vocational training carried out by the subsidiary itself is concerned, further training courses mainly designed for middle management are often organized with the help of special training staff from the parent company or, less frequently, from regional offices (in Europe, for example) or from other subsidiaries that have been established longer in the same geographical area and thus have more experience.

Nor must one overlook the part played by technicians coming on technical missions and providing practical training on the spot for those employed by the subsidiary.

In some cases the subsidiary sends its employees or allows them to attend courses in local training centers outside the firm. Thus in Brazil, a subsidiary in the petrochemicals sector regularly finances language, technical, and some-times university courses; in the last-mentioned case the employee undertakes to serve the firm for a definite period at the end of his studies.[4]

Opinions as to the quality of local training vary from country to country but broadly speaking it corresponds to the level of economic development.

Lastly, some subsidiaries (as for instance the three contacted in Brazil[5]) provide training courses for members of the universities, both undergraduate and postgraduate, which is an inter-esting method of selecting future employees. These are however isolated examples which do not reveal a significant trend.

In any case the host country does not really benefit from the training acquired by its nationals on the management of MNC except insofar as there is a fairly high rate of rotation of staff of the subsidiary within the host country.

Unfortunately, all the case studies show comparatively low mobility for qualified workers and almost none for management. The multinationals themselves sometimes raise institutional obstacles to such mobility, as when the subsidiaries make their management staff sign undertakings (as in Brazil[6]) to prevent them, if they leave, from being recruited by other competing firms. All vocational training work outside the group is closely connected with the requirements of a single firm; there is very little concerted work and still less real cooperation among the MNC, or between them and the host countries. Examples of multilateral vocational training as a joint

activity are rare. Mention may however be made of
the extremely successful experience of the Asian
Institute of Management (AIM) of Manila,[7] set up
in 1968 by local university bodies, public
authorities and national and multinational firms
(which finance it) in nine Asian countries. This
Institute, which provides training specially
concerned with the needs of the region and trains
top managers, has already acquired some prestige
as a vocational training school in Southeast
Asia. It is interesting to note that it is the
national industries which make the most use of the
trained staff.

Vocational training activities at the level
of the subsidiary, and in cooperation with the
scientific and technical potential of the host
country, raise two basic problems. The first
concerns *the willingness of the authorities of the
host country* to expand or even start such
activities; and the second, *the willingness of the
MNC* to intensify vocational training of locally
recruited managerial staff, especially those whose
activities would be decisive for the retention
and transfer of technology (both of management and
organization and of manufacturing processes).

So far as the first problem is concerned it
may be said that the positions of the host countries
are not really identical. Thus alongside countries
such as the Philippines, the Ivory Coast, and
Morocco, which complain of the small contribution
which the MNCs make to their higher education and
call for increased participation by them, many
Latin American countries have expressed definite
mistrust towards whatever comes from the multinationals. This mistrust has gone to such
lengths in Argentina that Law No. 20654/1974 on
the national universities prohibits MNC staff
(nationals or expatriates) from taking part in
local teaching or research activities;[8] and they
may also--when of Argentine origin--be deprived
of certain civic rights (standing for election,
for example), thus giving them the status of
potential "traitors" to the country. The paradox
lies in the fact that, as we shall see later, some
authors consider that the MNCs show an equally
suspicious attitude to this same personnel,
especially when they are in management posts.

Concerning the problem of the willingness of
the MNC to make a genuine transfer of its
technology by means of vocational training, the
small number of subsidiaries analyzed, and

236

consequently the absence of any statistical
significance in the sample taken, does not enable
us either to confirm or refute the assumptions
made by Franko[9] that the willingness of the MNC to
train nationals of the host country would depend
on (1) their policy on product diversification,
and (2) the oligopolistic position of the firm in
the sector of industry concerned.[10]

It is this same aim of the MNCs to preserve
their oligopolistic position, especially in the
technological field, which according to several
researchers guides their policy in regard to
management personnel.

Top Management and Control of the Activities of the MNC

The report by J. D. Peno[11] suggests that on
the whole the MNCs have avoided employing nationals
of the host country in top management positions[12]
both in parent companies and in subsidiaries
abroad, even at the regional coordination levels.
Professor Peno notes that the highest concentration
of expatriates is in the top engineering and technical posts in order to protect the firm's stock
of technical knowledge and know-how. According to
this author the transmission of such knowledge to
the subsidiary by using expatriates in the highest
technical and engineering positions enables the
MNC to protect its market position in the face of
competition from other firms and slow down the
diffusion of its know-how.

Thus the argument put forward to justify--or
rather explain--this attitude of the MNC is based
on the firms' preferences, and reflects their
desire to establish close control from headquarters
over foreign operations and especially over
everything affecting technology and know-how in
an uncertain political and commercial situation.

Clearly the background to this assumption is
the loyalty of locally-appointed higher management
to the firm, or rather the divided loyalty which
might come to light if there were conflicts of
interest between the MNC and the host country.
Thus, in addition to the mistrust of the national
community in regard to its nationals working in
the MNC, there is that of the firm itself,
leading to *mutual mistrust* rather than divided
loyalty.

The idea that management is dominated by
staff of the source country has been strongly

criticized by the directors of the MNC. The question of the nationality of the directors of a subsidiary is not in their view a fundamental one; the essential issue, they believe, is that the directors should have a common policy towards the total activities of the firm. The strength of an MNC lies in having a team working in a way that is closely linked to the firm's general philosophy, in order to be better able to defend the firm's interests. Non-acceptance of this results in a director who cannot accept this philosophy-- independent of his nationality, and who will eventually be rejected by the firm; in any event it will be difficult for him to climb the ladder of the hierarchy if he is not already impregnated with it.

We are thus seeing a trend towards internationalization of personnel--and towards a higher proportion of native staff where subsidiaries are concerned--at all levels, which, owing to the fact that they are trained within the firm (not only in the source country but also in the subsidiaries), tend to adopt attitudes that their values are linked with those of the firm.

The problem which arises in practice is that of knowing the extent to which power as regards major decisions depends on the nationality of the director. Directors of a subsidiary, though they have a comparatively wide margin of autonomy, are in constant contact with the parent company. All important decisions are taken in agreement with the parent company, or by it alone; and in effect, the country's papers show that while subsidiaries have a wide degree of operational autonomy in the firm's current activities (staff policy, production programming and control, commercial policy, etc.), they must have the parent company's approval to launch new products or make new investments. Control is exercised through the operations reports and balance sheets sent in periodically by the subsidiary. Thus, whatever the nationality of the board of directors, it remains very closely integrated in the parent company or the group. Control is a variable which appears to be independent of nationality, the essential point being that through its training, the staff comes to adopt the basic philosophy of the firm.

In practice, and in accordance with a recently noted trend towards regionalization of top management, there is some tendency for it to

become "denationalized" (through its training,
interests, and ability to move to other posts in
the region) in order to identify with the aims and
values of the firm.

EMERGING AREAS OF ACTIVITIES

Location of R & D

Whatever degree of technological autonomy a
developing country attains is achieved through
the formation of a local scientific and technical
infrastructure. The development of R & D
activities in the subsidiary is very important
insofar as the subsidiary may become independent
of the parent company as far as the production of
technology is concerned. In addition, these
relocated R & D units could in principle play an
important part in developing a local technical
base and training skilled staff. We may therefore
wonder how far it would be possible for the multinational firms to transfer some of their R & D
activities.

An analysis of the activities of subsidiaries
has shown that they only rarely have R & D units.
Taking the OECD definition of R & D,[13] it may be
seen that whatever the sector or country of
establishment, laboratories situated in the
developing countries rarely undertake basic or
applied research.

When a country possesses a raw material that
does not exist in the source country, part of that
research may be done locally. In Kenya,[14] for
example, some experimental research was being
carried on in a tea processing factory, but this
was confined to developing new growing techniques
involving the use of herbicides, which by their
nature could not be carried out in England.

Different conditions of environment may make
it difficult to carry out research in the source
country. In Brazil, for example,[15] a pharmaceutical
business is at present carrying on research in
the country before deciding on what raw materials
are required for medicines capable of curing
endemic diseases.

Finally, work on devising products specially
suited to certain markets may be entrusted to
subsidiaries. A local vehicle assembly subsidiary
in the Philippines, for example,[16] has produced,
with the help of its own R & D work, a car

designed for the Philippines market. This model
is being exported to other countries in the region.
In Spain,[17] in the case of a subsidiary
specializing in cosmetics, the local laboratory
is studying the preferences of the Spanish
clientele for perfumes, and has invented a new
product which is now being exploited at the level
of the group. Lastly, in Mexico,[18] R & D activity
in the Mexican food industries has been found to
be on the increase, particularly in developing
new production processes and products. This
branch of industry is in fact very market-conscious,
and the food products have to conform to local
consumers' habits.

Apart from these special cases, the country
studies showed that basic research is usually
centralized in the country of the parent company.
There are several reasons for this centralization
of R & D in the industrialized countries, according
to the directors of MNC:

1. R & D can be carried on only with the
   support of industry and through extremely
   close links with it, particularly where
   rapidly evolving technology is concerned.
2. There are threshold problems in R & D which
   mean that in order for a technology to be
   competitive internationally it must be
   produced in a small laboratory, the more
   so as it is difficult to coordinate on a
   decentralized basis.
3. R & D requires qualified and highly
   specialized manpower such as rarely exists
   in the developing countries.
4. At the level of the group it is not
   profitable to scatter research laboratories
   because of the difficulties of coordinating
   research on a decentralized basis.

Thus, generally speaking, subsidiaries have
only one specialized center dealing with the
problems of adapting processes and/or products to
local conditions, and with quality control of
raw materials and finished products.

Where adaptation work is done, however, it is
very closely supervised by the research centers of
the parent company. Thus work of the Greek and
Moroccan subsidiaries[19] of an American tire firm is
under the supervision of the group's R & D center
in Luxembourg.

Moreover, according to Kaplinsky,[20] who raises

the case of Kenya, the importance of technology as a means of control by the parent company over its subsidiaries is suggested by the fact that the former obtains rights of ownership of new technology created in the subsidiaries. Thus, in general, the latter depend on external sources for innovation, and do not have any real capacity to create or innovate.

The MNCs do nonetheless sometimes apply the principles of international specialization to their production of knowledge. Each laboratory may then be integrated into a worldwide basic or applied research program of which it does only a part. This type of research organization is marked by the absence of any organic links between the subsidiary and the laboratory, the latter being attached to the research center of the firm's head office. As an example we may take the case of IBM,[21] whose research is organized on this model of international specialization. This type of "pseudo-decentralized" laboratory is not geared to the needs of the local market, but mainly to the requirements of the policy for recruiting high-level staff at salaries well below those in the source country; in other words it is a "brain drain" *within the host country* and vocational training is thus in the last resort to the detriment of the developing host countries.

It is precisely because of this that the developing countries should be very careful when calling for the decentralization of R & D by the MNC. If the product of research does not directly and amply benefit the local, national, or regional economy, the small scientific potential of the host country is going to contribute to the scientific and technological development of the source country, to the detriment of its own development.[22]

The virtual absence of R & D activities at the level of the subsidiary in relation to the latter's technological lead over the host country is hardly an incentive to those responsible in the subsidiary or the parent company to develop links with local scientific centers, such links having no justification from a strictly economic point of view.

Where relationships of some importance with local laboratories have been found (as for instance in India, Mexico, Greece, and Spain), they mainly if not exclusively relate to quality-control work, not forgetting the few adaptation activities which have already been mentioned.

Clearly the educative value of these contacts is extremely limited, and their contribution to the setting up of a national capacity for innovation would seem to be very small. From the firm's point of view, the exchange cannot avoid being lopsided, the subsidiary offering more than it receives. It is even dangerous insofar as the retention of a technological lead is an important card in the game of competition. This leads to the formulation of the argument that the interests of the MNC run counter to the creation of an innovation capacity in the developing countries.[23] To the extent to which transfer of technology is one of the main instruments for maximizing the profits of the multinationals, scientific and technological process in the developing countries can be regarded as a potential danger for them, as it will enable the developing countries

1. to increase their bargaining power;
2. to improve their ability to imitate technology creatively; and
3. to promote the building up of a national scientific and technological system capable not only of producing a national technology but also of developing a critical approach to the relations between sciences and technology on the one hand and society on the other.

In these circumstances what are the factors which could encourage the establishment of R & D in the subsidiaries? Some relocation of research and development work might be justified by the benefits which the MNC can enjoy in local markets. "It is the opportunities for a profitable extension of market-linked activities which are the governing factor."[24] Nonetheless, for countries with a scientific potential and an abundant and low-priced technical workforce, such as India,[25] the scientific and technical resources available locally might encourage firms to transfer a part of their research and development activities. This relocation would certainly be cost-effective for them.

Relations of the Subsidiary
With Suppliers and Customers

Purchases by a subsidiary from local producers are another possible way of stepping up the local technical and industrial potential, inasmuch as the suppliers of the subsidiary have to meet a number of technical specifications. A particular way in which this can be done is a type of international subcontracting[26] and more specifically that one whereby a subcontractor manufactures components and parts which are then assembled in the local plant of the firm placing the contract which is a subsidiary of an MNC established in the country of the subcontractor.

The need to meet strict technical specifications involves direct control by the firm mainly concerned, namely the subsidiary awarding the contracts, which results in technical assistance given to the subcontractor. This technical assistance involves not only the assimilation of manufacturing techniques but also an initiation into those of management and organization.

It is also possible for a subcontracting arrangement--especially if it is a specialized one--to be based on the exploitation of local techniques, which could be improved by the sophisticated know-how of the main firm or at least by elements of this, resulting in the creation of *intermediate technologies*. This trend clearly depends on the branch of industry concerned, and is generally found as subcontractors expand their capacity.

Unfortunately, in the present state of affairs, relations between the MNC and local domestic suppliers are rather tenuous. The subsidiaries often prefer to subcontract to subsidiaries of other MNCs specializing in sub-contracting. The argument advanced is almost always the inability of the domestic firms to conform to the required standards, which implies-- on the assumption that the argument is sincere-- that the subsidiaries do not wish to dispense the technical assistance or vocational training needed to ensure compliance with those standards. While this argument might be valid for some countries such as the Philippines or Morocco, its weight is considerably reduced in the case of countries such as Spain or Greece (for which the argument has also been advanced) whose industrial capacity is comparatively large.

The use of local engineering capabilities could also contribute to further develop the technological potential of LDCs. However, the nonexistence or the weakness of these local capabilities makes the subsidiary rely on foreign engineering firms--if not on its own capacities-- and most often the local firms are restricted to the simpler tastes of civil engineering.

Lastly, sales of products of the MNC on local markets also convey technical knowledge. Thus the use of their products can lead to changes in behavior likely to encourage the incorporation of technical progress, as when capital goods are sold to local manufacturers.

"Education" of the consumer occurs with products having a high technological content, usually for collective use, and takes place not only through the traditional after-sales services, some of which are "personalized" (such as the permanent loan of technicians to a customer using the product) but also through training of the customer before purchase and sometimes even before he expresses the intention to buy. In the last-mentioned case the need is created by familiarizing the potential customer with the product and providing him with training which only a subsequent purchase of it could justify or make worthwhile. MNCs specializing in electronics (telecommunications equipment or computers), multicopying equipment, air transport, and military supplies are typical examples of this training and education of customers.

The relationship with customers may be indirect, the subsidiary not marketing its products but passing them through a distribution network. On this assumption (as in the motor vehicle and tire sector), the firm has an important function of helping and advising its approved agents. This function is very extensive, ranging from the organization of further training for mechanics to the laying down of accounting and stock management rules for storekeepers and checks on the existence of suitable tools.

A final question is that of the training given by the multinational groups on the occasion of delivery of capital goods.

The desire to move quickly has led some developing countries, especially those with substantial foreign currency surpluses (such as the oil-exporting countries) to abandon certain traditional principles of control of technology

transmitted to a developing country from abroad.
The aim of speed is in fact incompatible with the
undoing of the technological "package" which makes
it possible to ensure that each imported technology
is indispensable and could not be replaced by
local technology or is already available in the
country. Thus orders for turn-key plants have
become general. These are a result of the demand
of an industrial group, usually multinational, to
reproduce in the host country a large production
unit of the type which it operates in its country
of origin. The building and equipment of such a
plant does not, however, fully resolve the problem
of acquisition of technology: it is necessary
to have a work force capable of operating the plant.
Another notion has thus come into being which is
tending in some sectors to replace that of the
turn-key factory: the factory *"product-in-hand."*
The supplier is then required to deliver a plant
in full operation manned by staff capable of
making it operate at a profit and complying with
quality standards for the international market.
Most of the contracts for such plants, therefore,
include specific clauses covering vocational
training of workers and management.

The international industrial groups are
sometimes even asked to supervise the performance
of industrial plants supplied by them--what is
known as *monitoring*. This kind of after-sales
service goes well beyond the industrial clauses
of licensing agreements which provide for the
maintenance of relations between the two parties
so that each shall benefit from the changes made
by the other party to the original technology.

NOTES

1. See the report by C. A. Michalet,
"Multinational Corporations and Transfer of
Technology: A Comparative Approach of the Cases
of Greece, Ivory Coast, Morocco, and Spain,"
pp. 46-57.
2. C. A. Michalet, *op. cit.*
3. See the report by B. Villegas,
"Multinational Corporations and Transfer of
Technology: The Philippine Case," pp. 151-160.
4. See the report by Carlos de Faro Passos,
"Multinational Corporations and Transfer of
Technology: The Case of Brazil," pp. 192-218.
5. *Ibid.*

6. *Ibid.*

7. D. Germidis and T. Ohsu, "Industrialisation and Technical Co-operation in South East Asia: the Case of the Philippines," I.D.C. of Japan, Tokyo, February 1975.

8. See the report by José-Maria Dagnino Pastore, "Multinational Corporations and Transfer of Technology: The Case of Argentina," pp. 161-191.

9. L. Franko, "Obtaining Technological and Management Skills from Transnational Enterprises: Prospects and Problems for Host Countries and National Joint Venture Partners," CEI, Geneva, May 1975.

10. According to these assumptions, with an equal degree of market domination, the MNCs with a large range of products are likely to be more favorably disposed to training nationals, even those of national firms (under a long-term arrangement forming part of a joint venture, for example), than MNCs whose survival depends on defending a single product. In other words the diversified MNCs are not so threatened by the danger of creating competition as the "single-product" multinationals.

When an MNC feels itself comparatively immune from worldwide competition it is willing to train the personnel of the host country. On the other hand a firm whose share of the market is threatened might be tempted to protect its position by reinforcing secrecy, among other things. Newly established MNCs can use training of national personnel as an instrument for making a breach and entering that branch of industry in the host country. If they succeed in making this breach the MNCs that are already established will very probably be tempted to abandon secrecy in order to employ other means of maintaining their oligopolistic position.

11. J. D. Peno, "Multinational Corporate Behaviour in Host Country High-Level Manpower Markets: The Implication for Technology Transfer and Foreign Investment Control in Less-Developed Host Countries," OECD Development Center, November 1975.

12. These are the posts whose holders are responsible for deciding on the aims of the firm and on matters of planning and control. Operationally, these key posts embrace the functions of organization (managing director), finance, technology and engineering, and control of

production, sales, and marketing.

13.   According to OECD terminology, R & D covers basic research, applied research, and development research. Basic research includes all the work done mainly for the purpose of pushing back the limits of scientific knowledge without any specific practical application of it in mind. Applied research covers this work having at the same time a specific practical aim in mind. Lastly, development is defined as the use of basic and applied research to put to use unexploited materials or to improve those already in existence.

14.   See the report by R. Kaplinsky and S. Chishti, "Technical Change and the Multinational Corporations: Some British Multinationals in Kenya and India," pp. 77-150.

15.   Faro Passos, *op. cit.*

16.   B. Villegas, *op. cit.*

17.   C. A. Michalet, *op. cit.*

18.   See the report of A. Nadal "Transnational Corporations and Transfer of Technology: the Case of Mexico," pp. 219-250.

19.   C. A. Michalet, *op. cit.*

20.   R. Kaplinsky and S. Chishti, *op. cit.*

21.   C. A. Michalet, *op. cit.*

22.   The attitude of Japan to research done by the Japanese subsidiaries of foreign MNCs is based on this point of view and thus contrasts with the attitude of France, for example, which until recently was more receptive to foreign investment when the establishment of a new subsidiary was to be accompanied in the longer term by the establishment of an R & D laboratory (see N. Jequier "Le defi industriel japonais," European Research Center, Lausanne, 1970, pp. 138-140).

23.   A. Nadal, *op. cit.*

24.   C. A. Michalet, *op. cit.*

25.   R. Kaplinsky and S. Chishti, *op. cit.*

26.   The Development Center has recently undertaken research on international subcontracting and the strengthening of the technological absorptive capacity of the developing countries.

This selection is reprinted from Dmitri Germidis, ed., *Transfer of Technology by Multinational Corporations*, Vol. I. Paris: Development Center of the Organization for Economic Cooperation and Development, 1977, pp. 17-30. Reprinted by permission.

PART 3
IMPACT ON CONSUMPTION PATTERNS AND VALUES

Editorial Note

The three articles in this section examine the impact of TNEs on consumption patterns and values in the host developing nations. Michael B. Bader in the tenth chapter discusses the role of TNEs in the promotion of bottle feeding in developing nations and its consequences for the health and mortality of the affected children. According to him, faced with the declining birth rates in industrialized nations, TNEs which produce baby foods have been exploring new markets for their products. For this purpose they have undertaken all kinds of promotional activities in developing countries ranging from widespread advertising to personal visits by nurses to the mothers of the newly born. Bader shows that their efforts have not been in vain and an increasing number of mothers, especially in urban areas, are resorting to bottle feeding their children. However, because of their low levels of income, they over-dilute the baby food with the result that the child does not get proper nutrition. Moreover, the baby food often becomes infectious in the absence of refrigeration facilities. Therefore Bader argues that the activities of these TNEs are posing a serious threat to children in developing nations. He cites many studies which indicate that bottle feeding has been responsible for various diseases and even death in Latin America. The author sees the popularization of bottle feeding as yet another illustration of the changes in general consumption patterns which TNEs have been inducing to maximize their profits.

Karl P. Sauvant and Bernard Mennis in the next chapter examine the sociocultural effects of TNEs in the context of North-South relations. They conceptualize TNEs as "transmission belts"

248

through which sociocultural preferences and
attributes of their home countries are transmitted
to the host nations. Their primary focus is on
what they call "business culture" which consists of
a set of attitudes, values, and behavior patterns,
forms and patterns of corporate organization,
production processes, and consumption patterns. The
authors believe that the business culture diffused
by TNEs provides ideological justifications for
the economic domination of developing nations by
the industrialized ones. Therefore they suggest
that the economic emancipation of the South is not
possible without its emancipation from "inappropriate sociocultural patterns" imported from the
North through the instrumentality of TNEs.

Evelina Dagnino further elaborates the theme
of cultural dependence of developing countries,
which has been raised in the two preceding
articles. She suggests that the cultural dependence
of Latin American nations is not the outcome of a
deliberate, planned cultural invasion by a single
country. Instead, it is the product of a complex,
international capitalistic system led by TNEs,
whose center is located in the United States but
which is engulfing the entire world. This system
views the world as a world of commodities to be
sold and bought and is producing cultural produc-
tions which provide its own ideological justification. Dagnino believes that because of this
capitalistic system, the elites of Latin America
have learned to define development in terms of
capitalistic criteria rather than with reference to
those standards which are rooted in their own
cultural systems. And this explains to her the
role which they are playing in the perpetuation of
the present international system dominated by
TNEs.

10
Breast-Feeding: The Role of Multinational Corporations in Latin America

Michael B. Bader

Threatened by declining birthrates in the developed countries, multinational corporations look to the creation of infant formula markets in the developing countries to sustain long-term corporate profitability. Literally millions of infants in the developing countries are the unwitting victims of this myopic mentality, what pediatric nutritionist Derrick B. Jelliffe calls "commerciogenic malnutrition." This paper explores the complex matrix of factors related to the decline in breast-feeding in Latin America. Specifically, we review studies concerning the statistical decline in breast-feeding and the associated immunological, contraceptive, and economic costs. A case study of bottle-feeding and infant mortality in rural Chile is presented. Next, the question of cultural imperialism and dependency is addressed. Multinational corporate advertising tactics and current regulation attempts are covered in separate sections. Finally, some suggestions are made concerning public policy to ameliorate this problem, including a considera-tion of the capacity of nation-states to intervene in marketing channels.

THE DECLINE IN BREAST-FEEDING

Breast-feeding has declined precipitously in the developing countries during the last 30 years (Table 10.1). For example, 26 years ago, 95 percent of Chilean mothers breast-fed their children beyond the first year; by 1968, only 6 percent did so, and only 20 percent of the babies were being nursed for as long as two months. In

Singapore between 1951 and 1960 there was a
decrease from 79 to 42 percent of children in
low-income families who were breast-fed for at
least three months; by 1971 only 4 percent of the
babies were still nursed at age three months. In
the Philippines, 30 percent fewer mothers nursed
their babies for twelve months in 1968 than a
decade earlier. That manufactured milk formula
was substituted for human milk is evidenced in
the case of Colombia, where, as breast-feeding of
babies declined, milk imports increased rapidly;
in 1968, milk imports were seven times greater than
the 1964-1967 average.[1]

In most low-income countries, the abandonment
of breast-feeding is primarily an urban phenomenon,
often not so much because urban mothers work as
because bottle-feeding is one of the sophistica-
tions of city life which the urban migrant
adopts. In Guatemala, 98 percent of rural Indian
babies continue to be nursed after their first
birthday, compared with 57 percent of urban
children.[2] Yet, the efficacy of advertising
campaigns for Western-style goods means that urban

TABLE 10.1
Extent of Breast-Feeding in
Selected Countries and Years, 1946-1971[a]

Country	Year	Babies Breast-Fed %
Chile	1960	95
(at age 13 months)	1968	6
Mexico (at 6 months)	1960	98
	1966	41
Philippines	1958	64
(at 12 months)	1968	45
Singapore	1951	79
(at 3 months)[b]	1971	4
United States	1946	40
(on leaving hospital)	1966	18

[a]This table is adapted from a chart contained in
A. Berg, *The Nutrition Factor*, Brookings Institution, Washington, D. C., 1973. p. 91.
[b]Low socioeconomic class only.

habits and life-styles have an increased influence on rural societies. In rural Mexico, the decline in breast-feeding is already being felt; between 1960 and 1966 the percentage of babies under six months of age who were fed only breast milk in one rural Mexican community declined from 95 to 73.[3] The concentration of the loss of breast-feeding in urban environments is especially alarming because cities in developing countries are under-going mammoth growth. The urban populations in Venezuela and Mexico, for example, were projected to increase from 47.2 to 65.3 percent and 24.3 to 39.1 percent, respectively, of the total population between 1965 and 1975. This pattern is mirrored throughout Latin America and other parts of the developing world.

What are the causes of the dramatic decline in breast-feeding? Breast-feeding is often viewed as an old-fashioned or backward custom and, by some, as a vulgar peasant practice. Indeed, anthropologists, struck by the relationship of artificial feeding to societal change, have used the duration of nursing as an inverse measure of acculturation for some countries. In most developing countries, the bottle has become a conspicuous status symbol.

Failure of lactation is one of the responses to the stress of modernization. Among the tensions in a changing environment is the mother's anxiety about her capacity to breast-feed. Her failure to initiate or continue breast-feeding is rarely traced to a physical cause but often to psycho-physiological causes that interfere with the key "let-down reflex" which allows the milk to flow. As a study on lactation concludes: "Social and cultural factors and their psychological and emotional accompaniments were far more important determinants of lactation performance than dietary and nutritional factors."[4]

Changing social attitudes regarding the body reinforce the trend. In the United States, the breast has been gradually transmogrified from its nutritional role into a cosmetic and sexual symbol, and some women fear unjustifiably that breast-feeding will ruin the shape of their breasts. Nursing in public, a common sight a decade ago in most parts of the developing world, is rapidly disappearing, as the modesty accompanying changes in attitude grows. In an effort to reverse this dangerous trend, the Zambian government has issued an advertisement proclaiming that "Breast-Feeding

Is Best for Baby," in which a mother in traditional dress nurses her child.[5]

Convenience also is a factor in the abandonment of breast-feeding. To free themselves from the constraints of motherhood, women no longer bound by tradition have turned to artificial feeding. Although this is especially true for those who wish to join the organized work force, working mothers comprise only a small portion of those women who have forsaken breast-feeding. In Latin American countries, less than a fourth of women of child-bearing age hold jobs,[6] and in one study, conducted in an *urban* area, only 8 percent of the mothers worked outside the home.[7]

The health establishment has also encouraged the wholesale defections from breast-feeding. Large quantities of dried skim milk, a copious by-product of the butter industry, have been made available in developing countries under the "Food for Peace" and other international and state institutional feeding programs.[8] Medical advice from uninformed or Western-trained doctors and nurses, the provision of supplemental infant foods to new mothers at maternity clinics, and unregulated access to wall space for pro-bottle-feeding posters in clinics, have all exacerbated the problem. Furthermore, health personnel casually distribute free literature printed by infant food companies, literature whose bias is obvious.[9]

The most powerful agents of infant formula promotion are the multinational corporations whose profit statements reflect this trend. Aggressive sales promotion tactics persuade the new mother to change traditional infant feeding practices. In the West Indies, competitive representatives of baby food manufacturers visit the homes of new mothers and give free product samples.[10] And in Nigeria, women from commercial firms make the rounds of maternity clinics, distributing free samples, while doctors are given supplies for their own children.[11] Other methods, such as funding research aimed at establishing scientific acceptance or endorsement of various products, and the sponsoring of pediatric conferences, are usefully employed.[12] Finally, widespread advertising in professional journals, public newspapers, radio, and billboards has spurred sales growth. The multiplicity of promotional techniques has sparked Derrick Jelliffe to write:

> The pediatric nutritionist...is left
> increasingly frustrated by the well financed,
> steam roller, marketing techniques of the food
> industry to sell totally unaffordable and
> inappropriate infant foods in impoverished
> communities, while mouthing sanctimonious
> platitudes about their world role in
> improving child nutrition.[13]

Clearly, attempts to reverse this trend will
require attention to each of the promotional
approaches detailed above.

"IT'S NOT NICE TO FOOL MOTHER NATURE"

In the words of Oliver Wendell Holmes, "the
breasts were more skillful at compounding a
feeding mixture than the hemispheres of the most
learned professor's brain."[14] Holmes' analysis is
corroborated by a host of nutritional studies
conducted in recent years; these studies uniformly
conclude that mother's milk is in many ways the
perfect food for the infant. The most exhaustive
review of the scientific literature on breast-
feeding was conducted by Derrick B. and
E. F. Patrice Jelliffe of the University of
California at Los Angeles School of Public Health.[15]
The Jelliffes summarize studies on the biochemical
and immunological properties of breast milk as
well as the psychological and economic costs of the
trend away from breast-feeding.

Perhaps the most useful contribution of human
milk to the infant's long term health is in the
conferring of immunological defenses upon the
child. Not only is the bacteria level in breast
milk low, especially as compared to the bacteria
level in milk delivered from an unsterilized
formula bottle, but human milk has inherent anti-
infective properties as well. Immunoglobulins
transferred to the child through the colostrum, or
first few days of mother's milk, provide immunity
to certain infectious diseases and help create an
intestinal environment inimical to the growth of
undesirable pathogenic organisms. The "bifidus
factor" in human milk allows additional
protection against diarrheal disease by inhibiting
the growth of *Escherichia coli* bacteria.

To the extent that reliance on infant formula

based on cow's milk reduces the infant's ability to
fend off bacterial infection and facilitates the
development of diarrheal disease, it contributes
to high rates of infant mortality in the developing
countries. The results of a 1957-1960 study in
rural Punjab, India, showed that "at any age when
comparisons can be made, case rates for diarrheal
disease were lowest among children taking only
breast milk and highest for those with the more
complex diet of breast milk, other milk, and solid
foods."[16] Diarrhea occurred ten times more
frequently in a group of non-breast-fed Mexican
children than in a group of breast-fed children.[17]
Moreover, in the years 1950-1953, the Pan American
Sanitary Bureau found acute diarrheal disease to
be the leading cause of death in eight of seventeen
Latin American countries.[18] (This figure includes
older children and adults as well as infants.) The
compilation of data from this and other studies
led the World Health Organization to assert in
1964: "In large parts of the world deaths from
diarrheal disease in the general population
outnumber those from any other cause."[19]

Since diarrhea results in reduced absorption
of nutrients from food, it is commonly associated
with infant malnutrition. In 1963, J. E. Gordon
noted of his experiences in rural Guatemala: "An
episode of acute diarrheal disease commonly precedes
kwashiorkor by about four or six weeks."[20] It has
been estimated that there are ten to twenty million
young children with severe syndromes of kwashiorkor
at any one time.[21] And it has been amply documented
that malnutrition itself is a leading cause of
death in developing countries. The inter-
American investigation of mortality in childhood
showed that in deaths of 35,000 children under
five years of age in ten Latin American countries,
57 percent had malnutrition as either the underlying or associated cause of death.[22] In addition,
malnutrition and infectious disease have been
shown to have a synergistic relationship.

The protective functions of human milk are,
of course, of even greater importance in the
developing countries, where in many cases the
community is impoverished and where there are low
educational levels, highly contaminated environments, and insufficient culinary equipment for the
sanitary preparation and storage of food. To
prepare bottle formula requires a potable water
supply, unpolluted by sewage; in Latin American

countries, however, expenditures on water and sewerage are woefully inadequate.

In terms of national development, the most meaningful attribute of unimpaired and unsupplemented breast-feeding is its definite contraceptive effect. If, in the first four to six months the infant receives only human milk, the sucking stimulus appears to inhibit ovulation in the mother. In the lactating mother, menstruation and ovulation are delayed from ten weeks to as long as twenty-six months. In Taiwan it was estimated that lactation prevented as many as 20 percent of the births that would have occurred otherwise. In India the same ratio would mean prevention of approximately 810,000 births each year.[23] Jelliffe and Jelliffe conclude: "On a worldwide basis, lactation contraception probably has a numerically greater rate of protection from pregnancy than has currently been achieved by technological devices."[24]

Another consideration is the economic significance of declining breast-feeding, which has an impact at both the family and national levels. To purchase an adequate quantity of formula is impossible for the vast majority of families in the developing countries, as it requires one-quarter to one-third of a worker's income.[25] As a result the family often purchases too little of the milk formula, and overdilutes the mixture in the bottle. Since each feeding is too low in its content of calories and nutrients, the result is a slow but inevitable development of nutritional marasmus,[26] which demands prolonged, expensive treatment. Indeed, medical costs are usually ten times greater for bottle-fed babies than for those who are breast-fed.[27]

On the national level, the costs for individual families translate into enormous expenditures. For example, the recorded decline in breast-feeding in the Philippines in 1968 alone required the approximate expenditure of the equivalent of $33 million by families or agencies. And in Kenya, it was estimated that the $11.5 million loss in breast milk was equivalent to two-thirds of the health budget, or one-fifth the yearly economic aid.[28] In Tanzania, the value of human milk in terms of foreign exchange has been estimated at $22 million per year if substituted with powdered cow's milk or milk formula. This sum is considerably larger than the total budget

of the Ministry of Health in that year.[29]
Nutritionist Alan Berg totals the bill for bottle-
feeding on the international level with these
startling calculations:

> An estimated 87 percent of the world's babies
> are born in the developing countries, about a
> quarter of them in urban areas. If 20
> percent of the estimated 27 million mothers
> in urban areas do not breast-feed, the loss
> in breast milk is $365 million. If half of
> the other 80 percent do not continue to
> breast-feed after the first six months, the
> total loss reaches $780 million. These
> estimates, however, clearly understate the
> situation; losses to developing countries are
> more likely in the billions.[30]

Additionally, in a world of scarce energy and raw
materials, the costs in processing, distributing,
preparing, and refrigerating cow's milk formula
must be considered. In the United States alone,
70,000 tons of tinplate each year are consumed
in the canning of infant formula.[31]
     Because of its immunological, contraceptive,
and economic significance, human milk must be
considered as a resource priority in international
planning for health, food production, and family
planning. We turn now to the concrete example of
bottle-feeding and infant mortality in rural Chile.

BOTTLE-FEEDING AND INFANT MORTALITY IN CHILE

     One of the most carefully documented studies
of infant feeding and infant mortality in Latin
America was conducted by Plank and Milanesi of the
Harvard School of Public Health in rural Chile in
1960-1970.[32] Ninety-six percent of the women
between 15 and 44 years of age in fifteen rural
Chilean communities were interviewed in their
homes, comprising a sample size of 1712 women.
     Even though only 2 percent of the women were
not in favor of breast-feeding and more than two-
thirds felt it should be continued for at least
a year, in practice only 25 percent of the mothers
fed their children exclusively on breast milk by
the third month, and only 40 percent of the
children who had reached the age of one year were
receiving any breast milk at all by then. Employment of the mother, often cited as an important

reason for discontinuing breast-feeding, was an insignificant factor in the communities studied. Of the 17 percent who were gainfully employed, fewer than half worked outside the home, and less than 1 percent claimed that their jobs kept them from breast-feeding.

Infant feeding patterns in the population were largely determined by psychosocial factors, since breast-feeding decreased significantly as maternal education and paternal income rose. The least educated, poorest group (maternal education less than three years, paternal income less than 300 escudos) bottle-fed before age six months in only 35.5 percent of the cases; conversely, the most educated, wealthiest group (maternal education greater than six years, paternal income greater than 500 escudos) bottle-fed in 70.4 percent of the cases, almost twice the frequency of the former group.

Of the children being bottle-fed or partially bottle-fed, 66 percent received partially defatted dried milk regularly under the Chilean National Health Service's distribution program. It is important to note the complicity of the government health agency here, as other studies have shown that the availability of free milk substitutes is correlated with a decline in nursing.

The results of the study are remarkable. Post-neonatal deaths (i.e. deaths occurring after the first month of life) were three times more frequent among those who started bottle-feeding in the first three months than among those exclusively breast-fed during that time. Although the investigation did not draw specific correlations between qualitative and quantitative deficiencies associated with bottle-feeding, an investigation carried out by Mönckeberg in rural Chile found bacteriological contamination in 80 percent of bottles used for feeding babies.[33] Moreover, since bottle-fed children literally lack the intestinal fortitude to fend off bacterial attack, the Chilean study underscores the fact that bottle-feeding often leads to death as a result of diarrheal disease and malnutrition.

Paradoxically, higher income levels were associated with higher mortality rates in the Chilean study. The additional disposable income of these groups was apparently used to purchase milk formula, as higher-income groups tended to begin bottle-feeding at an earlier age. The proportion of infants receiving bottles but no additional foods at six months rose from 34 to 44 percent as income increased; this was paralleled by a rise in infant mortality from 42 to 54 per 1000 infants.

Another anomaly is that sanitary conditions--presumably because of their association with income and education--were better in the homes where infant deaths occurred. There were 48.1 post-neonatal deaths per 1000 infants in houses with running water (17 percent of the total) as compared with 32.3 in those without it; the rate was 36.0 in houses with some sort of sewage system (83 percent of the total) as compared with 30.0 in those that had none. The families affected lived in less overcrowded conditions than others, with fewer members per room and per bed, and their homes were more likely to be supplied with electricity.

Health personnel share directly in the responsibility for alarming infant mortality rates in Chile. The risk of postneonatal death was higher if mothers had visited a private physician or prenatal clinic during pregnancy than if they had professional care only at delivery or not at all: 37.5 as compared with 27.3 per 1000 infants. Ironically, the more contact a mother had with health establishments, the greater was the risk to her child's life. We may assume that this fact is in part explained by the distribution and promotion of infant formula by health personnel at the clinics.

This catalog of paradoxes is summarized by Plank and Milanesi in their concluding statement:

> The inverse relationships of the infant mortality rates to family income, environmental factors, and medical care reinforce the conclusion that the differential mortality observed was attributable to bottle feeding and neglect of supplementary foods.[34]

The Chilean case demonstrates that higher standards of living (as defined in conventional economic terms) are not necessarily associated with a better quality of life for individuals and families in developing countries. Next, we consider briefly the question of imperialism--political, economic, and cultural--as a background to multinational corporations' advertising practices in the infant formula industry.

THE "COCA-COLONIZATION" OF THE WORLD

In the midst of Lenin's classic work, *Imperialism, the Highest Stage of Capitalism*, lies a quotation from Cecil Rhodes, millionaire founder of the British colony of Rhodesia:

> ...We colonial statesmen must acquire new lands to settle the surplus population, to provide new markets for the goods produced by them in the factories and mines.

In Lenin's view, Rhodes was merely articulating an endemic feature of capitalism: the tendency to seek out new markets abroad in the face of declining profits at home.

The underconsumption hypothesis which underlies much of the modern analysis of imperialism, was first developed by Simonde de Sismondi, a Swiss historian, and later elaborated by Rodbertus. The basic argument was really quite uncomplicated: highly developed capitalist economies simply tended to produce more than they could consume. The solution to this problem seemed to lie in expanded foreign investment opportunities overseas, where new markets could take up the slack in consumption in the capitalist nations.

Although Karl Marx himself never developed a formal economic theory of imperialism, Marx's disciples, John Hobson and Rosa Luxemburg, did. These theories are critically examined by Benjamin J. Cohen in a recent work.[35] Cohen offers the following operational definition of imperialism: "Imperialism refers to those particular relationships between inherently unequal nations which involve effective subjugation and the actual exercise of influence over behavior."[36] Cohen examines the formation of patterns of tastes in the subjugated countries, as evidenced by the distribution of the public's total expenditure of income. This distribution of expenditures, according to Marxist and radical writers, does not reflect tastes which have been autonomously determined by their citizens and government, but rather reflects the configuration of ideals and values, styles and fashions, generally associated with the system of global capitalism.

Trade transmits the configuration through what is usually called the "demonstration effect": many people in poor countries (and often those that

can least afford it) attempt to emulate the
consumption patterns of rich nations about which
they are informed by the media. Tastes are
gradually oriented away from home-grown products
toward characteristically foreign types of goods.
Multinational corporations producing these goods
have an incentive to widen and consolidate the
market via investment in merchandising facilities
and sales promotion. Their aim is to facilitate
the spread of a preference for their output
throughout the whole of the local economy.

In the opinion of Marxists and radicals,
this practice is cultural imperialism, or the
destruction of local autonomy; it is often called
the "coca-colonization" of the world. The
distortion of consumer desires by multinational
corporations has a retarding effect on economic
development since it represents a misallocation
of scarce monetary resources from the standpoint
of the welfare of the community at large. These
concerns are echoed by Theotonio Dos Santos:
"The result of dependency is to limit the development of [the dependent nation's] internal market
and their technical and cultural capacity, as
well as the moral and physical health of their
people."[37] Furthermore, since high-income groups
initiate the consumption of infant formula in the
dependent countries, and lower-income groups
attempt to emulate their values, an internal
pattern of cultural imperialism develops. We
turn now to a comprehensive examination of the means
and motives of multinational advertising campaigns
to promote bottle-feeding.

THE PROMOTION OF BOTTLE-FEEDING BY MULTINATIONAL CORPORATIONS

United States infant milk companies, like
their big brothers, the adult food manufacturers,
have gone looking for business in developing
countries because of disappointing population
trends at home. The annual population growth
rate in the wealthiest countries of the world is
less than one-half the rate in the remainder of
the world (Table 10.2).

The low population growth in the 1960s has
limited the sales growth of food processing
companies in general. In fact, a business survey
published in 1973 stated that U.S. food processing
companies had reported the lowest annual rate of

estic sales growth (5 percent) of any industry in the survey. And a 1973 article in *Business Week* explained that food processers, "starving for profits," are looking both at overseas markets and at nonfood products and services at home, seeking "renewed opportunities for profitable business."[38]

Baby-related industries have been even harder hit by population trends in the United States, for although the population is still growing--albeit at a slower rate--the birthrate itself is in a substantial decline. From a 1957 peak of more than 4.3 million births, the annual number of births had declined in 1974 to about 3.1 million. The 1973 birthrate in the United States was the lowest in American history, a fact reflected in business publication headlines such as "The Baby Bust," and "Bad News in Babyland." The decline in the U.S. birthrate--what *Dun's Review* called "too few mouths to feed"--appears to varying degrees throughout the affluent world.[39]

Searching for opportunities to increase profits, then, some baby food companies have

TABLE 10.2
Gross national product, per capita gross national product, and population: 1970 levels and 1960-1970 annual growth rates[a]

Area	Per Capita GNP, 1970	Total GNP, 1970	Per Capita GNP Annual Growth Rate, 1960-1970	GNP Annual Growth Rate, 1960-1970	Popu-lation, 1970	Population Annual Growth Rate, 1960-1970
	$	$ bil	%	%	mil	%
Rich countries	2,790	2,570	4.4	5.5	920	1.1
Middle-income countries	870	270	4.5	6.5	310	2.0
Poor countries	300	155	3.2	6.0	520	2.8
Very poor countries	120	230	1.8	4.0	1,930	2.2
World	880	3,225	4.1	6.1	3,680	2.0

[a]Source, Richard Jolly, "International dimensions," in Hollis Chenery et al., *Redistribution with Growth*, p. 160, Oxford University Press for World Bank and Institute of Development Studies, University of Sussex, 1974.

diversified into new lines. Others, including the milk companies, have tried to expand markets for their traditional products in those areas of the world where population is still increasing: the Third World countries.

Abbott Laboratories, the pharmaceutical multinational whose Ross Laboratories division manufactures Similac and Isomil formulas for infant feeding, is expanding rapidly overseas, with the pediatric market a major focus. The overseas portion of Abbott's pediatric sales (including formula products and drugs) rose from 14.3 percent in 1969 (overseas pediatric sales of $12.5 million) to 22.2 percent in 1973($31.3 million). From 1972 to 1973, Ross expanded domestic sales for the fomula products it markets by 9 percent but foreign sales by 32 percent. In Abbott's 1973 annual report, marketing plans for the company's international division were confirmed: "In essence, our strategy for 1974 remains unchanged: maintain consistent growth in the pharmaceutical area, but exert major thrust at the newer, more dynamic hospital and pediatric markets."[40] This strategy appears to have been successful: pediatric sales were up 17 percent in 1974, with sales of two infant formula products up 38 percent. Latin American sales comprised 28 percent of total sales for Abbott in 1974.[41]

Bristol-Myers, whose Mead Johnson division manufactures Enfamil, Olac, and Prosobee, includes among its problems over the last five years "the sudden decline in the birthrate which affected Enfamil and other pediatric products." Bristol-Myers' international division, with sales up from just over $100 million in 1968 to $400 million in 1974, is the fastest-growing part of the company.[42] Infant formula constitutes an important segment of the division, according to the 1973 annual report, particularly in Latin America. Indeed, about 40 percent of the total sales of Enfamil is outside the United States. International sales grew 12-18 percent per year during the last decade, compared with 7 percent for domestic. Advertising and product promotion expenses in 1974 totaled $296 million.[43]

It is significant to note that Abbott and Bristol-Myers allegedly control 90 percent of the infant formula market, which constitutes a virtual monopoly. In December 1974, *Baker Laboratories* (subsidiary: Baker/Beech-Nut Corporation) went out of the infant formula business. On March 13, 1975,

Baker brought suit in federal court in Philadelphia against Abbott and Bristol-Myers, charging that they monopolized the infant formula market, and seeking treble damages and a halt to alleged unfair competition.[44] *Advertising Age*, March 1975, summarized additional allegations contained in the suit:

> Baker has charged the two companies with paying cash grants to hospitals as well as supplying free infant formula in return for the hospital staff feeding newborns these brands and recommending that mothers continue using them at home. The suit also notes that the hospitals distribute promotional literature.[45]

Another multinational involved in the infant formula business is *Nestle*, the world's second largest food company (the first is the Netherland's Unilever). While only 12 percent of its assets are located in developing countries, they account for 20 percent of its sales. Sales in Latin America, where Nestle began operating in 1920, comprise 35 percent of the total. Brazil, Mexico, and Nicaragua have requested Nestle to increase its activities there, especially with respect to the development of local dairying. Nestle's annual report for 1971 underscored the importance of sales in the developing countries: "In the developing countries, demographic growth, the rising standard of living and, generally, the endeavors to promote infant nutrition, offer good prospects for our products."[46] But Nestle has not gone without virulent criticism. Switzerland's "Third World Group" published a pamphlet delicately titled "Nestle Kills Babies," in June 1974. The following month, Nestle brought suit against the group for libel, and court proceedings were expected to ensue. The group intends to defend itself by establishing a clear cause-and-effect chain from bottle-feeding in poor countries to malnutrition and death, and by showing that Nestle's advertising has played a significant role in the switch to the bottle.[47]

ADVERTISING THROUGH THE MEDIA AND HEALTH PERSONNEL

The first noteworthy study of the role of the advertising and health professions in the

promotion of bottle-feeding was completed in 1975
by Ted Greiner. Greiner studied the distribution
of infant formula advertisements in public and
professional journals and magazines, and the
multinational firms' efforts to employ health
professionals directly in their sales campaigns.
    Greiner's statistics controvert the claim
the infant food companies that they direct
advertising toward more affluent audiences. He
writes: "There appears to be a tendency to
advertise selectively in low income publications.
This should come as no surprise, since advertising
funds are targeted toward maximum efficiency."[48]
In addition, broad-based media, such as radio,
outdoor displays, general publications, and recently
even television, are relied upon. Efforts at
reaching target groups (mothers) are confined to
promotion through clinics and hospitals, retail
outlets, and home visitations using hospital-
provided lists of new mothers.
    The advertisements themselves are misleading.
Many stress that infant formula are "ideal
substitutes for mother's milk," an assertion that
is directly contradicted by evidence concerning
breast milk's unique immunological properties.
Nestle even maintains that Pelargon provides
"extra-protection" and a "reduction in bottle-
borne infections caused by poor hygiene."[49] We
should recall, however, that 80 percent of the
bottles used for infant feeding in the Chilean
example were contaminated with bacteria.
    Mothers who are unsure if and when to bottle-
feed are encouraged by Similac advertisements to
use it "right on the first day," despite careful
scientific studies testifying to the initial
importance of mother's milk because of its special
immunological characteristics.[50] Finally, many
imported infant foods stress their origin from a
developed country, showing that the charge of
cultural imperialism has some justification.
    Advertising specifically directed toward
health professionals is particularly useful to
multinational firms, since 73 percent of physicians
find journal papers and articles "preferred sources
of information."[51] Surprisingly, this is reported
to be true of medical journal advertisements as
well. Greiner found that journals published in
developing countries contain "a higher number of
infant food ads per issue than journals of
comparable date and area of specialty from
developed countries."[52]

Free literature on infant care and feeding, distributed by pediatricians to new mothers as part of their child care services, is notorious for its biases. In a "content analysis" of twenty-two infant food publications, Greiner reports that "most receive uniformly low ratings with respect to both space given to and statements made about breast-feeding."[53] Ross Laboratories' free infant care and feeding literature, "Breast-Feeding Your Baby" makes twice as many negative statements as positive statements about breast-feeding, and devotes no fewer than one-third of its pages to promoting its formula.[54]

Two other aspects of health institutions are exploited to promote infant formula: milk nurses and milk banks. A study of the use of these "milk nurses" in Jamaica in 1974 detailed their questionable practices.[55] Fully trained nurses who also undergo training by the infant food companies are employed to visit all the new mothers whose names are given by area hospitals. The mothers visited often do not have adequate income to feed their children artificially, but, in general, milk nurses do not tell mothers about the costs involved in artificial feeding. The Jamaica Milk Products Nurse, who sells Nestle products, is allowed to enter maternity wards in public hospitals in order to talk to mothers directly. Other nurses make home visits and home deliveries, sometimes on a commission basis. Although they are supposed to give mothers moral support and child care information, the study revealed that "most mothers felt that the nurses had offered very little information unrelated to the company's products."[56]

Milk banks are sales outlets for commercial formula products set up in hospitals and clinics that serve the poor. The banks sell infant milk (sometimes imported tax-free) at discount prices to mothers of limited economic resources.[57] From information collected in 1974 on milk bank operations in Guatemala City and Santo Domingo, the banks seemed to be a marketing device-- generally introduced by the Swiss firm Nestle-- aimed at expanding the practice of artificial feeding among the poor without interfering with the normal commercial market.

Even at discount prices, however, commercial substitutes for breast milk are too expensive for the people the milk banks are designed to reach. At Robert Reid Cabral Hospital in Santo Domingo,

Nestle's Pelargon sells in a one-pound tin for
90 cents, a 40 percent discount off the retail
price. But very few mothers who go to the bank
purchase enough formula each month to feed an
infant adequately. Fifty mothers at this bank
were asked if they could affort to buy a tin of
formula every few days (the maximum feeding
duration for a one-pound tin); the most common
response was that they simply did not buy it
that frequently, that instead they "prepared the
bottles with less milk and more water and in
this way the milk lasted longer."[58] Of course,
habitual dilution of the formula causes chronic
malnutrition of the infant.

These sad facts make the nutritional firms
no less candid about their promotional tactics.
Abbott Labs' annual report for 1967 proudly
proclaims: "Not only quality of product, but
skillful promotion to pediatricians, general
practitioners, and hospitals have enabled
Similac to hold its market leadership."[59]
Briston-Myers' annual report for 1973 states:
"Mead Johnson [subsidiary of Bristol-Myers] is
frequently introduced to new parents by their
doctor or in the hospital with the Enfamil
Discharge-Pack."[60] *Business Abroad*, June 1970,
summarizes Nestle's marketing coups:

> In less developed countries, the best form
> of promoting baby food formulas may well be
> in clinics which the company sponsors, at
> which nurses and doctors in its employ
> offer child-care guidance service. One
> fruitful by-product of this operation is
> that at christenings and birthday parties
> Nestle products often are given as presents.[61]

Clearly, the multinational corporations have
sufficiently wooed the health profession to
implicate them in their promotional schemes. We
move now to an examination of current efforts to
monitor and control multinational advertising
practices in the infant formula industry.

EFFORTS TO REGULATE ADVERTISING OF BOTTLE-FEEDING

Two groups have been most active in
inveighing against the practices of multinational
infant food corporations. The Interfaith Center
on Corporate Responsibility (ICCR), a "sponsored

related movement of the National Council of
Churches," has encouraged stockholders' inquiries
into the marketing vehicles of Abbott Laboratories
and the Bristol-Myers Company. The Protein
Advisory Group (PAG) of the United Nations
System has been instrumental in drafting industry
codes of marketing ethics and publishing studies
related to the breast versus bottle controversy.

Bristol-Myers has responded to ICCR's charges
in a twenty-page report that, in the opinion
of this writer, is misleading, distorted, and self-
indicting. The report cleverly employs a PAG
classification scheme that places fifty countries
in twelve general development levels. Bristol-
Myers purposefully regroups these development
levels to buttress its claim that "over three-
fourths of Enfamil sales come from the more
'developed' countries."[62] Yet, a careful analysis
of the Bristol-Myers report reveals that those
countries which the corporation considers
"developed" include over 71 percent of the
population of Latin America, an area of the world
that is almost invariably regarded as part of the
"developing" world.[63] Such semantic manipulations
seriously undermine the credibility of Bristol-
Myers' defense of its practices.

The report then takes up the specific points
of information raised by stockholders. To the
question of what kinds of promotional programs are
employed, the report answers:

> Pediatricians and other medical professionals
> are the primary audience for technical
> promotional literature. The Company believes
> the physician--not the producer of infant
> formula products--should advise the mother
> about her infant's feeding and health care.[64]

Yet, in light of Greiner's study showing the
complicity of health personnel in infant formula
promotion, Bristol-Myers' response is at best
self-indicting. Also, with respect to the
labelling and the hygienic preparation of infant
formula, Bristol-Myers commments:

> Mead Johnson formula products throughout the
> world are labelled in accord with U.S. Food
> and Drug Administration labelling regulations
> for such products....The label of each infant
> formula product contains complete and
> explicit directions for the correct

storage, preparation, and use of this
product.65

In no way, however, does this comment deal with
the fact that in large parts of the developing
world, the "correct" storage and preparation
facilities (e.g., refrigerators and stoves)
simply do not exist, and large numbers of mothers
cannot even read these labels.

Finally, the company asserts that infant
formula products are not marketed to marginal-
income or illiterate families. Unfortunately,
Bristol-Myers neglects to provide statistical
proof of this assertion; they merely conjecture:

> In each country, regardless of the overall
> level of development, one segment of the
> population has sufficient affluence to seek
> medical services and to demand and pay for
> top quality products. It is believed that
> this segment accounts for essentially all
> Enfamil sales in the "developing" countries.66

In sum, the report smacks of the worst forms of
multinational corporate sophistry.

The United Nations Protein Advisory Group
has assumed leadership in the incipient
dialogue between multinationals and stockholders'
groups for which ICCR provides investigative
support. In 1972 and 1973, PAG held two international seminars for pediatricians and senior
representatives of the infant food industry. These
meetings led to the issuance of PAG Statement
No. 23, "Promotion of special foods (infant
formula and processed protein foods) for
vulnerable groups."67 One of the recommendations
made in the seminars was that PAG should
collaborate with industry, the medical and health
professions, and national governments to establish
regional industry councils that would assess and
act on problems related to inappropriate infant
and young child feeding practices. The first of
these seminars was held in Singapore in November
1974, and generated a number of useful
recommendations.

The recommendations included (a) clear
policy guidelines for feeding practices for young
infants, older infants, and young children; and
(b) general proposals to the medical and health
professions, industry, and government "for action
to promote desirable policies and practices."68

Moreover, the *PAG Bulletin* has faithfully
reproduced a host of studies relating to bottle-
feeding, malnutrition, and mortality rates, and
has significantly aided in the dissemination of
other relevant studies on nutrition.

One of the most interesting proposals
produced in response to these PAG efforts is the
"International Code of Marketing Ethics with
Reference to Infant Feeding," submitted by
Ross Laboratories. The code consists of guidelines
for ethical behavior that amount to a succinct
truth-in-advertising statement.[69] Although this
code could be dismissed as the work of wily public
relations men, it does seem to signal a heightened
awareness of the social responsibility of these
corporations in the face of alarming correlations
between bottle-feeding and infant mortality.

Unfortunately, PAG's efforts are weakened
by the voluntary nature of industrial participation.
Bristol-Myers, for example, is not participating
in the industry code.[70] And in the absence of any
legal jurisdiction to enforce these policy guidelines, PAG is effectively powerless to force
compliance. Moreover, can an industry so heavily
dependent on the growth of its markets in
developing countries honestly be expected to give
significant weight to a "code of ethics" in the
calculation of profits? It seems that we must
look elsewhere--to the power of individual or
associated nation-states for the capacity to
regulate the multinational infant food corporations.

PEOPLE BEFORE PROFITS--PUBLIC POLICY RECOMMENDATIONS

The decline in breast-feeding in Latin
America, in particular, and the developing countries
in general has been shown to be a trend whose
serious public health consequences mandate a
powerful state response. The urgency of the need
for strict regulation of marketing practices
of multinational infant formula corporations must
penetrate both the mass media and professional
journals in developing countries. Health personnel
training programs throughout the world should be
reoriented to emphasize the immunological and
nutritional value of breast-feeding. In addition,
the same advertising techniques that are responsible
for the increase in artificial feeding can be
used to counter the trend. Magazines and daytime
radio programs directed specifically to women

can serve as channels of information. Maternity
clinics can be staffed with specialists in infant
nutrition trained not by multinational corporations,
but by education centers established under the
auspices of the United Nations Protein Advisory
Group's regional councils.

Under existing international arrangements,
only the state has the legal jurisdiction and
political power to control product promotion
techniques. Each nation must first autonomously
determine which Western consumer goods--whether
they be automobiles, clothing, appliances, or
technology-intensive health products such as
pharmaceuticals and infant formula--are critical
to its national development plans, and then decide
which of these Western technologies should be
produced domestically, and which should be imported
and marketed under strict regulation.
Alfred C. Stepan has argued that direct foreign
investment for purposes of creating foreign
subsidiaries must be subject to a policy of
nonautomatic entry, with access to important
markets only selectively and conditionally granted
to multinational firms.[71] Since declining birthrates
in the industrialized countries make access to
markets in developing countries crucial to the
long-term profitability of infant formula concerns,
developing countries should be able to exact many
bargaining concessions from them. Among these
concessions is compliance with comprehensive
marketing codes drafted by local public health
officials and state planners. On the regional
level also, common market organizations such as
the Andean Pact must close existing loopholes with
respect to media access. Thus, the state can
employ a variety of bargaining maneuvers to
mitigate the harmful impact of multinational
corporations whose advertising efforts shape local
consumption patterns.

Stockholders' groups and "corporate
responsibility" centers should continue to press
industry for details concerning marketing practices,
and corporate responses to these inquiries should
be carefully scrutinized for misleading analysis
and obfuscatory statements. These groups may
work through existing legal structures throughout
the world to extend "truth in advertising"
precedents and to destroy monopolistic tendencies
of the food multinationals.

In the final analysis, however, what is needed
is the development of an awareness that human milk

is an invaluable natural resource uniquely
constituted by nature to protect and nourish the
infant. The health needs of the *people* in the
developing countries must be placed before the
cold requirement of healthy *profits* for the multinational infant formula corporations. The
"mother's milk" of politics may be money, but
money is immaterial when the health of human
beings is concerned.

Note Added in Proof--Since this article was written,
the Swiss court ruling on Nestle's charges of
libel against the Third World Working Group held
thirteen members of the Group liable for $130
each for damages. The Group plans to appeal this
verdict.

Acknowledgments--I would like to thank
Ann Crittenden, Leah Margulies, Ann L. Engelland,
and Eleanor M. LeCain for their invaluable
assistance in the preparation of this paper.

NOTES

1. A. Berg, *The Nutrition Factor*, pp. 89-106.
Brookings Institution, Washington, D. C., 1973.
2. *Ibid.*
3. *Ibid.*
4. *Ibid.*
5. N. Wade, Bottle feeding: Adverse effects
of a Western technology. *Science* 184:45-48,
1974.
6. *Ibid.*
7. F. Mönckeberg, Factors conditioning
malnutrition in Latin America, with special
reference to Chile. *Bibl. Nutr. Dieta* No. 14,
pp. 23-33, 1970.
8. Wade, *op. cit.*
9. T. Greiner, *The Promotion of Bottle
Feeding by Multinational Corporations: How
Advertising and the Health Professions Have
Contributed.* Cornell University International
Nutrition Monograph Series No. 2, Ithaca, New
York, 1975, p. 3.
10. Mönckeberg, *op. cit.*, p. 100.
11. C. A. M. Wennen-Van Der May, The decline
of breast feeding in Nigeria. *Trop. Geogr. Med.*
25:93-96, 1969.
12. Greiner, *op. cit.*, p. 33.

272

13. D. B. Jelliffe and E. F. P. Jelliffe, The urban avalanche and child nutrition. *J. Am. Diet. Assoc.* 57(8):111-118, 1970, p. 116.

14. Quoted by Berg, *op. cit.*

15. D. B. Jelliffe and E. F. P. Jelliffe, An overview. *Am. J. Clin. Nutr.* 24:1013-1024, August 1971.

16. J. E. Gordon, Weanling diarrhea. *Am. J. Med. Sci.* 245:345, 1963.

17. Mönckeberg, *op. cit.*

18. R. R. Puffer and C. V. Serrano, *Patterns of Mortality in Childhood.* Pan-American Health Organization, Washington, D. C., 1973.

19. Quoted in N. S. Scrimshaw, C. E. Taylor, and J. E. Gordon, *Interactions of Nutrition and Infection.* World Health Organization, Geneva, 1968, p. 217.

20. Gordon, *op. cit.*

21. D. B. Jelliffe and E. F. P. Jelliffe, Human milk, nutrition, and the world resource crisis. *Science* 188:557-561, May 9, 1975.

22. Puffer and Serrano, *op. cit.*

23. This figure assumes a population growth rate of 2.8 percent per annum. The data are taken from the Overseas Development Council, Washington, D. C., 1975, *The United States and World Development--Agenda for Action 1975*, (J. Howe, editor), p. 200.

24. Jelliffe and Jelliffe, Human milk, nutrition, and the world resource crisis, *op. cit.*

25. Scrimshaw *et al.*, *op. cit.*

26. Marasmus, the other main clinical form of protein-calorie malnutrition, usually occurs in the first year of life, and is characterized by wasting of muscle and subcutaneous fat and very low body weight (usually less than 60 percent of standard). It is almost always associated with diarrheal disease.

27. Berg, *op. cit.*

28. Wade, *op. cit.*

29. Greiner, *op. cit.*, p. ii.

30. Berg, *op. cit.*

31. Jelliffe and Jelliffe, Human milk, nutrition, and the world resource crisis, *op. cit.*

32. S. J. Plank and M. L. Milanesi, Infant feeding and infant mortality in rural Chile. *Bull. WHO* 48:203-210, 1973.

33. Mönckeberg, *op. cit.*

34. Plank and Milanesi, *op. cit.*

35. B. J. Cohen, *The Question of Imperialism.* Basic Books, Inc., New York, 1973.

273

36. *Ibid.*, p. 15.
37. T. Dos Santos, The structure of dependence. *American Economic Review* LX(2): 231-236, 1970.
38. Quoted in R. Ledogar, *Hungry for Profits*, pp. 127-145. IDOC, North America Publishers, New York, 1975, p. 128.
39. Quoted *Ibid.*
40. Quoted *Ibid.*
41. Greiner, *op. cit.*, p. 59.
42. Quoted in Ledogar, *op. cit.*, p. 129.
43. Greiner, *op. cit.*, p. 63.
44. *Ibid.*, p. 61.
45. Quoted in Greiner, p. 61.
46. *Ibid.*, pp. 71-72.
47. *Ibid.*, p. 72.
48. *Ibid.*, p. 6.
49. *Ibid.*, p. 10.
50. *Ibid.*, p. 7
51. *Ibid.*, p. 8
52. *Ibid.*, p. 9
53. *Ibid.*, p. 12.
54. *Ibid.*, p. 13.
55. Ledogar, *op. cit.*, pp. 137-138.
56. *Ibid.*, p. 138.
57. *Ibid.*
58. *Ibid.*, p. 139.
59. Greiner, *op. cit.*, p. 14.
60. *Ibid.*
61. Quoted in Greiner, *op. cit.*, p. 15.
62. The Infant Formula Marketing Practices of Bristol-Myers Company in Countries Outside the United States, pp. 12-17. Bristol-Myers Company, August 7, 1975 (mimeographed).
63. The following Latin American countries are grouped with the "developed" countries by the Bristol-Myers report: Mexico, Brazil, Paraguay, Peru, and Colombia. The total population of these countries (Overseas Development Council statistics, 1969) is 173.4 million, which is 71 percent of the total Latin American population of 244.5 million. The PAG classification scheme explicity calls the countries "developing countries."
64. Bristol-Myers Company Report, *op. cit.*
65. *Ibid.*
66. *Ibid.*
67. Protein Advisory Group of the United Nations System. *PAG Bull.* V(1):1-33, 1975, p. 1.
68. *Ibid.*, pp. 1-5.
69. *Ibid.*, pp. 23-25.

70. L. Margulies, Eco-justice task force, Interfaith Center on Corporate Responsibility. Letter to the author, p. 1, October 15, 1975.

71. A. C. Stepan, The state and foreign capital. In *The State and Society: Peru in Comparative Perspective*, Ch. 7. Princeton University Press, Princeton, N.J., 1977.

Manuscript originally submitted for publication, February 25, 1976.

11
Sociocultural Investments and the International Political Economy of North-South Relations: The Role of Transnational Enterprises

Karl P. Sauvant and Bernard Mennis

The current discussions about a new international information and communication order focus attention on an area that has hitherto remained largely ignored. But the problem is broader than these discussions lead one to believe. The issue is not only information and communication but rather the entire sociocultural dimension of development and north-south relations.

Increasingly it is being recognized that the sociocultural indifference curves of host countries are not only the result of internal processes but that they may also be derived from preferences imported or induced from abroad. This, of course, throws strong doubts on what has been an accepted dogma about the "immaculate conception of indifference curves,"[1] be they those of individuals or those of nations. The result is that questions are being raised about, for instance, what the main factors are in the development of sociocultural preferences and the extent to which certain indifference curves are desirable and appropriate. While the effect of foreign preferences may be seen in many developed countries, their impact on north-south relations is of greatest concern to us here.

A small but expanding literature is developing on this subject matter. Most of it focuses on the sociocultural effects of transnational business enterprises (TNEs), especially as they pertain to the relations between developed and developing countries.[2] In many cases, this literature pays special attention to the question of sociocultural dependency and domination. This aspect is particularly important for the developing

countries since a successful implementation of
their efforts to achieve economic decolonization
and development may depend, in no small measure,
on a recognition of the effects of sociocultural
realities and, ultimately, on their ability to
emancipate themselves from inappropriate sociocultural patterns imported from the developed
countries.

In this paper, we first place the relevance
of sociocultural effects into the broader context
of north-south relations. Then, conceptualizing
TNEs as transnational communication systems
that transmit sociocultural attributes, we examine
this process in terms of who says what through
which channel, to whom with what effect. In a
last section, we return again to the relationship
between economic development and sociocultural
patterns.

SOCIOCULTURAL EMANCIPATION

The emancipation of the developing countries
from colonial dependency is a historic process
that began with the end of World War II and that
encompasses at least three dimensions: political
emancipation, economic emancipation, and sociocultural emancipation.

Political emancipation involves what is
usually described as decolonization, i.e., the
achievement of political independence. Political
independence was largely obtained during the
1960s. The emergence of the movement of the
nonaligned countries during that decade signaled
the successful organization of the Third World as
an independent international political force.[3]

With the consolidation of political
independence by the end of the 1960s, it became
increasingly apparent that political decolonization
had to be complemented by economic decolonization
if a real change in the dependency relationships
of the developing countries was desired. The
result of this realization was the politization
of the development issue. In the 1950s and 1960s,
development issues were "low politics": they
were dealt with in the technical ministries of
economics, finance, planning, etc. Beginning with
the 1970s, however, development issues came to
be regarded as "high politics": they were
elevated from the ministerial level to the level of
heads of state or government.

This transformation was ratified by the fourth summit conference of the nonaligned countries in Algiers in September 1973. That summit's "Economic Declaration" and "Action Program for Economic Cooperation" made the reorganization of the international economic system one of the main objectives of the Third World. And from there it was only a small step until the quest for the New International Economic Order (NIEO) was brought before the world community as a whole.[4] This occurred with the Sixth Special Session of the United Nations General Assembly which adopted, in May 1974, the "Declaration on the Establishment of a New International Economic Order" and the "Action Program on the Establishment of a New International Economic Order."[5]

The purpose of these resolutions was to include development among the main objectives of the international economic system, a system that had developed without the active participation of the developing countries and whose institutions had primarily been created to serve the needs of the developed countries. The NIEO program is an effort to outline the required changes in the main areas of north-south interaction: trade and commodities, money and finance, science and technology, industrialization, and food and agriculture.

Whether or not the NIEO program can actually be expected to bring about the desired structural changes is certainly a question that needs serious analysis. But the developing countries' commitment to it indicates that economic emancipation has become a priority concern for them.

However, during the colonial period, the countries of the Third World were not only subjected to political and economic but also to sociocultural colonization. The values and behavioral patterns of important segments of Third World societies had been transformed to reflect those of the metropolitan countries. After independence, infused patterns have been maintained and, in fact, reinforced through a variety of mechanisms. This is particularly apparent in the area of consumption patterns which do not reflect the needs and absolute poverty of the developing countries but rather the wants and the relative abundance of the developed countries. And these consumption patterns, together with other factors, determine to a certain extent the production apparatus of the developing countries, i.e., the types of

products that are being produced and the types of
processes that are being used for their production.
To the extent to which the satisfaction of these
consumption patterns--or, more generally, the
goals embodied in the sociocultural system imported
from the developed countries--requires continued
inputs from abroad, dependency on countries and
their institutions (especially TNEs) that can help
to fulfill these aspirations becomes unavoidable.

Hence, just as it had been realized that
political independence cannot be achieved without
economic emancipation, it also has to be realized
that economic emancipation is a function of sociocultural emancipation.

TNEs AS TRANSNATIONAL COMMUNICATION SYSTEMS

Given the important role of TNEs as transnational actors, the increasing realization of the
significance of the sociocultural dimension of
north-south relations has given rise to a number of
questions concerning the sociocultural impact of
these enterprises. What is the role of TNEs in
changing or reproducing global sociocultural
structures? To what extent do they foster or hinder
the sociocultural decolonization process of the
developing countries? What direction do they give,
through their sociocultural impact, to the development process of the Third World? And what can be
done about those aspects of their impact that
are thought to be undesirable?

Too little empirical research has thus far
been undertaken to allow definite answers to these
questions. In fact, even the conceptualization of
the processes involved is still at a preliminary
stage.

We hope to advance the understanding of these
processes by conceptualizing TNEs as transnational
communication systems which function as transmission
belts through which sociocultural (or even broader:
sociopolitical and economic) attributes and preferences of home countries are disseminated to
other countries. The basis of this conceptualization is the recognition that foreign direct
investment not only involves capital, technology,
and similar resources but is usually also accompanied, intended or not, by sociocultural investments.
Where this occurs, the sociocultural profile of
host countries tends to lose its national
characteristics and to acquire those of the home

countries involved. In these processes, TNEs are mere transmission belts, even if they take an active part in the promotion of home-country related sociocultural investments and even if they played a central role in the original formation of the sociocultural profiles involved.

The concept of a communication system allows us to examine systematically the possible effects of TNEs in terms of the principal aspects of such a system. Following Harold D. Lasswell[6] these are:

Who
Says What
In Which Channel
To Whom
With What Effect?

The "who" refers to the organization, the sender of the transmission, the unit that is in control of the process. The "what" deals with the content of that which is being transmitted--the message, in other words. In communication theory, the "channels" through which the messages are sent are, of course, the media; in our context, these media also have to include the foreign affiliates of TNEs. Through the various channels, sociocultural investments are passed on to host societies (including those host-country nationals working in foreign affiliates)--the receptors of the message, the "whom" in Lasswell's formulation. The effect of the message on the host society constitutes the final link in the communication process.

In the following, we examine the sociocultural effects of TNEs in terms of these five aspects.

Who

Obviously enough, the "who" in the framework of our paper are the headquarters of TNEs (as proxy for the home country). And, also obviously enough, we include not only those in primary and secondary industries (on which most of the past and current discussions surrounding TNEs have centered), but especially those in tertiary industries. Twenty to thirty thousand TNEs control some eighty thousand foreign affiliates which represented (in 1977) a book value of over $300 billion. As a result, TNEs have become the main stratifiers of the present international economic system (and, one may add, the main manifestation

of the laissez-faire character of the system). For
instance, TNEs are the main agents for the
delivery of goods to foreign markets, either
through traditional trade (a substantial part of
which consists of intracompany transactions, i.e.,
is channeled through the enterprises' transnational
networks) or through the production of their
foreign affiliates (the volume of which--estimated
at $830 billion in 1976--has already surpassed
that of the aggregate exports of developed
market economies). They are in the forefront in
research and development and the transfer of
technology. Especially in the form of transnational
banks and through the provision of investment
capital, they are crucial for the provision of
financial resources, be it for the financing of
international trade, for development, or for other
objectives. And they play a key role in the
industrialization of developing countries.

It is not intended here to document the
importance of TNEs and their role in host
countries, home countries, and the international
system. For such a documentation, the reader is
referred to the expanding literature on TNEs.[7]
However, four characteristics of international
direct investment are of particular relevance to
the topic of this paper and therefore require
mention.

The first concerns the limited number of home
countries and headquarters (our "senders") from
which foreign direct investment originates.
Although all developed market economics, and even
a number of developing and socialist countries,
have outward foreign direct investment, nearly
half of it originates directly in the United States,
and nearly another one-third in the United
Kingdom, Japan, the Federal Republic of Germany,
and Switzerland combined. Concentration in
international direct investment extends, however,
beyond the country level: although we mentioned
that there are 20,000 to 30,000 TNEs, only
about 150-200 of them--virtually all of them
headquartered in the five countries just listed--
are estimated to account for approximately one-
half of international direct investment. In the
context of this study, this degree of concentration
is important for two reasons: (1) it means that
the number of important "senders" is relatively
small, and (2) since the major home countries
in which this limited number of enterprises is
located share essentially the same culture, the

content of the transmitted sociocultural messages
can be expected to be relatively similar.

The second relevant characteristic of
international direct investment concerns the
concentration of ownership of foreign affiliates
(an important part of our "channels") as well
as the pattern of their locational distribution.
As to the first point, approximately four-fifths
of all foreign affiliates are controlled by parent
enterprises headquartered in the five major
investor countries mentioned above. As to the
second point, the pattern of distribution of
foreign affiliates (mirroring the distribution of
book value) across developing countries, while
changing, still strongly reflects the past
colonial ties or hemispheric interests of the main
investor countries involved: the overwhelming
majority of the foreign affiliates of these
investor countries in the Third World is located
in countries that at one point or another were
formally or informally dependent on them. In
fact, these investor countries (especially the
United Kingdom, France, the United States) are the
dominant foreign-direct-investment suppliers in
most of their (former) dependencies. The relevance
of this pattern for the topic of this paper is
that at the level of the host country, the number
of sending cultures is often reduced to one, and
the concentration of actual senders is reduced to a
few TNEs from that culture.

The third relevant characteristic concerns
the ownership and control of parent enterprises.
By definition, TNEs are transnational in scope.
For many of them, a substantial part of their
profits, assets, production, and employment is
located outside their home country. But with few
exceptions, virtually all parent enterprises are
nearly exclusively owned and managed by home country
nationals. In fact, in a number of countries,
legal provisions make the takeover of TNEs by
non-nationals very difficult, if not impossible.
And where multinational ownership or control
exists, it is virtually entirely limited to
nationals of a few developed countries.[8] In other
words, control over the most important senders and
their networks is fully in the hands of nationals
of a very limited number of headquarter countries.

Finally, the fourth characteristic concerns
the situation in a number of specific tertiary
industries that are of particular importance to the
transmission of sociocultural investments. In

them, the characteristics observed above are even
more pronounced than in international direct
investment in general. To illustrate, only three
news agencies with global scope exist (the
United States agencies AP and UPI and the British
Reuters) and virtually all market economies
(with the exception of Japan) are heavily dependent
on them for their foreign news--and their
selection of what is newsworthy.[9] Similarly, a
high percentage (between one-third and two-thirds,
a percentage that is even higher during prime
time) of the television programs of most countries
is imported from a few countries, mainly the
United States, the United Kingdom, and France.[10]
And finally in international advertising--a key
industry when it comes to sociocultural messages--
21 of the 25 largest agencies in the world are
United States agencies (or strongly linked to
them) and most of them generate about half of their
billings abroad. Agencies with majority foreign
ownership are the largest in 44 of 73 developed
and developing countries; in 39 of these countries,
these affiliates are connected with North American
parent agencies. In an additional six countries,
United States parents have acquired an often
substantial minority interest in the largest agency.
If the aggregated 5 largest agencies in each of the
73 countries are examined (information is available
on a total of 261 of these agencies), nearly
three-fifths of them (151) are majority foreign-
owned; and more than half of these 151 are
controlled by 5 parent agencies, all of them
North American or strongly related to them.[11]

What

Given these characteristics of international
direct investment, the content of the messages
transferred has to be sought in the culture of
the main headquarters countries and particularly
in the business culture of the leading TNEs of
these countries (and especially of the United
States).[12] Actually, a comprehensive analysis of
the "what" would have to go beyond business culture
since more than that is being transmitted
(e.g., artistic tastes) and since business culture
itself is embedded in the sociocultural totality
of the home country. However, in the context of
this paper, with its emphasis on TNEs, the business
culture related content of the transmission process
is the main focus of interest.

We conceive of the concept of business culture as referring especially to the following four components: (1) attitudes, values, and patterns of behavior; (2) forms and patterns of (corporate) organization; (3) production patterns and processes; and (4) consumption patterns.

The first component includes attitudes, values, and patterns of behavior which are learned, shared, and generationally passed on in one society (the home country) and that are being transmitted to another society (the host country). Their scope is obviously broader than business culture and includes, for instance, general ideological preferences; "attitudes and life styles" may be an appropriate shorthand for describing them in the aggregate. In the more restricted context of foreign affiliates, this aspect would include all attitudes, values, and patterns of behavior specifically associated with foreign affiliates-- for short, the "foreign affiliate experience."

The second component of business culture includes structures of corporate organization, with special emphasis on selected functions (e.g., marketing), types of control mechanisms, corporate strategies, and also preferences concerning the role of business in society (e.g., ideological opposition to state intervention and collective bargaining rather than general legislation to achieve certain social goals). "Business philosophy" may be a term that captures most of these elements.

The third component is of particular concern to primary and secondary industries. Especially relevant in this context are the mechanisms of the product cycle through which production patterns and processes (including technological know-how) are introduced and/or promoted in host countries.[13] Reflecting the relatively high consumer incomes and labor costs in home countries, as well as their emphasis on technological advance, expansion of output and increased consumption, these production patterns are often geared towards the production of luxury and advanced consumption goods. They tend to be characterized by capital-, skill-, and energy-intensive processes, product innovation and differentiation, as well as packaging and branding. Furthermore, they tend towards (wasteful) planned obsolescence and use hard-sell advertising for want creation and consumption expansion.

As can be seen, inherent in the mechanisms of

the product cycle are implications for consumption
patterns--identified above as the fourth component
of business culture. In the framework of the
product cycle, TNEs have a nature incentive to
replicate in host countries products and processes
already successfully tested and introduced elsewhere (i.e., in home countries)--and in shaping
host country consumption patterns to obtain
acceptance of these products. Partially, this can
be done through forward and backward linkage
through which foreign affiliates may be able to
prescribe demand and supply patterns; partially,
this can be done through public relations,
marketing, and advertising aimed directly at the
preference profiles of consumers.[14]

Channels

Advertising is one of the main channels which
tramsmits the messages that contribute to the
formation of consumption patterns. But preference
profiles are not shaped by advertising alone.
They are also formed by general attitude-and-life-
style messages that are part of a broader
sociocultural transmission process. The channels
for these general transmissions are particularly
the various communication industries (most
notably the mass media), including television,
films, news agencies, newspapers, magazines,
professional journals, books, broadcasting, records,
and video tapes. Other relevant channels are
educational institutions, including business
schools,[15] expatriate managers, individuals
participating in exchange programs, tourism,
governmental cultural programs,[16] and even
language. Since the controllers of these channels
are, as a rule, located in a few headquarter
countries, the messages carried by them can be
expected to be similar.
In the context of business culture, the
foreign-affiliate networks of TNEs are, apart from
advertising, the main channel for sociocultural
investments. The effectiveness of this channel
rests on the managerial control of foreign
affiliates by their headquarters: foreign
affiliates are integrated into hierarchical
transnational organizational structures. Managerial
control is assured by the fact that foreign
affiliates are, as a rule, majority-owned by their
parent enterprises or otherwise tightly linked to
them. The effectiveness of the channel is further

reinforced by the presence of expatriate managers
in key positions of foreign affiliates and it is
complemented (as reported above) by the virtual
absence of non home-country nationals in the
headquarters of TNEs. The combination of these
factors, together with modern high speed
communication technologies, makes the foreign
affiliate networks of TNEs indeed a dynamic
global communication system.

Several intracountry channels of communication
link foreign affiliates to host countries. They
are important since through them sociocultural
investments associated with foreign affiliates are
disseminated into the host society. Three types
of linkages can be distinguished. The first one
involves interinstitutional connections related
to foreign affiliates. Thus, for instance, the
government bureaucracy may change educational
institutions to adapt to skill requirements of
foreign affiliates. As educational institutions
undergo such changes, they may, in turn, encourage
changes in the family, for example as regards
attitudes towards type and length of schooling
for both sexes. A second linking mechanism is
the "organization-set"[17] of foreign affiliates.
It consists of the complement of organizations
with which the affiliates have recurrent interactions in the course of obtaining its inputs
from suppliers, banks, etc., and channeling its
output to wholesalers, distributors, etc. (i.e.,
forward and backward linkages). A third linking
mechanism is finally the "status set"[18] of
employees of foreign affiliates. Since employees
simultaneously occupy roles, directly or
indirectly, in most societal institutions or
subsystems (e.g., the family, the economy, the
polity, educational institutions), they can
potentially transmit the foreign affiliate
experience to them. This linkage is growing since
the number of employees working in foreign
affiliates is increasing with the expansion of
international business.

Whom

It should be clear from the course of the
preceding discussion that the main receptors are
those host society groups particularly exposed
to sociocultural messages from abroad. As far as
attitudes and life styles as well as consumption
patterns are concerned, the receptor is the host

society as a whole. As far as business philosophy
as well as production patterns and processes are
controlled--messages that are, by their very
nature, somewhat more specialized--the main
receptor is the economic subsystem of the host
country. But because of the linkages of this
subsystem with the system as a whole, they do not
remain confined to it.

Employees in foreign affiliates are obviously
one of the special groups. In addition to being
tuned into the general sociocultural channels that
penetrate host societies, they are also exposed
to the foreign affiliate experience. The upper
and upper-middle classes (especially in developing
countries) are also particularly exposed, since
many of the messages are directed to them and
since their already existing sociocultural
preconceptions predispose them favorably to such
messages. These elites, in turn, have a model
function for other societal groups.

Effects

The extent and magnitude of effects can be
expected to be a function of a number of conditions
suggested by each of the individual aspects of the
communication process discussed above. Without
attempting to be exhaustive, we can identify a
number of these conditions before dealing with the
effects themselves.

As far as the originators of sociocultural
transmissions are concerned, they have to be strong
in the sense of being important transnational
actors that permeate as many facets of host
countries as possible. In addition, clear control
as well as clear authority structures appear to
be important preconditions for clear messages.
As we have seen above, these conditions are well
fulfilled.

As far as the content of the transmission is
concerned, the critical condition is the degree
to which it differs from the prevailing sociocultural environment (including the business
culture) of the receptors. If the messages
received are more or less "in tune" with this
environment, one could hardly expect any effects.
Under such a condition, added special exposure
(like the foreign affiliate experience) of some
host-country groups to such messages will probably
not make a difference. To illustrate this point:
it is very unlikely that employees living in the

Walloon part of Belgium and working in an affiliate of a TNE headquartered in Paris would, on account of differences in sociocultural variables, exhibit attitudes, values, or patterns of behavior which are different from those of their colleagues in a local company.

Thus, a prerequisite for the operation of sociocultural investments appears to be an appreciable difference between the sociocultural environments of home and host countries. On the basis of this condition alone, the impact is probably most pronounced in developing countries.[19]

Other content-related conditions are the clarity of the message, its frequency, and the extent to which it is convincing, appealing, or seductive. Messages originating in the same or similar sending cultures, reaching host societies constantly and through many channels, and depicting powerful images such as success and modernity thus promise to have the greatest impact. Our earlier discussion--in particular concerning the characteristics of international direct investment-- has shown that the sociocultural diffusion associated with TNEs fulfills these conditions.

As far as channels are concerned, their actual number is probably a variable that influences effect. This also applies to foreign affiliates--the more there are in a host country, the higher the potential for transmission. In the case of affiliates, the tightness of the various linkages--both between headquarters and foreign affiliates on the one hand and foreign affiliates and host societies on the other--can also be assumed to play a role.

Finally, when it comes to receptors, two key variables appear to be the degree of exposure and the vulnerability of the indigenous sociocultural system. The higher exposure to a clear and convincing message, by as many individuals and institutions as possible, in a vulnerable host-country sociocultural system, the greater the effects. A high degree of predisposition on the part of receptors (e.g., the elites in developing countries) towards the message would be an added supportive condition. According to our earlier discussion, all these conditions appear to be met in many developing countries. In developed countries, as well as in a number of developing ones, however, resistance to change by indigenous sociocultural systems can be expected to be a significant mitigating factor.

In sum, it appears that the combination of key conditions most favorable for pronounced effects to occur is given when a different and vulnerable sociocultural system is highly exposed to a clear and strong message emitted by convincing senders. The situation of many developing and a number of developed countries vis-a-vis the sociocultural investments of TNEs appears to fit almost exactly this combination of conditions. For a number of them, however, a main source of resistance may be a strongly developed indigenous sociocultural system. On the other hand, for a number of countries (i.e., those which are characterized by far-reaching similarities in their sociocultural systems and whose particular cultural modalities are relatively resistant)-- especially developed ones--effects may be marginal as far as the general sociocultural system (including lifestyles) is concerned. Nevertheless, they may be appreciable in some of its specific subcomponents, e.g., corporate organization. In fact, they may even reach individual issues pertaining to lifestyle, such as language, fashion, or reading habits. These propositions, as all the others suggested earlier, require of course empirical testing for conclusive answers.

As already indicated, the effects of sociocultural investments can be expected to be most pronounced in developing countries--with respect to their general sociocultural systems as well as with respect to all components of their business-culture subsystem. The basic effect is the absorption of home country related socio-cultural investments by host country nationals, which leads to a change in the sociocultural profile of these nationals towards that of home countries.[20]

When the aggregate of such individual changes is linked with parallel changes in the other components of the indigenous business culture (especially regarding production patterns and processes), they can have profound economic and political implications.[21] Sociocultural investments maintain or introduce in developing countries sociocultural patterns that are frequently based on want creation and thus may be highly undesirable.[22] They reflect the factor endowments and income levels of the developed and not the developing countries.

The issue is, therefore, the proper allocation of scarce resources: should they be used for the

establishment of a production apparatus geared
primarily to the consumption wants of the small
upper and upper-middle classes or be used for
the establishment of a production apparatus geared
primarily to the satisfaction of the basic needs
of large portions of the population? Under
conditions of very scarce resources, the adoption
of sociocultural systems and especially the
consumption patterns of the rich home countries
means first of all that the provision of basic
food stuffs, health services, clothing, housing,
drinking water, education, reliable transportation,
and the like is neglected. It furthermore means
that production processes tend to be utilized which
actually may increase unemployment and underemployment and that, in fact, resources are
wasted in products subject to planned obsolescence.
Moreover, as observed earlier, to the extent that
foreign-oriented consumption wants depend for
their satisfaction on inputs from abroad (and on
foreign institutions, like TNEs, that provide
these inputs), host countries actually keep
themselves in economic dependence--or even increase
it.

The adoption of foreign-oriented consumption
patterns may also have ramifications for the
social stratification of developing host countries
since production patterns that depend on
relatively rich population segments may represent
an obstacle to efforts aimed at the redistribution
of income. In fact, they may even further aggravate
existing income inequalities.[23] The result of
these processes is that the (small) upper and
upper-middle classes in the developing countries
and the corresponding (larger) sectors in developed
countries tend to become integrated into one
transnational sociocultural system and tend to be
more closely linked with each other than with the
other segments of their own societies. To quote
Osvaldo Sunkel:

> These sectors share a common culture and
> "way of life" which expresses itself through
> the same books, texts, films, television
> programs, similar fashions, similar groups
> of organization of family and social life,
> similar style of decorations of homes,
> similar orientations to housing, building,
> furniture, and urban design. Despite
> linguistic barriers, these sectors have a
> far greater capacity for communication among

themselves than is possible between integrated and marginal persons of the same country who speak the same language....For this international community, inhabiting different countries--developed and underdeveloped--to have similar patterns of consumption it must also have similar patterns of income.[24]

But the existence of such a transnational sociocultural system cannot conceal that the linkages in it are strongly unidirectional. Preferences are formed in a very limited number of headquarter countries. From there they are disseminated to the rest of the world. Possibilities for feedback or synthesis are very limited. The system is thus hierarchically structured, with the associated uneven distribution of autonomy and (direct and indirect) benefits.

CONCLUSIONS

This hierarchical structure of the international sociocultural system mirrors that of the international economic system. And in both systems, the same actor plays a key role in reproducing these structures. Although the two systems are analytically distinct, they are, in reality, mutually reinforcing. They are part of the existing international dominance system in its north-south dimension.

Our discussion of the sociocultural effects of TNEs links up here again with our introductory observations about the emancipation process of the developing countries: it may well be that sociocultural emancipation is a prerequisite for economic emancipation and the choice of an appropriate development path.[25]

The current discussions about the New International Information and Communication Order indicate that the importance of this link is gradually being appreciated--at least for one aspect of the overall problem. To quote from the "Declaration" of the 1976 Ministerial Conference of the Non-Allligned Countries on the Press Agencies Pool: "Just as political and economic dependence are legacies of the era of colonialism, so is the case of dependence in the field of information which in turn retards the achievement of political and economic growth....The Conference reaffirmed... that the establishment of a New International

Order for Information is as necessary as the
New International Economic Order."[26]
The nonaligned countries have taken the
lead in this field. After their 1973 Algiers
summit and their 1975 Lima Conference of Foreign
Ministers, the nonaligned countries have taken
a number of organizational measures (including the
establishment of a Press Agencies Pool of the
Non-Aligned Countries) to assure that this subject
matter receives continued attention. The
nonaligned movement has also played a key role in
introducing these questions into UNESCO, the main
forum in which sociocultural questions related to
development are currently being considered.[27]

Certainly, these efforts have greatly
contributed to focusing more attention on an area
hitherto neglected. But the full scope of the
issue at stake has yet to be recognized and
acknowledged. And, what might be equally important,
this recognition and acknowledgment has to occur
at the highest political level. Perhaps what is
needed is an equivalent of the Algiers Economic
Declaration and Action Program in order to set into
motion the process of sociocultural emancipation.

One important final point has to be made. Many
of the phenomena discussed here--e.g., hard-sell
advertising, excessive product differentiation--
are probably unavoidable concomitants of socio-
economic development as pursued by profit-oriented
institutions in market economies. In other words,
they are systemic outcomes and not outcomes that are
associated with particular countries and their
institutions. From this general point of view,
it is therefore in principle not important whether
an enterprise is transnational or local in origin,
as long as it is a profit-oriented enterprise.

Still, TNEs do play a special role. The
main reason is that they as the main stratifiers
of the international economic system and with
world-wide financial, technological, and human
resources at their command, frequently are in a
position to influence strongly the character of
indigenous production patterns and processes and,
more generally, the specific variation of the
socioeconomic development path of the host
countries in which they operate. In other words,
TNEs are in an unusually favorable position to
promote their particular variation of the market-
economy system in host countries. Thus--and
assuming no major systemic changes--the question
becomes whether (within the constraints of the

market system) the variation offered by TNEs at the present time is the optimal one for host countries.

While it is possible to delineate such variations at the conceptual level, the researcher who attempts to measure the sociocultural impact of TNEs is faced with the problem of empirically isolating the specific TNE impact and to distinguish it from that of any profit-oriented institution, that of messages sent through channels other than the foreign-affiliate networks of TNEs, and that of progress in industrialization in general (i.e., systemic characteristics).

Unquestionably, this is not an easy task. But it has to be undertaken if the exact nature of the role of TNEs in the formation of the socio-cultural indifference curves of host countries and the importance of these indifference curves for the development process are to be understood.

NOTES

1. The expression is Kenneth Boulding's.

2. For current research and literature in this area, see, respectively, the listings under classifier 72 of United Nations, Center on Transnational Corporations, *Survey of Research on Transnational Corporations: Report of the Secretariat.* ST/CTC/3, and *Bibliography on Transnational Corporations,* ST/CTC/4.

3. The documents of the nonaligned countries are contained in Odette Jankowitsch and Karl P. Sauvant, eds. *The Third World without Superpowers: The Collected Documents of the Non-Aligned Countries* (Dobbs Ferry, N. Y.: Oceana, 1978), 4 vols.; for a discussion of the non-aligned movement, see Leo Mates, *Non-Alignment: Theory and Current Policy* (Dobbs Ferry, N. Y.: Oceana, 1972).

4. For analysis of the role of the on-aligned countries, see Odette Jankowitsch and Karl P. Sauvant, "The Origins of the New International Economic Order: The Role of the Non-Aligned Countries," in Karl P. Sauvant, ed., *The New International Economic Order: Changing Priorities on the International Agenda* (Oxford: Pergamon Press, forthcoming).

5. General Assembly resolutions 3201 (S-VI) and 3202 (S-VI) of 1 May 1974. Basic to the program for the New International Economic Order

is also the "Charter of Economic Rights and Duties
of States," adopted as resolution 3281 (XXIX) by
the Twenty-ninth Regular General Assembly on
12 December 1974, and resolution 3362 (S-VII)
entitled "Development and International Economic
Co-operation," adopted on 16 September 1975 by
the Seventh Special Session.

6. Harold D. Lasswell, "The Structure and
Function of Communication in Society," in
Lyman Bryson, ed. *The Communication of Ideas*,
(New York: Harper, 1948), p. 37.

7. Main data sources are United Nations,
*Transnational Corporations in World Development:
A Reexamination* (New York: United Nations, 1978),
OECD, *Pénétration des entreprises multinationales
dans l'industrie manufacturière des pays membres*
(Paris: OECD, 1977), and J. P. Curhan,
W. H. Davidson, and R. Suri, *Tracing the Multina-
tionals* (Cambridge: Ballinger, 1977).

8. See Karl P. Sauvant and Bernard Mennis,
"Corporate Internationalization and German
Enterprises: A Social Profile of German Managers
and Their Attitudes Regarding the European
Community and Future Company Strategies," mimeo.
See Jeremy Bacon, *Corporate Directorship Practices:
Membership and Committees of the Board* (New York:
The Conference Board, 1973).

9. See Juan Somavia, "The Transnational
Power Structure and International Information:
Elements of a Third World Policy for Transnational
New Agencies," *Development Dialogue*, No. 2, 1976,
pp. 15-28, and the related study by
Fernando Reyes Matta, "The Information Bedazzlement
of Latin America: A Study of World News in the
Region," *Development Dialogue*, No. 2, 1976,
pp. 29-42.

10. See Tapio Varis, *International Inventory
of Television Programmes' Structure and the Flow
of TV Programmes between Nations* (Tampere:
University of Tampere, 1973). It should be noted
that these figures refer to the supply of programs
and not to the ownership of TV stations.

11. See Karl P. Sauvant, "The Potential of
Multinational Enterprises as Vehicles for the
Transmission of Business Culture," in *Controlling
Multinational Enterprises: Problems, Strategies,
Counterstrategies*, ed. by Karl P. Sauvant and
Farid G. Lavipour (Boulder, Col.: Westview Press,
1976).

12. The dominance of United States business
culture is not only grounded on that country's

share in international direct investment but also
in the fact that United States business schools and
their affiliates abroad train an important part of
non-United States managers; see Sauvant, "Transmission of Business Culture." See also,
Theodore D. Weinshall, "Communication, Culture and
the Education of Multinational Managers," in *The
Multinational Company in Europe: Some Key Problems*,
Michael Z. Brooke and H. Lee Remmers, eds.
(London: Longman, 1972) and his "Changing the
Effects of Culture on Problem-Solving in Management
Education," *Management International Review* 13
(1973), pp. 145-166.

13. See Raymond Vernon, "International
Investment and International Trade in the Product
Cycle," *Quarterly Journal of Economics* 80 (May
1966), pp. 190-207 and his *Sovereignty at Bay*
(New York: Basic Books, 1971).

14. Relevant material on consumption patterns
is contained, *inter alia*, in Richard J. Barnet and
Ronald Müller, *Global Reach: The Power of
Multinational Corporations* (New York: Simon and
Schuster, 1974); Thomas J. Biersteker, "Distortion
or Development? Transnational Corporations and the
Transfer of Patterns of Consumption" (New Haven:
Yale University, 1977), mimeo, and "Multinational
Investment in Underdeveloped Countries: An
Evaluation of Contending Theoretical Perspectives,"
Ph.D. dissertation, MIT, 1976; and
Robert J. Ledogar, *Hungry for Profits* (New York:
IDOC/North America, 1975).

15. See footnote 12. It should also be noted
that many developing countries base their education
on material imported from the metropoles. See,
for further references, André Cartapanis,
William Experton, and Jean-Luc Fuguet, "Transnational Corporations and Educational Systems in
Developing Countries: An Annotated Critical
Bibliography" (Paris: UNESCO, 1977), mimeo.

16. See e.g., Hans Arnold, *Kulturexport
als Politik? Aspekte deuscher auswärtiger
Kulturpolitik* (Tübingen: Erdmann, 1976).
According to Hildegard Hamm-Brücher, Minister of
State in the Foreign Office of the Federal Republic
of Germany, "Foreign cultural policy is a
supporting pillar of our foreign policy" and has
a status comparable to that of foreign policy's
other two "supporting pillars," political and
economic policy. Quoted in *The Bulletin*,
March 30, 1977, p. 52.

17. See, William M. Evan, "The Organization-Set: Toward a Theory of Interorganizational Relations," in *Approaches to Organizational Design*, ed. by James D. Thompson (Pittsburgh: University of Pittsburch, 1966).

18. R. K. Merton, *Social Theory and Social Structure* (New York: Free Press, 1957).

19. Possibly, degree of economic development could be used as a first approximation of socio-cultural differences. It should be kept in mind, however, that sociocultural differences are only one condition for effects to occur.

20. Some of the changes introduced may also be understood in terms of Talcott Parson's pattern variables, i.e., as changes in the direction of "modernity."

21. This has long been argued by a number of scholars. Nevertheless, empirical research that systematically examines this subject matter hardly exists.

22. It should be noted that many of the socio-cultural attributes discussed here may also be undesirable for the majority of the people in the developed countries.

23. If a causal relation exists between an inequitable distribution of income and high-income goods consumption patterns, then governmental policy may actually aim at the creation of a skewed income distribution in an effort to stimulate industrialization and especially also foreign direct investment.

24. Osvaldo Sunkel, "Transnational Capitalism and National Disintegration in Latin America," *Social and Economic Studies* 22 (March 1973), pp. 132-176. For Sunkel, the result of the disintegration of national sociocultural systems is a polarization in them, with those not included in the transnational system adopting consumption cultures that are different from the consumeristic culture promoted by TNEs and that, in the longer run, may lead to a reintegration of the individual national cultures.

25. The concept of individual and collective self-reliance--lately gaining more currency among developing countries--could advance movement in this direction.

26. In Jankowitsch and Sauvant, *The Third World without Superpowers*, Vol. 3, pp. 1554-1555.

27. See especially International Commission for the Studies of Communication Problems

("MacBride Commission"), *Interim Report on Communication Problems in Modern Society* (Paris: UNESCO, 1978) and the various documents prepared for this Commission and issued by UNESCO. See in this context also Breda Pavlić, "UNESCO on Transnational Corporations," *Review of International Affairs* 17 (September 20, 1976), pp. 27-30, and UNESCO, *Moving towards Change: Some Thoughts on the New International Economic Order* (Paris: UNESCO, 1976).

12
Cultural and Ideological Dependence: Building a Theoretical Framework

Evelina Dagnino

This paper examines the characteristics of cultural and ideological systems in dependent societies. That is, it deals with questions concerning the nature and dynamics of a super-structure that is the expression of a dependent economic system. The cultural aspects of dependence have been given small attention in comparison with economic factors in the effort to produce a theoretical framework adequate for the analysis of structures of dependency. Yet, the importance of culture and ideology as agents in the maintenance and reproduction of dependent relationships cannot be denied. Thus, part of the effort here is to provide some conceptual tools that may prove useful in understanding this set of phenomena.

Dependence may be seen as a general framework that qualifies the inclusion of a country in the international capitalist system, at present under the hegemonic power of the United States. The internal elites of these countries, in order to implement their own interests as a class, adopt as their own project (i.e., as a deliberate option), the inclusion of their countries in this system, within which they occupy a subordinate role.[1] Inclusion in this international capitalist system brings with it the sharing of a whole style of life, values, and beliefs that express a determinate material condition, accessible only to the privileged sectors integrated into that part of the system. In this sense, the major referent of the national model adopted by dependent elites is this international system to which they are committed.

Integrated into this international capitalist system is the majority of the population in the

United States, the hegemonic center, and a small
part of the population of the peripheral, underdeveloped, dependent countries, chiefly their
ruling elites. Excluded from this system, that is,
sharing minimally in its benefits, is that small
part of the United States' population formed by
racial minorities and poor white and the majority
of the population in underdeveloped countries.
Other members of the system might be included in a
more complete representation, e.g., the advanced
industrialized countries that share (and at some
points challenge) the dominant power of the United
States. There exists a double polarization in
this system. At the international level, there is
a stratification of nations in an international
economy whose basic characteristics, as pointed out
by Sunkel, is "the penetration of the underdeveloped
economics by the economies of the developed countries through the extractive, manufacturing,
commercial, and financial transnational conglomerates."[2] Connected with this and according to
the degree of penetration, another dimension of
stratification, internal to each dependent country,
draws a vertical cleavage across activities, social
groups, and regions within countries. There is
a set of activities, social groups, and regions
that are developed, modern, and integrated into the
international capitalist system. And there is
another complex of activities, social groups, and
regions that are backward, underdeveloped, excluded
from the global system, forming the marginal
sectors that surround the first. This cleavage
cuts across different classes dividing each of
them in a way that hinders the formation of
national classes. Thus, entrepreneurs, middle
classes, and workers are absorbed in different
proportions by the integrated sector. This determines their internal differentiation and limits
their expression as national formations.

Underlying this double polarization there is
a relationship of domination that is expressed at
both levels: between nations in the context of
the international system and between classes within
each country. This domination expresses at the
political level a relationship of economic
exploitation in which the privileged position of
certain nations, sectors, and classes is due to the
marginalization and exclusion of others.

In order to preserve and maintain this
relationship of domination, the dominant elites of
each country have to deal with the pressures posed

by the contradiction opposing privileged, integrated
sectors to marginalized ones. Within the United
States, the internal cleavage is handled mainly via
minority programs, including jobs, education, and
social security, and welfare programs for poor white
people. In the dependent countries, the resources
available are fewer and, in addition, given the
great proportion of the population not integrated
into the internationalized sector of the system,
the risks and challenges involved are much greater.
It is in this context that the cultural and ideological system assumes major importance. For it must
fulfill a strong need for holding together a system
that is heavily divided by inequalities in the
distribution of resources.

Thus, in order to cope with potential pressures
from marginalized sectors--whose very marginalization makes possible the privileged position of the
internationalized elites--the capitalist system had
to engender an ideology that provides its own
justification as *the* ideal system for all human
beings. The internationally shared set of values,
the "way of life" adopted by these elites is then
erected as a model for the society as a whole.
Dependent elites enthusiastically embrace a
capitalist culture, a capitalist ideology, as
substitutes for their national cultures, in an
attempt to achieve a *cultural homogenization* that
is crucial for the maintenance and strengthening
of the international capitalist system.

From the point of view of dependent countries,
this cultural homogenization implies a limitation
of the options open to their people. There is an
increasing narrowing of the range of alternatives
available, a consequence of a specific "way of
life," a determined set of attitudes and beliefs,
and a certain ideology. Latin American people
are thus being enfolded in a "modern" world, in
which one type of modernization is defined and is
being accepted as modernization itself, without
consideration of alternative conceptualizations.
In this process people play a passive role: their
whole life is molded from the outside, not as a
result of their own choice but as part of the model
adopted by their elites in seeking integration into
the international capitalist system.

The climate of prosperity brought to the
country by this type of development helps to
explain its attraction and the passivity or even
active enthusiasm it evokes. The fact that this
prosperity actually reaches only small sectors of

the population does not diminish its appeal. For
people living at striking levels of poverty for
decades, a mere hope of sharing in the new development of the country can nourish their support for a
long period of time.

Yet, Latin American ruling elites are not
consciously "selling the country" to international
powers. This is not their intention. What they
are looking for is to achieve national development
through association with these international powers.
But here arises the basic question of dependence--
cultural, political, as well as economic: how
large is the range of alternatives available to
Latin American countries within the international
system? In other words, what are the possibilities
of autonomy within the scope of this association,
an association between international powers such
as the super-developed countries and poor, underdeveloped countries like those in Latin America?

What seems to be true is that the structural
conditions underlying this kind of integration do
not justify the use of the word "association,"
not if the word is taken to imply similar
bargaining powers and similar ranges of autonomy.
The concrete experience of underdeveloped countries
has been that of a subordinate role within the
international system; the idea of partnership on
an equal footing seems to constitute an illusion or
a rationalization fostered by dependent national
elites. Those promoting the model of dependent
development must face squarely the consequences of
the kind of relationship on which it is based.
Once the game is entered, economic, political, and
cultural decisions are subordinated to the needs
and interests of the global system, as defined by
those who control this system.

What we want to suggest here is that the
effects of cultural dependence on the lives of
Latin Americans are not a consequence of an "invasion" led by a foreign "enemy," but of a choice
made by their own ruling class, in the name of
national development. Through this choice,
national life and national culture are subordinated
to the dynamics of the international capitalist
system, submitting national cultures to a form of
homogenization that is considered a requirement
for the maintenance of an international system.
To the same extent that the economic and political
alternatives available to each country are limited
by its very inclusion in this broader structure,
and by the very conditions that define this

inclusion, cultural and ideological choices begin
to disappear from the minds of people. Entire
peoples are subordinated to choices made elsewhere
through a constant, efficient, and subtle spreading
of contents and meanings appropriate to those
choices.

What is posed here as a problem then is the
manipulation of people, the control over the
alternatives open to them, the inexorable transformation of Brazilians, Argentinians, and
Venezuelans into consumers, when they should have
the right and the opportunity to become something
else. In the name of modernization and development,
a particular model of man is being implemented:
anything that does not add to the making of this
new internationalized capitalist man, that does
not reinforce the "*homo homini mercator*," is
considered as having no use and will be supressed
and replaced by something more efficient.

While the implications of this massive
process of cultural penetration are by no means
fully clear, its scale and intensity require that
it be given attention. Latin American popular
music, for instance, is being gradually transformed
under the influence of American music. Even in
Brazil, recognized as having a strong musical
tradition, genuine manifestations of Brazilian
rhythm are decreasing and being replaced by a more
Americanized, internationalized style. Latin
American social scientists conform their intellectual production to the requirements and models posed
by American social science. Latin American children
spend long hours in front of TV sets looking at
Bonanza, *FBI*, *Mission Impossible*, *Maverick*,
Disneyland, *Rin Tin Tin*, and *Julia*. Latin American
consumers are being bombarded with massive
quantities of advertising, through all the mass
media, praising the advantages of sophisticated
products manifestly at odds with the wage levels
and the subsistence needs of the vast majority of
the population.

Even if one accepts the world definition
contained in each one of these channels of cultural
homogenization, still a claim for personal self-
determination and some degree of freedom of choice
may be advanced. Individual needs have to be
defined by the individuals themselves, but only
when and if they are free to provide their own
definition. To the extent they are manipulated
their choices cannot be considered autonomous:
they are imposed from the outside. In the

dependent countries, a capitalist ideology is
providing the definitions. No individual effort
is required. Needs, values, beliefs, and attitudes
come in packages: ready to use.

Cultural dependence in Latin America is,
of course, not new. Yet it definitely assumes
new forms with the evolution of the international
capitalist system. From colonial times, the
influence exerted by the metropolis--first Europe
and then United States--is a constant in Latin
American history. Cultural life was directly
connected to the main tendencies within European
intellectual circles; the internal pole of this
connection was the small group of native intellectuals attracted by metropolitan styles of thought
and life. Early critiques of these "alienated
and mentally colonized" intellectuals were
advanced by figures such as José Enrique Rodó in
his *Ariel*, José Carlos Mariátegui and José Marti
with his *Nuestra América*.

After the Second World War the international
system suffered transformations. World stratification became more apparent and the United States
assumed a new importance within the international
scene. In the most recent period the process of
development in Latin America has been characterized
by new features such as the emergence of the
multinational corporation and the international
production for local markets. As Fernando
Henrique Cardoso has pointed out, an "internaliza-
tion of the anti-nation" replaces small groups
of Europe-oriented intellectuals with more
differentiated and larger groupings of internal
elites actively committed to the international
system. In addition, the technological advance
of the mass media and the new class composition
with its new institutional settings make culture
and ideology accessible to large portions of the
population generalizing a type of consumption
previously reserved to a small privileged
sector.

THE CONTENTS OF CULTURAL DEPENDENCE

An attempt to define the main features of
capitalist culture and ideology would be beyond
the scope of this paper. A comprehensive treatment
would require a careful examination of the works
of a number of authors: from Galbraith and his
"affluent society" to Marcuse and his "one-

dimensional man," from Lukács and the concept of reification to Lefèbvre and the terrorist society, and on to include Ronald Laing and Philip Slater and their critique of the "civilized" world, as well as Parsons with his indicators of modernity. Still, accepting the risks of oversimplification, an effort to specify and make clear some basic aspects of capitalist ideology and culture is necessary here.

The set of values and beliefs that constitute capitalist ideology is based on some fundamental principles designed to ensure the maintenance and propagation of the capitalist mode of production. First of all, the capitalist system is presented as a truth in itself, unquestionable and inevitable. This principle expresses itself in what Lukács called the contemplative nature of man under capitalism. Here, man is a spectator of his own life:

> For the essence of rational calculation (the basis of capitalism) is based ultimately upon the recognition and the inclusion of one's calculation of the inevitable chain of cause and effect in certain events--independently of individual "caprice"....[3]

> ...Man in capitalist society confronts a reality "made" by himself (as a class) which appears to him to be a natural phenomenon alien to himself, he is wholly at the mercy of its "laws," his activity is confined to the exploitation of the inexorable fulfillment of certain individual laws for his own (egoistic) interests. But even while "acting" he remains, in the nature of the case, the object and not the subject of events.[4]

The advanced capitalist society has achieved a "robotization" of man. Circumstances outside himself, presided over by an increasing "rationality" supported by scientific and technological advancement, determine, condition, and prefabricate man.

This principle is recurrently recognized both by Lefèbvre and Marcuse. The first asserts the "programmed everyday life" of man under capitalist society. But most important, this is viewed as a "voluntary, programmed self-regulation." For even submitted to this conditioning from the outside, man "sees himself none the less as more than ever self-sufficient and dependent only on his own spontaneous conscience even under robotization."[5]

This existence as a subject is not questioned
as long as the appearance of "free" choice is
maintained. The quantitative and qualitative
range of these choices is taken as given:
inevitable and unquestionable with its mask of
objective rationality. As Marcuse points out,
we are "sublimated slaves," characterized by being
manipulated instruments, things: "This is the pure
form of servitude: to exist as an instrument, as
a thing. And this mode of existence is not
abrogated if the thing is animated and chooses its
material and intellectual food, if it does not
feel its being-a-thing, if it is a pretty, clean,
mobile thing."[6]

In the second place, and intimately related
with the first principle, the world is seen as a
world of commodities. As a legitimating rationale
of the mode of production that generated it,
capitalist ideology presents a world of goods, a
world made of things to be sold and bought, things
that are defined by their exchange value, where men
are buyers and sellers before being users. This
is a world in which the Hobbesian wolf has assumed
other forms and where *"homo homini mercator,"*
i.e., man merchandises man. In line with this
basic assumption, a whole set of attitudes and
patterns of behavior are considered to be the
most appropriate to the best possible performance
of this fundamental activity: to buy and to sell.
Thus we see the cult of efficacy, competitiveness,
achievement, affective neutrality, individualism,
sense of time--just to mention a few examples.

The following quotation from Marcuse summarizes
these principles and gives us an accurate picture of
capitalist ideology:

> We live and die rationally and productively.
> We know that destruction is the price of
> progress as death is the price of life, that
> renunciation and toil are the prerequisites
> for gratification and joy; that business
> must go on, and that the alternatives are
> Utopian. This ideology belongs to the
> established societal apparatus; it is a
> prerequisite for its continuous functioning
> and part of its rationality.[7]

The idea of a capitalist ideology and culture,
spreading throughout the world along with the
imperialist expansion of capitalism--being, at the
same time, a consequence of and condition for this

expansion--poses new issues for a theory of
cultural domination. For seen in this light what
we are witnessing is not the invasion and dominance
of one national culture by another national
culture, as in colonial times. We see, rather,
national cultures being invaded, distorted, and
suffocated by a capitalist ideology. The internal
elites of these countries themselves share in the
production of this ideology; the process is a
result of a project partly promoted from within
and is considered as essential to the development
of the subordinate country.

In this sense, there is no confrontation
between national cultures, in which one has to
dominate and absorb the other. There is, rather,
a capitalist ideology seeking to impose itself
over national elements that could represent alternative options to the economic model that capitalism
seeks to institute, preserve, and reinforce. In
this connection American culture is identified
with capitalist ideology only to the extent that the
United States is the power center of the international capitalist system, the fertile ground where
American values contributed to forge the supreme
expression of capitalism and, in the same process,
were through the years molded and transformed by
it. Moreover, the domination of capitalist
ideology is being contested from within the United
States, not only by minorities seeking to
preserve their cultural identity but also by
disaffected whites resisting capitalist manipulation of their own lives. In this sense, the
organization of movements of resistance within each
national unit is linked by its common reference
to similar processes of domination.

Thus, it is not American culture as such,
as a national culture, that is homogenizing the
world. There is not a new "Romanization" of the
world, as in the times of the Roman Caesars. The
complexity and sophistication of the new international capitalist system, in which, speaking
analogically, the multinational corporations could
be seen as the new Caesars, does not allow an
analysis based on an outdated colonial model.

The cultural and ideological homogenization
of the world is being pursued not by a single
nation but by an integrated system of different
national sectors, committed to a specific form of
socio-economic organization. This basic assumption
has important implications for the discussion of
the role played by elements of national cultures

in the struggle against this form of cultural
and ideological domination. They will be examined
when the internal cultural systems and their
dynamics are considered.

THE PROCESSES OF CULTURAL DEPENDENCE

The importance assumed by this process of
cultural and ideological homogenization in the
latest phase of international capitalism--in which
the technological revolution makes possible the
"global village" that McLuhan talks about and
imperialist expansion requires a stronger control
apparatus--brings with it the rise of "ideological
industry." This ideological industry undertakes
the role of production and distribution of the
ideological elements--representations, images,
and beliefs--destined to pervade all sectors of
the society and integrate them around a set of
common values and goals. The ideological industry
has its specific social space in the mass media--
radio, television, and cinema--at work 24 hours
a day in an intensive and constant activity directed
to each individual during each moment of his everyday life, wherever he lives.[8]
But ideological production pervades the entire
capitalist economic apparatus as well. For
Marcuse, "today, the ideology is in the process of
production itself."[9] In this sense, each economic
element of the capitalist mode of production carries
with it the ideological elements that it needs for
its preservation. From its own economic performance
an ideological action is released. If we analyze,
for instance, the operation of a multinational
corporation in Latin America, we see that by simply
producing and selling its product in a Latin
American market, it is creating and reinforcing a
need the satisfaction of which is the reason for the
corporation's own survival there. That is, it
creates a need in order to make profits, assuring
the consumption of its production. The extent to
which this need is adequate to the conditions of
life of the people involved or corresponds to their
real needs is a secondary consideration. In this
process, specific consumption patterns are established that inform people as to what they should
drink, eat, and wear, and what their lives should
be like. To this extent these corporations act as
ideological agents engaged in reinforcing a
specific form of economic organization and the life

style it generates. Bauman elaborates on the idea
of how elements of the organization of production
function as producers of ideology and culture, and
as distributors and agents of cultural homogenization.[10] He analyzes the role of three components:
market, organization, and technology.

Dependence on the market is a characteristic
of modern societies. Today everybody is involved
in the market, either as sellers or buyers, in the
labor market, or in the commodities market. The
market is the mediator in the satisfaction of human
"needs" and, in this sense, it has the power of
culturally modeling these needs. Thus, the
circulation of commodities is exposed to the
culture-forming influences of the market. It is
easy to understand that these culture-forming
influences correspond to the interests of those who
dominate the market in each concrete situation.

Dependence on technology, just like dependence
on the market, culturally shapes human needs. The
use of technology conditions and controls the range
of options available to man, in addition to
increasing his alienation from alternative options
since he cannot easily understand the connections
between new technological events and his personal
situation. Technology is far from being a neutral
tool, and an extensive theoretical analysis of the
point has been developed, especially by Marcuse
and Habermas, two of its leading theorists.[11]

Ideological production permeates each and
every component of the capitalist system with
different degrees of specificity and efficacy
according to the specific functions to be performed
by these components. With respect to infrastructural components like the ones discussed
above, one can observe that their ideological
efficacy is directly related to the scope of their
performance in each concrete situation considered
in terms of the number of people involved and the
intensity of their participation in the economic
activity in question. In other words, if an
individual's participation in the market, to take
one case, is restricted to subsistence goods, the
ideological success of the market will be severely
limited.

In the same way, superstructural elements
whose specific tasks are the production and
distribution of ideology have their efficacy
conditioned by the extent of people's exposure to
them. Acting as a connecting element between these
different types of ideological processes,

advertising plays an important role in establishing
relationships among the various factors of
ideological production. In his "Theses on
Advertising," Paul Baran[12] suggested that, given
the multiplicity of functions performed by
advertising, it operates by reinforcing the
performance of other operative factors, by filling
up existing gaps, in short, by giving unity to the
ideological system as a whole. Thus, if an
individual does not use shaving lotion because he
does not have enough money to buy it--that is, if
he does not participate in the market of shaving
lotions--a persuasive advertisement on television
is available, steadily at work until he can get
enough money and decide to become a shaving lotion
consumer and enjoy the privileges offered by this
particular form of consumption.

THE AGENTS OF CULTURAL DEPENDENCE

     In analyzing the processes through which
ideological production operates, one is able to
identify its agents in terms of classes and social
groups. Who are the producers of capitalist
ideology? What groups lead in promoting cultural
homogenization? Considering the picture of the
international capitalist system presented to this
point one must distinguish between internal and
external agents of this process.
     On the one hand, there is an external agent,
the United States, that at the hegemonic center of
the system, is also the generating hub of the
capitalist ideology and culture that is being
diffused. At the cultural level, unlike the
economic and political spheres, the center seems
to exert an uncontested leadership. On the other
hand, the internal ruling elites adopt and
incorporate these cultural patterns, retransmitting
them throughout their own country. Their functions
are making adaptations and adding new elements
when needed and redistributing these patterns.
     At this point the double dependence or double
alienation assumed by cultural and ideological
production in Latin American countries comes
clearly into view. First, because these nations
are included in the international capitalist
system, they are also subject to a capitalist
ideology that sees the world by definition as a
capitalist world, as a truth to be accepted without
any questioning. This means that the

representations of the concrete reality produced
by this ideology are to be seen as exhaustive,
leaving no room for alternative options. As in
the quotation from Marcuse, "alternatives are
Utopian." Second, this truth that is to be
accepted is not defined by the social unit for
itself but at the power center of the global
system, the United States, which imposes its own
particular model upon dependent countries. In
this sense, a dependent country has its options
externally limited from the outside in a double
sense: as a social system and as a nation.
    Having examined the international context
wherein the phenomenon of cultural homogenization
is running its course, the processes through which
it operates, and the agents of these processes,
a closer look at the functions of this homogenization within the global system is in order.

THE FUNCTIONS OF CULTURAL DEPENDENCE

    The role of ideological and cultural
homogenization has been characterized throughout
this paper as one of preservation and reinforcement
of the capitalist system. According to
Hans Magnus Enzensberger, this "nonmaterial
exploitation is the *sine qua non* for the continuing
of material exploitation."[13] Thus, the relationship
of domination inherent to the structure of the
capitalist system has to be masked and justified
in some way in order for it to appear acceptable
to dominated as well as dominant individuals. It
is not necessary to impute evil motives to the
dominant classes. They seldom are conscious of
relations of domination and especially of their
roles in it. It is because their roles appear as
benevolent and respectable to them that the whole
process can be perpetuated.
    But within this broad role, at a deeper level,
there are very specific and crucial functions
performed by the ideological system in a capitalist
society. They refer to the reproduction of the
relations of production on which capitalism is
based. To cite Althusser, "...in order to exist,
every social formation must reproduce the conditions
of its production at the same time it produces,
and in order to be able to produce. It must therefore reproduce (1) the productive forces, (2) the
existing relations of production."[14] The reproduction of productive forces includes the reproduction

of the material means of production, such as raw materials, machines, etc., and the reproduction of labor power. The ways in which the system takes care of this last task can be seen as follows.

First, reproduction of labor power is assured by providing the material means needed for it, that is, wages. A worker needs to earn enough money in order to be able to be present at his work every day, alive and well, and in addition, to raise and educate his children so that they can occupy his place in the future.

Second, besides wages, it is necessary for the reproduction of labor power to provide the different skills, the "know-how" needed for production. This is the function of the capitalist educational system, at its various levels.

Third, in addition to the reproduction of skills through the learning of techniques and knowledge, at the same time, there is a set of rules that has to be reproduced through learning. These are the rules "of respect for the socio-technical division of labor and ultimately the rules of the order established by class domination."[15] The reproduction of these rules which constitute the ruling ideology of society implies not only the learning of *submission* to them but also the learning of their *practice*. This means that people are trained to occupy a certain position in the relations of production and to behave adequately in the performance of their functions, either the role performances of the dominant or those of the dominated. In this sense, exploitation is learned at the same time and as part of the skills needed for production and is seen as natural and appropriate. It is because a worker is trained and conditioned to accept exploitation as natural that he cannot see the reality of his own exploitation. To the extent to which this happens and continues to happen the preservation of exploitative relations of production is assured.

It is this reproduction of relations of production that constitutes the specific function of ideology within the capitalist system. According to Althusser, this function is performed by the Ideological State Apparatuses, the ISAs. Distinguished from the State Apparatus as such insofar as the latter functions predominantly *by repression*, the Ideological State Apparatuses function massively and predominantly *by ideology* and present themselves in the form of distinct and specialized institutions such as the church, the school, the family, communications, trade unions, etc. There is a unity among these Ideological State Apparatuses that is given precisely by the ruling ideology, the ideology of the ruling class that holds state power and, consequently, has all state apparatuses at its disposal.

The assertion of the function of ideology and cultural homogenization within the global system (performed through the ISAs) leads to the analysis of the internal dynamics of the cultural system. Up to now we have been discussing a process of transformation within the cultural system that points to a cultural homogenization based on dependent patterns and led by the internationalized elites in each country. In other words, we have been examining the expression at a superstructural level of a relationship of domination originated in the infrastructure of society, in the class struggle.[16] In this sense, when we refer to cultural and ideological homogenization we are referring to the *dominant tendency* within the cultural system. Thus, to the extent that class struggle--that is, dominant against dominated--expresses itself at the ideological level, we have to recognize the existence of *dominated tendencies* within the cultural system that provide confrontation and resistance to ideological domination. The cultural and ideological system is not a homogeneous and solid block, but a contradictory one, expressing the contradictions in the infrastructure of society and those generated within itself, with internal dynamics of its own. It is to the analysis of these contradictions that the next section of this paper is dedicated.

THE INTERNAL DYNAMICS OF THE CULTURAL SYSTEM

For the purposes of this analysis the cultural system is seen as the superstructure of a social formation, the ways in which the infrastructure expresses itself through men's minds. These two elements, infrastructure and superstructure, must be seen as organic components of a totality, interdependent on each other and united by a dialectical relationship.

Thus, in a very broad sense, we consider culture as being the result of man's mental

production, that is, the ways in which he expresses
his relationship to reality, to nature, and to
other men. Within this comprehensive framework,
we include a number of institutions and systems of
abstraction that can also be seen as "cultural
fields" or "regions": art, science, technology,
religion, tradition, folklore, mass media,
education, advertising, law, political values, and
also a set of broader values and attitudes.

The basic idea here is that each one of these
cultural components is pervaded by two kinds of
cleavages. That is, there are two levels of
internal contradictions within each one of them.

In the first place, there is a *class contradiction*. In a class society we have cultural
expressions that are produced by dominant classes
and cultural expressions produced by dominated
classes. Dominant and dominated see and represent
reality in different ways to the extent that they
live different realities due to different material
conditions of life, i.e., different class positions.
Yet it is important to keep clear that the cultural
expressions of the dominated are subordinated, i.e.,
always framed and limited by the dominant culture
within the society that, as Marx pointed out, is
the culture of the dominant classes. In addition,
these dominated expressions are not to be considered
as valid in themselves just because they come from
oppressed classes in society. They are still
ideological manifestations that constitute mis-
representations of reality. The point to be made
here is that they originate within the cultural
universe of these classes, are limited by the
dominant culture but still represent genuine
contributions that add to the heterogeneity of
the cultural process.

Contradictions that bring into opposition
distinct perceptions of the world can be
identified in the concrete manifestations of each
cultural component. For instance, in religion, we
have at the same time the Catholic Church, a
cultural expression of the dominant classes, and
the sects of African origin that constitute in
Brazil the so-called "low spiritualism"--*"baixo
espiritismo"*--called "low" exactly because it is
practiced by lower classes. In the same sense,
we see within tradition and folklore, customs and
usages that are generated and practiced by
dominant classes and others that are proper to
dominated classes. In different degrees, this

class contradiction can be identified in each
cultural component.

In the second place, because there is a
class structure, an economic exploitation that
underlies a structure of domination, there is also
a need to mask this domination, to present it as
natural and desirable to dominated and dominant
as well. This function of mystification of
reality, as has been mentioned, is performed by the
component of ideology that is present in each one
of the cultural fields.

At this point we are giving a precise
meaning to a concept that has been used up to this
point in a rather undefined manner: ideology.
The reason why a more precise definition was
delayed until this point instead of being approached
at the beginning is that we considered that the
analysis and discussion being carried out throughout
this paper would clarify the concept of ideology in
a natural manner, through a sort of "theoretical
praxis," slowly and deliberately bringing a
spontaneous understanding of the concept through
the examination of the processes in which it is
involved.

We consider ideology as a set of representations of the world, a representation that is false
by definition. Ideology is a refraction of reality, a
mystification that presents false images of it as
being the reality itself. In this sense ideology
identifies itself with false consciousness or with
unconsciousness, a "knowledge which is unconscious
of its dependence," as defined by Horkheimer.[17] A
disguised version of reality is provided and affirms
itself as reality in order to preserve the existent
order.

Carrying this concept of ideology further,
Ludovico Silva[18] suggests that in the advanced
stage of international capitalism the pervasive
and efficient action of the "ideological industry"--
to which men are exposed during every minute of
their lives--produces constant pressures that are
internalized by the individual and transformed
into a sort of "internal police." This internal
repression is stored in the *preconscious*, one of
the regions of the psychic structure as conceptualized by Freud, located in an intermediate zone
between the *unconscious* and the *conscious*. From
the preconscious these internalized pressures
act as conditioned reflexes, as mechanical responses
which prescribe the individual's reactions to

stimuli presented by reality. Therefore, ideology
is received and stored in the preconscious,
conditioning from there the individual's behavior
which is then alienated from his consciousness to
the extent that this "internal police" impedes
any manifestation that opposes or contradicts
its directions. Ideology thus provides the
individual with an opaque, nonproblematic image
of "everyday life" which comes to be seen as
reality itself.

To the extent that we recognize the existence
of a fundamental and primary contradiction at the
level of the infrastructure, the one between the
means of production and the relations of production
(where the one who works does not possess the
product of his work), a contradiction which
expresses itself in the class struggle, we also
recognize the existence of elements that confront
ideology, forces of negation that *deny* the version
of reality that is being presented as reality
itself.

Thus we are faced with the second internal
contradiction present in the components of the
cultural system: they may contain ideological
elements that constitute an affirmation of the
status quo but they may also display elements of
a critical consciousness that *negates* the status
quo.

Critical consciousness as opposed to ideology
can be seen as an effort toward liberation from the
pressures imposed by capitalist ideology, a process
of unmasking reality. By confronting ideology,
critical consciousness confronts the dehumanization
of man who lives in submission to something else
which is not him but, at the same time, is
inside him, determining his behavior and restrict-
ing his options.[19]

Ideology and critical consciousness are in
this way seen as *attributes* that can be identified
in each one of the cultural components. Culture
can contain ideology as well as it can embody
elements of critical consciousness. This means
that it can be used as an instrument for
intensifying cultural and ideological dependence
but can also be used against it, as an instrument
of resistance and negation.

By examining concrete instances of cultural
construction we can see more clearly the manifestations of this contradiction. For instance, in
science it is possible to identify ideological
elements that contribute to a justification of the

status quo and adopting an acritical attitude
towards reality. A good example can be seen in
the theory of modernization that preempts the term
development for a specific and particular model of
development: the one advocated by the advanced
capitalist societies. On the other hand, we can
mention another scientific production--the theory
of dependence--as an attempt to uncover the ideological character of "scientific" models such as
the one mentioned above by criticizing its alleged
inevitability and "goodness."

In the same sense, the educational system
subordinates itself to the dominant ideology
reproducing and reinforcing its basic values
through learning and adjusting itself to the
constantly renewed demands of capitalist society
by elaborating pertinent, specific skills and
behavior. For this reason Althusser considers
the education system as the "ideological State
apparatus which has been installed in the
dominant position in mature capitalist social
formations as a result of a violent political
and ideological class struggle against the old
dominant ideological State apparatus (the
Church)."[20]

Still we are able to point to examples, such
as the experience of Paulo Freire in the
Brazilian Northeast with his method of adult
literacy or the role of the University in some
countries of Latin America during certain periods,
as instances of education fostering the development of critical elements of negation of the
status quo.

As another example, we can identify within
religion two opposing elements: on the one hand
we see in Latin America the traditional Catholic
Church involved in the maintenance of dominant
interests and acting to encourage resignation and
conformism and the hope for a transcendental
justice; on the other hand, the new "rebel"
Catholic Church leads a struggle against repression
and injustice and calls for "*conscientização*" of
the people.

It is clear through these examples that the
contradiction between ideology and critical consciousness that exists within all cultural
components expresses itself in different degrees
of intensity in each one of them. As with class
contradictions, each concrete historical situation
defines the limits for the manifestation of these
contradictions. One last example can be mentioned

in order to show the diversity in which this contradiction manifests itself in different concrete situations. The legal system of society can be considered as a sort of unconquerable redoubt of the dominant classes: it exists with the precise function of assuring respect for law and order, as defined and established by the ruling classes. What we want to suggest is that a contradiction between ideology and critical consciousness within the legal system is being highlighted by the Tupamaros in Uruguay to the extent that they have been proposing to society an alternative legal system. In very limited terms, of course, they have been denying the justice of the "official" legal system as an ideological one, utilized to protect and legitimize the present structure of domination in the country. When an unfair and oppressing boss is put on trial by the Tupamaros and sentenced to return to his employees the money that resulted from their exploitation, Critical Justice and Ideological Justice confront one another in a process that uncovers domination.

The importance of an adequate analytical framework for the study of the cultural system derives from a basic assumption that is, as Althusser puts it:

> ...to understand that the Ideological State Apparatuses may be not only the *stake*, but also the *site* of class struggle and often of bitter forms of class struggle. The class (or class alliance) in power cannot lay down the law in the ISAs as easily as it can in the (repressive) State apparatus, not only because the former ruling classes are able to retain strong positions there for a long time, but also because the resistance of the exploited classes is able to find means and occasions to express itself there, either by the utilization of their contradictions, or by conquering combat positions in them in struggle.[21]

By superimposing these two contradictions, one opposing dominant to dominated classes and the other opposing ideology to critical consciousness, we obtain a complex picture of the cultural system at the same time that we present a redefinition of cultural heterogeneity in dependent countries. Through the analysis of this double

contradiction in a concrete situation it is
possible to try to identify the different forces
that confront themselves, the social groups
involved in this struggle, and the content of this
confrontation.

RESISTING CULTURAL DEPENDENCE

In Latin American countries we are able to
identify dominant classes as the internationalized
elites, specific agents and reinforcers of cultural
dependence, urging and working for cultural
homogenization. In this sense, their cultural
expressions, in addition to being the dominant
culture in the country, are instruments of the
capitalist ideology promoting its spread throughout
all society.

In addition, we can see social groups that
would also be considered part of the dominant
classes, because they are the elite of the country,
but who represent elements of negation with
respect to the dominant culture. These can be
identified with what could be called *critical
factions* within the system: mainly intellectuals,
students, and a part of the priesthood, who were
able to overcome their original class position and
engage themselves in a process of formation of
critical consciousness. The role of the dominated
classes is also ambiguous. On the one hand, their
cultural expressions may be distinct from the
dominant culture but remain refractions of reality,
myths and representations that are an expression
of their own life experience but that do not contain elements of a critical approach to this
experience. In short, they constitute a dominated
ideology. On the other hand, we are able to
identify dominated groups that manifest themselves
critically with respect to the dominant culture
in a process of formation of a class consciousness
that brings together their actual position as an
oppressed class and a critical approach to their
own reality.

We consider the process of formation of
critical consciousness of the dominated classes as
the crucial element in the struggle for liberation.
This assumption points to a more careful analysis
of the subject that can only be initiated here.

In the first place, dominated classes are
seen by the dominant ones as *resources* that can
and must be manipulated and controlled. Their

position within the system as the productive forces
and their numerical strength in underdeveloped
countries account for this perception. To this
extent, the cultural expressions that represent
their "world view" are constantly snatched from
them by the dominant classes and incorporated into
the dominant culture as a mechanism of cooptation
of the dominated. One example of this is the
utilization of elements of the popular folklore
in advertising campaigns as incentives for
consumption, like the big *"Fiesta del Joropo,"*
a sale carried out by Sears in Caracas.

As a counterpart of this tendency we have
experiences like the one led by Paulo Freire that
we mentioned above, that have as main actors the
members of the critical faction engaged in an
effort toward *"conscientização"* of the masses.
Part of this effort consists of a search for
elements of the dominated culture, elements that
are part of the dominated day-to-day life and
that have a real meaning for them, that are
susceptible to being put to use for the development
of a critical consciousness. Paulo Freire himself
has tried to do this in his literacy method.

However, this kind of approach is still an
intermediate step toward alternative strategies
and still retains residues of the main tendency
in Latin American political movements, viz. a
"conscientização" "from above" that implies an
elitist conception of the processes of liberation
where "enlightened" elites show the masses the
correct path to be followed.

The second point that we want to emphasize
here refers to the role played by national elements
in the resistance against the dominant culture.
We have discussed before the problem of the
confrontation between a capitalist culture that is
the dominant one in dependent countries, and a
national culture. Since this is the real
confrontation--and not the one between two national
cultures--the elements of the national culture
constitute potential instruments that can lead to
critical consciousness to the extent that they
represent a negation of the capitalist ideology
embodied in the dominant culture. This is not to
defend nationalism against internationalism, but
it is important to recognize its strength in the
struggle against international capitalism.

But here again the voracity of the dominant
culture is present and nationalism and national
development have been taken over and transformed

into the favorite slogan of dominant classes in
some countries of Latin America. "National
development" is to be understood as "dependent
capitalist development." Despite some misconcep-
tions in his approach to the national question,
Lenin in this case goes right to the point:

> The *elements* of democratic and socialist
> culture are present, if only in rudimentary
> form, since in *every* nation there are
> toiling and exploited masses, whose conditions
> of life inevitably give rise to the ideology
> of democracy and socialism. But *every* nation
> also possesses a bourgeois culture...in the
> form, not merely of "elements," but of the
> dominant culture....In advancing the slogan
> of the international culture of democracy and
> of the world working class movement, we take
> *from each* national culture *only* its democratic
> and socialist elements; we take them *only* and
> *absolutely* in opposition to the bourgeois
> nationalism of *each* nation....Combat all
> national oppression? Yes, of course! Fight
> *for* any kind of national development, *for*
> "national culture" in general? Of course
> not.[22]

What is clear from these passages is that a
"bourgeois nationalism" has to be distinguished
from nationalism approached as an instrument of
raising critical consciousness with respect to
capitalist ideology. Not a national culture
"in general," not a national culture that confronts
other national cultures, but one that opposes
capitalist domination both at internal and international levels. And a national culture that
relates to other national cultures also involved
in the struggle against the common enemy which
is capitalist penetration.
   We are thus able to identify two potential
fronts in the struggle for liberation from the
oppressive processes of cultural and ideological
domination in which people of the dependent
countries are enmeshed. Cultural elements whose
manifestations are of the dominated culture and
which are national are seen as potentially valid
as instruments of resistance because they are
part of a cultural universe that is very close
to the individual, part of his own genuine
perceptions and feelings toward the reality in
which he lives. In this sense, they may constitute

his defense against the penetration of perceptions and meanings which are alien to him but that make their way through the processes of ideological domination discussed before and become internalized by and stored in his preconscious.

The ways in which those elements may become useful as defenders of autonomy and freedom of choice of individuals and countries have to be discovered in each particular situation and by its own actors. Yet, any kind of chauvinism must be confronted and rejected: what has been advocated here is precisely the enlargement and enrichment of the space given to individuals and societies so that they are able to exercise their own options.

The achievement of this goal will require a process of decolonization and reconstruction which will extend to the society as a whole. The circle of domination which encompasses dependent countries is not to be broken at one point or another but it has to be weakened in its entirety. At the cultural and ideological levels this task has to rely on creativity and social invention which will frame the search for new alternatives. Along these new paths and through a building practice, man will redefine the meaning of his humanity.

NOTES

1. The term "project" here, as in Sartre, "emphasizes the element of freedom and responsibility in historical determination: it links autonomy and contingency." Quoted by H. Marcuse in *One-Dimensional Man*, Boston: Beacon Press, 1964, p. xvi.

2. O. Sunkel, "Transitional Capitalism and National Disintegration in Latin America," paper presented in a conference on Dependence Theory at Lake Arrowhead, California, Winter 1971, and published in *Investigación Económica*, Mexico, Vol. XXXI, No. 121, January-March, 1971, p. 18.

3. Georg Lukács, "Reification and the Consciousness of the Proletariat," in *History and Class Consciousness*, Cambridge: MIT Press, 1971, p. 98.

4. *Ibid.*, p. 135.

5. Henri Lefèbvre, *Everyday Life in the Modern World*, New York: Harper and Row, Publishers, 1971, p. 66.

6. H. Marcuse, *One Dimensional Man*, p. 33.

7. *Ibid.*, p. 145.

8. Zigmunt Bauman, a Polish sociologist, asserts the peculiarities of the modern mass media in the following passage from his article "On Mass Culture," published in *The Polish Sociological Bulletin*, No. 2 (14), 1966, p. 60, "(i) the communication of the same unit of information to very many people at one and the same time, with no differentiation introduced into it according to the status of the addressees; (ii) the communication of this unit of information in one irreversible direction and the virtual exclusion of the possibility of an addressee to reply, leaving aside any discussion on an equal footing; a sharp polarization of the system of communication into those sending and those receiving it; (iii) the remarkable persuasiveness of the information being passed on, based on the exalted social authority of the sources, their semi-monopolistic position, and the conviction, of much psychological significance, that "everybody" is listening--and listening with respect--to the same message."

9. H. Marcuse, *op. cit.*, p. 79.

10. Z. Bauman, *op. cit.*

11. The problem of technology in advanced societies is dealt with in almost all of Marcuse's works. But it is mainly in *One-Dimensional Man* that a specific approach to the problem is found. Jurgen Habermas presents a very good discussion of the question in "Technology and Science as Ideology," in *Toward a Rational Society*, Boston, Beacon Press, 1971. *The Technological Society*, by Jacques Ellul, also has to be mentioned here as useful to the discussion.

12. Paul Baran, "Theses on Advertising," in *The Longer View*, New York: Monthly Review Press, 1969.

13. Hans M. Enzensberger, interview in *Casa de Las Américas*, No. 5, 1969, p. 118.

14. Louis Althusser, "Ideology and Ideological State Apparatuses," in *Lenin and Philosophy and Other Essays*, London: New Left Review Editions, 1970, p. 124.

15. L. Althusser, *op. cit.*, p. 127.

16. When we mention class struggle in the context of dependent countries we are considering the particular dimensions of this class struggle as made explicit through the thesis of double polarization discussed before. This means that

the concept expresses a much more complex reality than the one used by conventional Marxist theory, even if its fundamental content is maintained. Still, concerning class struggle and class structure, we recognize the need for a theoretical elaboration of class categories more adequate to their application in different historical contexts. This includes a differentiation, among classes, fractions of classes, social strata, social categories, that reflects social reality in more adequate ways. An important contribution in this connection is Nicos Poulantzas's *Poder Político y Clases Sociales en el Estado Capitalista*, México: Siglo XXI, 1969.

17. Max Horkheimer, in *Ideología y Acción*, in T. Adorno and M. Horkheimer, *Sociologica*, Madrid: Taurus Ediciones, 1966, p. 64.

18. Ludovico Silva, *La Plusvalia Ideólogica*, Caracas: *Universidad Central de Venezuela*, 1970. The original reference can be found in Theodor Adorno, "*L'Industrie Culturelle*" in *Communications*, No. 3, 1964. And "*El Sueño Insomne*," in *Teoría y Practica de la Ideología*, Mexico: Editorial Nuestro Tiempo, 1971.

19. A significant part of the work done on the conceptualization of critical consciousness is found in the works of Frantz Fannon, *Black Skin; White Masks*, New York: Grove Press, 1967, and *The Wretched of the Earth*, New York: Grove Press, 1968; Albert Memmi, *The Colonizer and the Colonized*, Boston: Beacon Press, 1967; and Paulo Freire, *Educação como Práctica de Liberdade*, Rio de Janeiro, 1967, and *Pedagogy of the Oppressed*, New York: Herder and Herder, 1972.

20. L. Althusser, "Ideology and Ideological State Apparatuses," *op. cit.*, pp. 144-145.

21. *Ibid.*, p. 140.

22. V. I. Lenin, "Critical Remarks on the National Question," in *Collected Works*, Vol. 19, p. 355.

This selection is reprinted from Frank Bonilla and Robert Girling, eds., *Structures of Dependency*. E. Palo Alto, Calif., distributed by Nairobi Bookstore, 1972, pp. 129-148. Reprinted by permission.

PART 4
SELECT BIBLIOGRAPHY

Adam, Gyorgy. 1971. *The World Corporation Problematics: Apologetics and Critique.* Budapest: Hungarian Scientific Council for World Economy.

Altbach, Philip. 1975. "Literary colonialism: Books in the Third World," *Harvard Educational Review.* Vol. 45(2) May, pp. 226-236.

Anderson, Michael H. 1978. "Transnational advertising agencies," paper presented for the East-West Communication Institute Summer Seminar on "Transnational Communication Enterprises and National Communication Policies," August 6-19, 1978.

Annerstedt, Jan, and Gustausson, Rolf. 1975. *Towards a New International Economic Division of Labor? Patterns of Dependence and Conditions for Liberation in the Periphery of Capitalism.* Roskilde: RUC Boghandel og Forlag.

Apter, David D. 1976. "Charters, cartels, and multinationals--some colonial and imperial questions," *The Multinational Corporation and Social Change.* New York: Praeger, pp. 1-39.

Arrighi, Giovanni. 1971. "International corporations, labor aristocrats, and economic development in tropical Africa," *Imperialism and Underdevelopment: A Reader.* New York: Monthly Review Press, pp. 220-267.

Asian Regional Conference on Industrial Relations. 1975. *Foreign Investment and Labor in Asian Countries: Proceedings of the 1975 Asian Regional Conference on Industrial Relations, Tokyo, Japan, 1975.* Tokyo: Japan Institute of Labor.

Bader, Michael B. 1976. "Breast-feeding: The role of multinational corporations in Latin

America," *International Journal of Health Services*. Vol. 6(4), pp. 609-626.

Ball, George. 1974. "Citizenship and the multinational corporation," *Social Research*. Vol. 41(4), pp. 657-672.

Barnet, Richard J., and Muller, Ronald. 1974. *Global Reach: The Power of Multinational Corporations*. New York: Simon and Schuster. pp. 123-210, 363-388.

Basche, James. 1974. *U.S. Business Support for International Public Service Activities Part II: Support From Foreign Affiliates-- Brazil*. New York: The Conference Board.

Basche, James. 1974. *U.S. Business Support for International Public Service Activities Part II: Support from Foreign Affiliates-- Colombia*. New York: The Conference Board.

Basche, James. 1974. *U.S. Business Support for International Public Service Activities Part II: Support from Foreign Affiliates-- Mexico*. New York: The Conference Board.

Bechtos, Ramona. 1975. "International advertisers change consumer ways," *Advertising Age*. Vol. 46(20), pp. 1-38.

Behrman, Jack. 1972. "Social investment issues raised by foreign operations of multinational enterprises," in *People/Profits: The Ethics and Investment*, edited by Charles W. Powers. New York: Council of Religion on International Affairs.

Beltran, L. R., and de Cardona, E. Fox. 1976. "Latin America and the U.S.: Flaws in the free flow of information," paper presented to the Conference on Fair Communication Policy for the International Exchange of Information held in Honolulu, March-April 1976, East-West Communication Institute, East-West Center.

Bienefeld, Manfred, and Martin, Godfrey. 1970. "Labor and export of jobs," *IDS Bulletin*. Vol. 8(3), pp. 33-36.

Bilsborrow, Richard. 1977. "Effects of economic dependency on labor force participation in less developed countries," *Oxford Economic Papers*. Vol. 29(1), pp. 61-83.

Biokemjioks, Robert, and Basekpi, R. 1974. "Center and periphery news in African newspapers: Testing some hypotheses on cultural dominance," *Kroniek Von Africa*. No. 3, pp. 243-271.

Bonilla de Ramos, Elsy. 1972. Las agencias internacionales de noticias y sus procesos

informativos; il estudio de un caso.
Documento presentado al Seminario Inter-
nacional. "Il Papel Socio-politico de los
Medios de Communicacion Colectiva para la
Sociedad de Cambio en America Latina," San
Jose, Costa Rica, 19-25 de Noviembre 1972.
Bonilla, Frank, and Girling, Robert (eds.). 1973.
Structures of Dependency. E. Palo Alto,
Calif.: Distributed by Nairobi Bookstore.
Braungart, Richard G. 1975. "Multinational
corporations: A new agendum for community
power research," Paper presented at the 25th
annual meetings of the Society for the Study
of Social Problems, San Francisco, California.
Broadcasting. 1977. "The U.S. as T.V.
programmer to the world." *Broadcasting*.
Vol. 92, April 18, pp. 48-58.
Brundenius, Claes. 1972. "The anatomy of
imperialism: The case of the multinational
mining corporations in Peru," *Journal of
Peace Research*. Vol. 9(3), pp. 189-207.
Bulatao, Edmundo. 1973. "Wage effects of foreign
investments," *Philippine Economic Journal*.
Vol. 12(1 & 2), pp. 271-293.
Burbach, R. 1977. "Union busting: Castle & Cooke
in Honduras," *NACLA'S Latin America & Empire
Report*. Vol. 11(10), pp. 40-41.
Business International. 1977. "ILO notes MNC
role in training workers, creating new jobs,"
Business International. Vol. 24(9),
March 4, p. 71
Business Week. 1970. "Madison Avenue goes
multinational," *Business Week*. No. 2141,
Sept. 12, pp. 48-58.
Cardona, Elizabeth. 1975. "Multinational
television," *Journal of Communication*.
Vol. 25(2), pp. 122-127.
Chomsky, Noam, and Herman, Edward S. 1977. "Why
American business supports third world
fascism," *Business and Society Review*. No. 23,
Fall, pp. 13-21.
Clark, Norman. 1975. "The multinational corpora-
tion: the transfer of technology and
dependence," *Development and Change*.
Vol. 6(1), pp. 5-21.
Cockcroft, James D., Frank, Andre Gunder, and
Johnson, Dale. 1972. *Dependence and Under-
development: Latin America's Political
Economy*. New York: Anchor Books.
Creamer, Daniel B. 1976. *Overseas Research and
Development by United States Multinationals*,

326

1966-1975; Estimates of Expenditures and a Statistical Profile. New York: The Conference Board.

Dagnino, Evelina. 1973. "Cultural and ideological dependence: Building a theoretical framework," in *Structures of Dependency*, edited by F. Bonilla and Robert Girling. E. Palo Alto, Calif.: Distributed by Nairobi Bookstore, pp. 129-148.

Daniels, John. 1974. "The non-American manager, especially as third country national in U.S. multinationals: A separate but equal doctrine?" *Journal of International Business Studies*. Vol. 5(2), pp. 25-40.

Dehner, W. J. 1974. "Multinational enterprise and racial non-discrimination: United States enforcement of an international human right," *Harvard International Law Journal*. Vol. 15(1), pp. 71-125.

Duerr, Michael G., and Green, James. 1968. *Foreign Nationals in International Management*. (Managing International Business No. 2). New York: The Conference Board.

Ebel, Karl H. 1976. "Socio-economic aspects of multinational mineral mining," *International Labor Review*. Vol. 113(1), pp. 53-65.

Egea, Alejandro Nadel. 1975. "Multinational corporations in the operation and ideology of international transfer of technology," *Studies in Comparative International Development*. Vol. 10(1), pp. 11-29.

Emmanuel, Arghiri. 1976. "The multinational corporations and inequality of development," *International Social Science Journal*. Vol. 28(4), pp. 754-772.

Estes, E. M. 1974. "General Motors and South Africa," in *The Multinational Corporation and Social Policy*, edited by Richard A. Jackson. New York: Praeger, pp. 81-108.

Evans, Peter B. 1971. "National autonomy and economic development: Critical perspectives on multinational corporations in poor countries," *International Organization*. Vol. 25(3), pp. 675-692.

Evans, Peter B. 1974. "The military, the multinationals and the 'miracle': The political economy of the 'Brazilian model' of development," *Studies in Comparative International Development*. Vol. 9(3), pp. 26-45.

Evans, Peter B. 1976. "Industrialization and imperialism: Growth and stagnation on the periphery," *Berkeley Journal of Sociology*. Vol. 20, pp. 113-145.

Fayerweather, John. 1972. "Elite attitudes towards multinational firms: A study of Britain, Canada, and France," *International Studies Quarterly*. Vol. 16(4), pp. 472-490.

Fayerweather, John. 1972. "Nationalism and the multinational firm," *The Multinational Enterprise in Transition*. Princeton: Darwin.

First, Ruth. 1972. *The South African Connection: Western Investment in Apartheid*. London: Maurice Temple Smith.

Frank, Andre Gunder. 1972. *Lumpenbourgeoisie and Lumpendevelopment: Dependence, Class and Politics in Latin America*. New York: Monthly Review Press.

Germidis, Dmitri. 1976. *Multinational Firms and Vocational Training in Developing Countries*. Paris: United Nations Educational, Scientific and Cultural Organization. SHC.76/CONF.635/COL. 7.

Girvan, Norman. 1970. "Multinational corporations and dependent underdevelopment in mineral-export economies," *Social and Economic Studies*. Vol. 19(4), pp. 490-526.

Girvan, Norman. 1975. "Economic nationalists v. multinational corporations: Revolutionary or evolutionary change?" in *Multinational Firms in Africa*, edited by Carl Widstrand. New York: Africana Publishing Company, pp. 26-56.

Godfrey, Martin. 1975. "International market in skills and transmission of inequality," *Development and Change*. Vol. 6(4), pp. 5-22.

Goodman, Louis Wolf. 1976. "The social organization of decision making in the multinational corporations," in *The Multinational Corporation and Social Change*, edited by David Apter and Louis Wolf Goodman. New York: Praeger, pp. 63-95.

Greenberg, Stanley. 1976. "Business enterprise in a racial order," *Politics and Society*. Vol. 6(2), pp. 213-240.

Greene, James. 1975. *Foreign Investment and Employment: An Examination of Foreign Investments to Make 58 Products Overseas: A Research Report From the Conference Board*. New York: The Conference Board.

Greiner, Ted. 1975. *The Promotion of Bottle Feeding by Multinational Corporations: How Advertising and the Health Professions Have Contributed.* Ithaca, New York: Program on International Nutrition and Development Policy, Cornell University (Cornell International Nutrition Monograph Series, No. 2).

Gunnemann, Jon P. 1975. *The Nation-State and Transnational Corporations in Conflict: With Special Reference to Latin America.* New York: Praeger.

Gunter, Hans. 1976. "Multinational corporations and labor: A worldwide theme with variations," *Foreign Investment and Labor in Asian Countries.* Tokyo: The Japan Institute of Labor, pp. 22-42.

Haden-Guest, Anthony. 1972. *Down the Programmed Rabbit Hole: Travels Through Muzak, Hilton, Coca-Cola, Walt Disney and Other World Empires.* London: Hart-Davis, MacGibbon Ltd.

Hartmann, Heinz. 1963. *Amerikanische Firmen in Deutschland: Beobachtungen über Kontakte und Kontraste Zwischen Industriegesellschaften.* Cologne and Opladen: Westdeutscher Verlag.

Helfgott, Roy B. 1973. "Multinational corporations and manpower utilization in developing nations," *Journal of Developing Areas.* Vol. 7(2), pp. 235-246.

Heller, Heinz Robert, and Heller, Emily. 1973. *The Economic and Social Impact of Foreign Investment in Hawaii.* Honolulu: Economic Research Center, University of Hawaii.

Heller, Heinz Robert. 1974. "The Hawaiian experience," *Columbia Journal of World Business.* Vol. 9(3), pp. 105-110.

Hirono, Ryokichi. 1976. "Industrial relations in foreign corporations--case of Thailand," *Foreign Investment and Labor in Asian Countries.* Tokyo: The Japan Institute of Labor, pp. 164-187.

Hymer, Stephen. 1972. "The multinational corporation and the law of uneven development," *Economics and the World Order: From the 1970's to the 1990's,* edited by Jagdish N. Bhagwati. London: Macmillan, pp. 113-140.

Hymer, Stephen. 1976. *The International Operations of National Firms.* Cambridge: MIT Press.

Iida, Tsuneo. 1976. "Some observations on the manpower development and the role of foreign

investment in Southeast Asian countries,"
*Foreign Investment and Labor in Asian
Countries*. Tokyo: The Japan Institute of
Labour, pp. 53-61.

International Labor Office. 1973. *Multinational
Enterprises and Social Policy*. (Studies
and Reports, New Series, No. 79) Geneva.

International Labor Office. 1976. *The Impact of
Multinational Enterprises on Employment and
Training*. Geneva.

International Labor Office. 1976. *Wages and
Working Conditions in Multinational Enterprises*. Geneva.

International Labor Office. 1972. *Employment,
Income and Equality: A Strategy of Increasing
Production Employment in Kenya*. Geneva.

Jackson, Richard A. (ed.). 1974. *Multinational
Corporations and Social Policy: Special
Reference to General Motors in South Africa*.
New York: Praeger.

Jelliffe, D.B. 1972. "Commerciogenic malnutrition," *Nutrition Reviews*. Vol. 30(9),
pp. 199-205.

Jequier, Nicolas. 1972. "Science policy in the
developing countries: The role of the
multinational firm," in *The Gap Between Rich
and Poor Nations*, edited by Gustav Ranis.
London: Macmillan.

Kaplun, Mario. 1973. *La Communicacion de Masas
en America Latina*. Bogota: Associacion de
Publicaciones Educativas. (Educacion Hoy
No. 5).

Kassalow, Everett M. 1976. "The impact of the
multinationals on industrial relations
practice," *Labor Gazette*. Vol. 76(11),
pp. 582-592.

Kean, Geoffrey. 1968. *The Public Relations
Man Abroad*. New York: F.A. Praeger.

Kerdpibule, Udom. 1974. "Thailand's experience
with multinational corporations," Bangkok:
Dept. of Economics, Kasetsart University
(unpublished).

Kitazawa, Yoko. 1975. *From Tokyo to Johannesburg*.
New York: Inter-Faith Center on Corporate
Responsibility.

Kobrin, Stephen. 1976. "Foreign direct investment, industrialization and social change,"
Journal of Conflict Resolution. Vol. 20(3),
pp. 497-522.

Kreye, Otto. 1977. "World market-oriented
industrialization of developing countries:

330

free production zones and world market
factories," in *Die neue internationale
Arbeitsteilung. Strukturelle Arbeitslosigkeit
in den Industrieländern und die Industrial-
isierung der Entwicklungsländer.* By
Folker Frobel, Jurgen Heinrichs and Otto Kreye.
Hamburg: Rowohlt Taschenbuch Verlag.
Kujawa, Duane (ed.). 1975. *International Labor
and the Multinational Enterprise.* New York:
Praeger.
Kumar, Krishna (ed.). 1979. *Bonds Without
Bondage.* Honolulu: University Press of
Hawaii.
Kumar, Krishna. 1979. *Social and Cultural
Impacts of Transnational Enterprises.* Trans-
national Corporations Research Project.
Sydney: The University of Sydney.
Kumar, Krishna. 1979. "Multinational Corporations
and the Transnational System," *Journal of
Political and Military Sociology.* Vol. 7(2),
Fall 1979.
Kumar, Krishna. "Economies Falls Short: The Need
for the Study of Social and Cultural Impact
of TNEs" in *Functioning of Multinational
Corporations in the Global Context,* edited
by Anant R. Negandhi. New York: Pergamon
Press (forthcoming).
Lappe, F. M., Collins, J., and McCallie, E. 1977.
Banana Hunger. Oakland: Institute for Food
and Development Policy.
Ledogar, Robert J. 1975. *Hungry for Profits:
U.S. Food and Drug Multinationals in Latin
America.* New York: IDOC North America.
Lester, Mark. 1978. "Criticism of multinational
advertising in developing countries,"
Honolulu: East-West Center (unpublished).
Leys, Colin. 1974. *Underdevelopment in Kenya:
The Political Economy of Neo-Colonialism,
1964-1971.* Berkeley: University of California
Press.
Lim, David. 1977. "Do foreign companies pay
higher wages than their local counterparts in
Malayasian manufacturing?," *Journal of
Development Economics.* Vol. 4(1),
pp. 55-66.
Loxley, John, and Saul, J.S. 1975. "Multina-
tionals, workers, and the parastatals in
Tanzania," *Review of African Political
Economy.* Vol. 2(Jan./April), pp. 54-88.
Maisonrouge, Jacques G. 1975. "How a multina-
tional corporation appears to its managers,"

in *Global Companies: The Political Economy of World Business*, edited by George Ball. Englewood Cliffs: Prentice Hall, pp. 11-20.

Margulies, Leah. 1977. "Cracks in the bottle," *New Internationalist*. No. 50, April, pp. 20-22.

Marsh, Robert M., and Mannari, Hiroshi. 1976. "A new look at 'lifetime commitment' in Japanese industry," in *Asian Business and Environment in Transition: Selected Readings and Essays*, edited by A. Kapoor. Princeton, New Jersey: Darwin Press, pp. 195-214.

Mascarenhas, Oswald A. 1976. "Towards measuring the technological impact of multinational corporations in the less-developed countries," Ph.D. dissertation, University of Pennsylvania.

Matsuo, Kei. 1977. "The working class in the Masan free export zone," in *Free Trade Zones & Industrialization of Asia*. Tokyo: Pacific-Asia Resources Center, pp. 67-78.

Mattelart, Armand. 1976. "Cultural imperialism in the multinationals age," *Instant Research on Peace and Violence*. Vol. 6(4), pp. 160-174.

May, Stacy. 1958. *The United Fruit Company in Latin America*. (NPA series on U.S. business performances abroad, number 7). Washington: National Planning Association.

Mazrui, Ali. 1979. "The Impact of Transnational Corporations on Educational Processes and Cultural Change: An African Perspective," in *Bonds Without Bondage*, edited by Krishna Kumar. Honolulu: University Press of Hawaii.

Meggers, B. J. 1971. *Amazonia: Man and Nature in a Counterfeit Paradise*. Chicago: Aldine.

Meier, R. L. 1977. "Multinationals as agents of social development," *Bulletin of the Atomic Scientists*. Vol. 33(9), pp. 30-32.

Mercer, G., and Forsyth, David. 1974. "Multinational corporations and graduate migration," *Vocational Aspects of Education*. Vol. 26(4), pp. 73-79.

Moran, Theodore H. 1974. *Multinational Corporations and the Politics of Dependence: Copper in Chile*. Princeton: Princeton University Press.

Morris, Roger, Mueller, Shelly, and Jelin, William. 1974. "Through the looking glass in Chile: Coverage of Allende's regime," *Columbia Journalism Review*. Vol. 13(4), pp. 15-26.

Muller, M. 1974. *The Baby Killer*. London:
War on Want Pamphlet.

Negandhi, Anant R. (ed.). *Functioning of
Multinational Corporations in the Global
Context*. New York: Pergamon Press
(forthcoming).

National Academy of Sciences. 1973. *U.S.
International Firms and R, D and E in
Developing Countries*. Washington, D.C.

Nickel, Herman. 1978. "The case for doing
business in South Africa," *Fortune*.
Vol. 97(12), June 19, pp. 60-74.

Nordenstreng, Kaarle, and Varis, Tapio. 1974.
Television Traffic--A One-Way Street?
Paris: UNESCO.

Nzimiro, Ikenna. 1975. "The political and social
implications of multi-national corporations
in Nigeria," in *Multinational Firms in
Africa*, edited by Carl Widstrand. New York:
Africana Publishing Company, pp. 210-243.

Ohara, Ken. 1977. "Bataan export processing
zone: Its development and social implications," in *Free Trade Zones & Industrialization
of Asia*. Tokyo: Pacific-Asia Resources
Center, pp. 93-120.

Ottaway, Marina. 1976. "Social classes and
corporate interests in the Ethiopian
revolution," *Journal of Modern African
Studies*. Vol. 14(3), pp. 469-486.

Overseas Development Institute. 1975. "Industry,
employment, and the developing world: the
contribution of private foreign business to
the employment objectives of developing
countries: The report of the seminar jointly
sponsored by IBM (United Kingdom) and ODI in
Oxford, Nov. 20-22, 1974. London.

Palvic, Breda. 1976. "Transnational companies and
mass communication among the non-aligned,"
Review of International Affairs. Vol. 27(621),
pp. 14-17.

Pang, Eng-Fong, and Tan, Chwee-Huat. 1976.
"Foreign investment, unions, and the govern-
ment in Singapore," *Foreign Investment and
Labor in Asian Countries*. Tokyo: The Japan
Institute of Labor, pp. 124-133.

Porteous, J. Douglas. 1974. "Social class in
Atacama company towns," *Association for
American Geographers Annals*. Vol. 64(3),
pp. 409-417.

Ramos, Elias T. 1976. "Filipino trade unions and
multinationals," *Foreign Investment and Labor*

in Asian Countries. Tokyo: The Japan
Institute of Labor, pp. 72-87.

Rangel, Dias Eleázar. 1967. *Pueblos Subinformados:
Las Agencias de Moticias y America Latina.*
Caracas, Universidad Central de Venezuela
(Cuadernos de Nuestro Tiempo No. 3).

Read, William H. 1975. "Multinational media,"
Foreign Policy. No. 18, Spring,
pp. 155-167.

Reyes Matta, Fernando. 1975. "América Latina,
Kissinger y la UPI: Errores y omisiones desde
México," in *Comunicación y Cultura* (Argentina)
Septiembre 1975, No. 4, pp. 55-72. Also,
Stanford, Calif: Institute for Communication
Research, 1975, 24 pages.

Reyes Matta, Fernando. 1976. "The information
bedazzlement of Latin America: a study of
world news in the region," *Development
Dialogue.* No. 2, pp. 29-42.

Rogers, B. 1976. "Apartheid for profit,"
Business and Society Review. No. 19,
pp. 65-69.

Ronstadt, Robert C. 1975. "R & D abroad: The
creation and evolution of foreign research
and development activities of U.S.-based
multinational enterprises," Ph.D. dissertation,
Harvard University, 1975.

Sauvant, Karl P. 1976. "The potential of multinational enterprises as vehicles for the
transmission of business culture," in
*Controlling Multinational Enterprises:
Problems, Strategies, Counterstrategies,*
edited by Karl P. Sauvant and
Farid G. Lavipour. Boulder: Westview Press.

Sauvant, Karl P. 1976. "Multinational enterprises
and the transmission of culture: The international supply of advertising services and
business education," *Journal of Peace
Research.* Vol. 13(1), pp. 49-65.

Sauvant, Karl P. 1976. "His master's voice,"
CERES. Vol. 9(5), pp. 27-32.

Schiller, H. I. 1969. *Mass Communications and
American Empire.* Boston: Beacon.

Schiller, H. I. 1973. *The Mind Managers.* Boston:
Beacon.

Schiller, H. I. 1976. *Communication and Cultural
Domination.* New York: International Arts
and Sciences Press.

Schiller, H. I. 1976. "Advertising and international communications," *Instant Research on
Peace and Violence.* Vol. 6(4), pp. 175-182.

Seidman, A., and Seidman N. 1977. *South Africa and the U.S. Multinational Corporations*. Westport, Conn.: Lawrence Hill.

Sepulveda, Bernardo, and Churnacero, Antonio. 1973. *La Inversion Extranjero en Mexico*. Mexico: Fondo de Cultura Economica.

Sklar, Richard L. 1975. *Corporate Power in an African State: The Political Impact of Multinational Mining Companies in Zambia*. Berkeley: University of California Press.

Sklar, Richard L. 1976. "Postimperialism: a class analysis of multinational corporate expansion: review essay," *Comparative Politics*. Vol. 9(1), pp. 75-92.

Smith, Keith B. 1975. "Who controls book publishing in Anglophone middle Africa?" *American Academy of Political and Social Science Annals*. Vol. 421, pp. 140-150.

Smith, Keith B. 1976. *The Impact of Transnational Book Publishing on Intellectual Knowledge in Less-Developed Countries*. Paris: UNESCO. SHC-76/CONF.635/COL.6.

Smith, Timothy. 1977. "U.S. firms and apartheid: Belated steps analyzed," *Africa Today*. Vol. 24(2), pp. 29-33.

Smith, Timothy. 1977. "Whitewash for apartheid from twelve U.S. firms," *Business and Society Review*. No. 2, pp. 59-60.

Snow, R. T. 1977. "Dependent development and the new industrial worker: The case of the export processing zone in the Philippines," Ph.D. dissertation, Department of Sociology, Harvard University.

Somavía, Juan. 1976. "The transnational power structure and international information," *Development Dialogue*. No. 2, pp. 15-28.

Spandau, Arnt. 1978. *Economic Boycott Against South Africa--Normative and Factual Issues*. Johannesburg: University of Witwatersrand.

Stauffer, Robert B. 1973. *Nation-Building in a Global Economy: The Role of the Multinational Corporation*. (Sage Professional Paper in Comparative Politics 01--39) Beverly Hills, Calif.: Sage.

Stauffer, Robert B. 1978. "Transnational corporations and host nations: Attitudes, ideologies, and behaviors," paper prepared for a conference on Transnational Corporations, sponsored by the Asian and Pacific Development Administration Center (APDAC), Kuala Lumpur, Malaysia, July 1978.

Stauffer, Robert B. 1979. "Western values and the case for third world cultural disengagement," in *Bonds Without Bondage*, edited by Krishna Kumar. Honolulu: University Press of Hawaii.

Stephenson, Hugh. 1973. *The Coming Clash: The Impact of Multinational Corporations on Nation States*. New York: Saturday Review Press.

Subido, Chita. 1973. "Employment effects on direct foreign investments," *The Philippine Economic Journal*. Vol. 12(23), pp. 251-270.

Sunkel, Osvaldo. 1973. "Transnational capitalism and national disintegration in Latin America," *Social and Economic Studies*. Vol. 22(1), pp. 132-176.

Sunkel, Osvaldo, and Faivovich, Edmundo. 1976. "The effects of transnational corporations on culture," Paris: UNESCO, SHC-76/CONF.635/COL.5.

Taira, Koji. 1976. "Foreign direct investment, personnel structure, and working conditions in less-developed countries in Asia," in *Foreign Investment and Labor in Asian Countries*. Tokyo: The Japan Institute of Labor, pp. 136-163.

Tak, Hi-Jun. 1976. "Foreign investment and industrial relations in Korea," *Foreign Investment and Labor in Asian Countries*. Tokyo: The Japan Institute of Labor, pp. 43-52.

Takeo, Tsuchiya. 1977. "South Korea: Masan--an epitome of the Japan-ROK relationship," *Free Trade Zones & Industrialization of Asia*. Tokyo: Pacific-Asia Resources Center, pp. 53-66.

The Conference Board. 1975. *The Multinational Union Challenges the Multinational Company*. New York.

Toyne, B. 1976. "Host country managers of multinational firms--evaluation of variables affecting their managerial thinking patterns," *Journal of International Business Studies*. Vol. 7(1), pp. 39-55.

Tsuda, Ey Mamoru. 1977. "The social organization of transnational business and industry: a study of Japanese capital--affiliated joint-ventures in the Philippines," M.A. thesis submitted to the College of Arts and Sciences, University of the Philippines.

Tunstall, Jeremy. 1977. *The Media are American*.
New York: Columbia University Press.
Turner, Louis. 1976. "The international division
of leisure, tourism, and the third world,"
World Development. Vol. 4(3), pp. 253-260.
United Church Board for World Ministries, *et al.*
1977. "Report to the Eleventh General Synod
of the United Church of Christ on 1975-1977
Corporate Social Responsibility Actions, with
Special Emphasis on Southern Africa," New York.
United Nations. 1977. *Activities of TNC's in
Southern Africa and the Extent of their
Collaboration with the Regimes in the Area*.
New York: United Nations, Economic and
Social Council, Commission on Transnational
Corporations.
United Nations Department of Economic and Social
Affairs. 1973. *Multinational Corporations
in World Development*. New York: United
Nations, ST/ECA/190.
United Nations Department of Economic and Social
Affairs. 1974. *The Impact of Multinational
Corporations on Development and on Interna-
tional Relations*. New York: United Nations,
E/5500/Rev.
United Nations, Economic and Social Council,
Commission on Transnational Corporations.
1976. *Research on Transnational Corporations*.
Lima: United Nations, E/C.10/12.
United Nations, Economic and Social Council,
Commission on Transnational Corporations.
1978. *Transnational Corporations in World
Development: A Re-examination*. New York:
United Nations, E/C.10/38.
Vaid, Kanwal N. 1976. "Personnel practices of
multinational corporations in India," *Foreign
Investment and Labor in Asian Countries*.
Tokyo: The Japan Institute of Labor,
pp. 88-99.
Vaitsos, C. V. 1974. "Employment effects of
foreign direct investments in developing
countries," *Tecnologia para el Desarrollo*.
Mexico City.
Varis, Tapio. 1973. *International Inventory of
Television Programme Structure and the Flow of
TV Programmes between Nations*. Tampere,
Finland: Institute of Journalism and Mass
Communication, University of Tampere.
Varis, Tapio. 1976. "Aspects of the impact of
transnational corporations on communication,"

International Social Science Journal.
Vol. 28(4), pp. 808-830.

Vernon, Raymond. 1971. *Sovereignty at Bay*.
New York: Basic Books.

Vernon, Raymond. 1977. *Storm Over the Multinationals*. Cambridge, Mass.: Harvard
University Press.

Vetterli, Richard R. 1972. "The impact of the
multinational corporation on the power
structure of Mexico and a Mexican border
community," Ph.D. dissertation, University
of California, Riverside.

Watanabe, Susumu. 1972. "International subcontracting, employment, and skill
promotion," *International Labor Review*.
Vol. 105(5), pp. 425-449.

Wells, Alan Frank. 1972. *Picture-tube
Imperialism? The Impact of U.S. Television
on Latin America*. Maryknoll, New York:
Orbis Books.

Wolfe, Alvin W. 1977. "Supranational organization
of production: An evolutionary perspective,"
Current Anthropology. Vol. 18(4),
pp. 615-635.

Yoshino, Michael. 1968. "Administrative attitudes
and relationships in a foreign culture,"
MSU Business Topics. Vol. 16(1), pp. 59-66.

Zeira, Yoram. 1975. "Some structural and cultural
factors in ethnocentric multinational
corporations and employee morale," *Journal
of Management Studies*. Vol. 12(1), pp. 66-82.